Agapanthus care notes

Remember not all agapanthus are fully hardy, in general most deciduous forms and species are hardy, whilst the evergreen types are mostly tender and only established clumps with good leaf cover may withstand cold winters but much depends on where you live and what facilities you can provide for the winter time

Planting in the Garden

Agapanthus prefer any well drained ordinary soil in a sunny open position where your plants will not be continually over hung by trees and shrubs or other vigorous leafy herbaceous perennials. Good deep soil cultivation and preparation by adding organic matter will always give better results. Plant in spring or early summer, when the ground is warmed up, 30cm - 60cm (12" – 24") apart, depending on the cultivar. Water in after planting and enjoy.

In late autumn/early winter, when the leaves of deciduous forms have turned yellow and died down, weed and mulch over the crowns with loose organic material. However should you be planting evergreen types then straw around the crowns to a depth of 10cm – 15cm (4" – 6"), leaving the upper leaves exposed, this will provide some protection in severe frost.

Planting in Pots

Whilst the very best plants are produced by growing them in the ground, excellent results and flowering can be achieved by cultivation in containers. We prefer the traditional clay pot that must be brought into the cold greenhouse or cold conservatory before the onset of cold winter frosts, that may not only damage the plants but could crack and destroy pots, especially if they are waterlogged at the time. Evergreen types with attractive succulent leaves are the most attractive displays and are best suited to pot culture, being more drought resistant. Use composts containing loam, such as John Innes No. 3, potting on annually until after a few years large specimens will be the result. These will require liquid feeding after the first year and left in the large pots until flowering declines, after which they should be split up and re-potted. Containerised plants may be plunged (not planted) in a border for the summer, but lifted in autumn. For winter storage, simply aim to keep just frost free and moist. If you don't have a greenhouse, move the pots against a warm wall of your house and protect with bubble wrap or fleece.

Lack of flowering

The most frequent question by far is "Why are my Ags. not flowering". Possible reasons are as follows:- **1)** Poor flowering strain (genetical, cannot be improved by cultivation methods) **2)** Planting in too shady a position – lack of sunlight necessary for flower initiation. Keeping containerised plants in too much shade. **3)** Overcrowding of rhizomes and root system in pot. Re-pot into larger container or maintain health and vigour by liquid feeding. Overcrowding in the ground after too many years in the same position, lift in spring, divide and re-locate. **4)** Overfeeding with too much nitrogen may result in vigorous growth and lack of flowering. **5)**Too cold. Too much frost may destroy flower initials, followed by leafy growth with no flowers. **6)** Too cold and wet – Agapanthus are best in well drained conditions.

DIPLADENIA SUNDAVILLE

(MANDEVILLA)

YOUR GARDEN IN SPAIN

PRACTICAL IDEAS FOR GARDENS THAT SUIT YOUR SPANISH LIFESTYLE

BY CLODAGH AND DICK HANDSCOMBE

SANTANA BOOKS

Designed by Chris Fajardo
Illustrations by the authors

Your Garden In Spain
is published by Ediciones Santana S.L.,
Apartado 422, 29640 Fuengirola (Málaga).
Phone 952 485 838. Fax 952 485 367.
Email: info@santanabooks.com
www.santanabooks.com

Printed in Spain by Gráficas San Pancracio S.L.
Depósito Legal: MA-895/2005
ISBN 84-89954-42-9

DEDICATION

To all experienced and inexperienced gardeners who take the opportunity to develop their Gardens of Eden under the Spanish sun.

ACKNOWLEDGEMENTS

At last the book is ready to share with new and experienced gardeners in Spain and it is time to acknowledge those who have helped make the book rich in ideas and practical. We would like to thank:

- Those expatriate and Spanish friends who have shared their experience and problems, and helped evaluate our ideas.
- The many readers of our weekly columns and previous book, who have sent problems into our Greenfingers CBN Help Line. At times they made us dig deep for solutions, some of which are reflected in this book.
- The Directors of Santana Books for their faith in selecting us to produce this special book.
- The designer for his diligent pagenation especially, for Section Four.
- Our parents and grandparents who stimulated an early and ongoing interest in gardening and the dedication to overcome a variety of soils, climates and situations.
- Each other, for the continuous encouragement and mutual support, while working day after day during a "lost summer" to reach the publisher's deadline.

CONTENTS LIST

SECTION FIVE – GARDENING IN DIFFERENT SITUATIONS - 176

SECTION SIX – CARING FOR YOUR PLANTS - 208

SECTION SEVEN – HOME GROWN ORGANIC VEGETABLES - 252

FOREWORD

We enjoy gardening and helping others with practical solutions to their problems. Within this book we share our combined 35 years of gardening in Spain, the last sixteen together. We hope that our ideas help you envisage, design or redesign, construct and maintain an attractive garden, wherever you have settled. Whatever you do, design your garden for tomorrow – a garden to live in and enjoy for the rest of your lives.

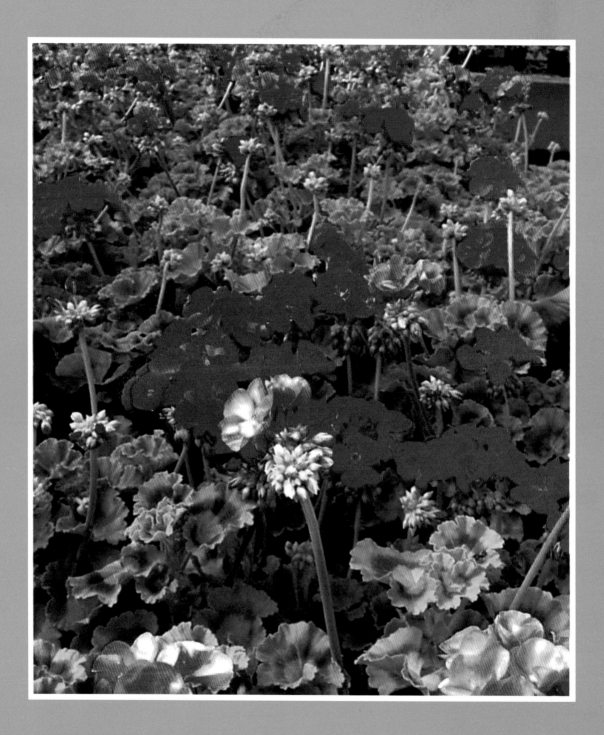

INTRODUCTION

Spain is a wonderful country in which to garden, whether designing and developing a new garden from scratch or maintaining a long-established one. The favourable year-round climate, the sun and bright light, the warm balmy nights make it possible for you, the amateur gardener, to achieve the garden of your dreams – an oasis in a stressful world in which flowers, vegetables and fruit can be harvested on every day of the year. Yes, it does rain, at times like monsoons, but nothing grows without water!

Over the last 25 years, hundreds of thousands of northern Europeans have purchased homes in Spain for full-time or holiday residency. The flow continues, with Eastern Europeans and North Africans adding to the diversity of peoples as well as the styles of gardens.

We, like many newcomers, knew little about the depth of the opportunities for gardening here, especially the wide variety of flowering, perfumed and edible plants that can be raised with care. We knew little of the challenges of enriching hard, sunbaked soils, of nursing plants through the high summer temperatures that can rise above 40 degrees, or in the frost belt with temperatures falling well below zero in the winter.

We both learned the hard way, at first in developing our own gardens on the coastal plain and in the coastal mountains, and then in helping others take over neglected wilderness gardens.

Twenty years ago there existed little written material to guide newcomers to gardening in Spain and few knowledgeable garden centres. Since joining forces as gardening partners eight years ago, we have walked 10,000 kilometres and driven 100,000 kilometres around the Spanish mainland and islands observing countless gardens and noting what grows successfully in a wide variety of locations.

Having seen many newcomers struggle, at least in their early years, we started to write columns in a number of newspapers and magazines to share our experiences. Some of our early columns were published in our first book, Practical Gardening on the Costa, which undoubtedly helped many, but only went so far.

We were therefore delighted to be invited to write this more comprehensive guide, which appears 400 years after a book called *Agricultura y Jardines por Vivo* (Agriculture and Gardens for Life) was first published in 1605, which summarised what was known at that time about establishing attractive gardens and growing productive crops, and served as a guide to many communities that moved from inland and northern Spain to the depopulated provinces along the Mediterranean coast and the Islands after the moors left Spain.

In writing this book, we aimed to do the same for today's new settlers, helping them create and maintain their gardens and select the right plants, shrubs and trees at the local garden centres.

We have included advice and ideas for gardens of all shapes and sizes, from large plots to a dozen flowerpots on an apartment balcony, and in all locations, from coastal areas to inland valleys, plains and mountainsides.

We aim to inspire creative ideas as well as provide solutions to problems. Above all, we aim to help you establish a garden that matches the lifestyle you had in mind when you came to Spain.

The authors.

SECTION ONE
THE SPANISH
GARDENING
CHALLENGES

1.1 YOUR NEW GARDENING OPPORTUNITIES

FOR MANY OF YOU, gardening in Spain will be very different to your previous gardening experiences. Luckily, many of the differences are positive and you will have every chance of creating a spectacular and practical garden, a garden that will satisfy your aspirations whether you are a keen gardener or a reluctant one.

You will have the opportunity to create a garden that is in flower and perfumed and yielding fruit and vegetables every day of the year, and a garden that is comfortable to work in for much of the year.

The favourable climate enables you to grow an amazingly wide range of temperate, sub-tropical and even tropical plants, provided the local microclimate of your garden is sufficiently warm and sheltered during the winter months. Naturally there are high and low extremes of temperature that can create occasional problems.

If retired and fit you will now have, at last, all the time in the world to enjoy designing and developing a garden in one of the best climates in the world. You will also have the chance to contribute to the greening of urbanized coastal areas by using natural organic practices where mules, oxen, manures and compost have been largely replaced by tractors, rotovators and chemicals.

No wonder gardening is such a popular hobby for many in Spain, not only for expatriates but also for the increasing number of Spaniards moving from city apartments to suburban houses.

Against this background, the horticultural industry has transformed itself in the last 20 years and new gardeners should have little difficulty in finding the supplies and services they need, such as:

- New nurseries and garden centres staffed by knowledgeable assistants, many of them offering garden design,

landscaping and maintenance services.
- An ever-expanding range of plants – with planes and pantechnicons bringing millions of plants monthly into Spain from all over the world.
- More organic material for enriching soils, such as improved peat substitutes, manure-based organic compost/ fertilizers, composted garden waste and seaweed from municipal Eco parks, and horse manure from the growing number of riding stables.
- More and more trained, professional gardeners and jobbing gardeners to help with some of the creative and heavier landscaping and maintenance tasks.

The opportunities are there for all and the Spanish soil awaits your creativity and hard labour. Success can be yours if you have the imagination, physical fitness, time and determination to overcome the several problems (discussed in the next chapter) that most gardeners face during their early years in Spain.

Most importantly, do grasp the opportunity to design a garden that matches your planned lifestyle and ensures that you are able to enjoy the wonderful climate that prompted you to come to Spain in the first place.

The list below summarises those things that could help you realise your dream, so bear it in mind as you read through the chapters that follow. An ideal Spanish garden should:

1. Suit your lifestyle, whether you are a resident or absentee owner.
2. Be a garden to live in, enabling an outdoor lifestyle.
3. Make good use of site and surroundings.
4. Match your interest or disinterest in gardening.
5. Provide space for working on hobbies.

6. Require minimum maintenance and watering once it matures.

7. Give year-round colour, perfume and interest.

8. Contain appropriate plantings for its microclimate.

9. Produce flowers, fruit and vegetables 365 days a year.

10. Include open spaces and cosy restful corners.

11. Provide areas of cool summer shade and warm, sheltered, winter sun.

12. Give shelter from winds and frost in colder situations.

13. Have good internal and external views.

14. Allow space for al fresco cooking and eating.

15. Ensure privacy and security.

1.2 TYPICAL PROBLEMS AND RISKS

Many foreigners buy properties in Spain with dreams of their own "Garden of Eden" with views of the sea, virgin mountain-sides, colourful orange orchards and picturesque olive groves. But these dreams are not always realised, either in the short or long-term, because there are a number of problems and risks newcomers have to face, whether they are resident or absentee gardeners.

Below is a list of some typical problems and risks to help you make the right decisions and be more realistic in the plans for your garden. For convenience, they are presented as a checklist with suggestions for practical preventive or corrective actions.

TYPICAL PROBLEMS AND RISKS

TYPICAL CURRENT PROBLEMS OR FUTURE RISKS	TICK WHICH YOU HAVE OR COULD HAVE	TYPICAL PREVENTIVE/ CORRECTIVE ACTIONS
Poor quality soil.		Immediately improve your soil. See Chapter 6.1.
Shallow soil over bedrock.		Buy soil and build raised beds. See Chapters 2.5 and 6.1.
Steep, terraced or rocky plot.		Incorporate terraces and rockeries in garden design. See Chapters 3.1, 5.10 and 5.11.
Shortages and cost of water.		a. Plant least thirsty plants and install economic irrigation system. See Section 4 and Chapter 6.5. b. Aim to collect/store rainwater. See Chapter 2.16. c. Maximize areas of paths and terraces. See Chapter 2.4.
Exposure to winds and gales.		a. Plant hedges and boundary trees. See Chapters 2.9 and 2.10. b. Ensure posts and ties are firm and do not strangle trees. See Chapter 6.4.
Very high summer temperatures for persons and plants as illustrated in the following "Typical Temperature Patterns" table.		a. Retain existing or plant new trees for shade. See Chapter 2.8. b. Avoid dark coloured terraces. See Chapter 2.4.
Gardens exposed to winter frosts, even if only every five years. Occasional snow on Mediterranean beaches.		Don't plant frost tender plants unless knowingly experimenting and protecting in the winter. See Section 4 and Chapter 6.15.
Heavy spring and autumn rains turn clay gardens into a quagmire.		a. Cover plot as soon as possible with paths, terraces and areas of stone chippings. See Chapters 1.3, 1.5 and 2.4. b. Channel water to where flower beds will be. See Chapter 2.16.
Loss of initial views from garden due to new construction.		Retain or plant high hedges and spreading trees. See Chapter 2.9.

TYPICAL CURRENT PROBLEMS OR FUTURE RISKS	TICK WHICH YOU HAVE OR COULD HAVE	TYPICAL PREVENTIVE/ CORRECTIVE ACTIONS
Security problems in fast expanding areas.		Build high walls or fences (good for climbing plants), plant thick hedges and install strong gates. See Chapter 2.9.
No shade, all trees felled by builder.		Purchase and plant one or two mature trees before the first summer or plant younger trees for the future. See Chapter 2.8.
Shortage of time to prepare bare plot for lettings.		Take on a gardener fast. See Chapters 1.5 and 9.2.
Will only be an absentee gardener for the first few years.		a. Don't be over ambitious. See Chapter 1.5. b. Keep the garden simple to minimise maintenance. c. Plant only drought resistant plants.
Swimming pool dominates the current garden.		Redesign the swimming pool area as a secluded mini garden. See Chapter 3.3.
Very hard sun baked soil.		a. Dampen before attempting to dig, move or plant. b. Add compost to lighten soil. c. Use Spanish mattocks instead of a spade and fork. See Chapter 9.5.
New Spanish lifestyle doesn't allow much time for garden maintenance.		Design/redesign for minimum maintenance. See Chapter 2.17.
Geraniums decimated by geranium moth.		a. Plant more resistant trailing varieties. b. Spray preventatively weekly. See Chapter 6.7.

TYPICAL PROBLEMS AND RISKS

TYPICAL CURRENT PROBLEMS OR FUTURE RISKS	TICK WHICH YOU HAVE OR COULD HAVE	TYPICAL PREVENTIVE/ CORRECTIVE ACTIONS
No gap left by builder between swimming pool terrace and boundary walls for plants.		Build raised beds around the boundary. See Chapter 2.5.
Plot too large to ever cope with in retirement.		a. Maintain a central controllable garden and develop the rest as a wild garden. See Chapter 3.8. b. Take on a gardener. See Chapter 9.2.
Saline soil		a. Wash through with good water. b. Plant salt compatible plants. See Chapter 5.13.
Over exertion in the Spanish sun.		a. Have a realistic garden development plan. See Chapters 1.3, 1.4, 1.5, 1.6, 1.7, 2.1 and 2.5. b. Work early in the summer before the sun comes up. c. Design the garden to match your lifestyle. See Chapters 2.1 and 2.17. d. Wear a sun hat.

Above all else, find out about your local microclimate, not just the average temperature and average rainfall but also the minimum and maximum. Most Spanish gardens love the average climate, provided they are watered, but the extremes can often be hostile and surprising to newcomers.

During our nearly 20 years in Spain, our garden has experienced temperatures between 47 and -5°C, no rain for periods up to five months, non-stop pouring rain for six days, a maximum rainfall of 69cm in a day and 24cm in an hour, and on several occasions almost hurricane winds. But our love of Spain as a wonderful place for gardening is still strong, even if at times the conditions are rather challenging.

TYPICAL TEMPERATURES PATTERNS

Codes: Very high (over 35°C) = VH: High (30 – 35°C) = H: Warm (20 – 30°C) = W.
Cool (10 – 20°C) = C: Cold (0 – 10°C) = Cd: Fr =below zero.

AREA	DAY TIME TEMPERATURES				NIGHT TIME TEMPERATURES				Chance of frost inland
	W	S	S	A	W	S	S	A	
Costa del Sol	W	W/H	VH	H/W	Cd	C	W/H	C	Low/medium
Costa Blanca	C/W	W	H/VH	W	Cd	C	W	Cd	Medium/high
Costa Brava	C	W	H/VH	W	Fr	C	C/W	Cd	High
Madrid	C/CD	C/W	H/VH	W/C	Cd/Fr	C/Cd/Fr	C/W/H	C	High
Balearics	C	C	W/H	W/C	Cd	Cd	C/W	Cd	Medium/high
Canaries	W	W	W/H	W	C	C	C/W	C	Low

The above table illustrates temperatures you might expect to experience. Both the hottest and lowest temperatures need special attention when designing and planting your garden. Both shelter from northerly winds and shade are very important in Spanish gardens if the more tender plants are to be grown successfully.

1.3 ESTABLISHING A GARDEN FROM SCRATCH

You have now moved into your new Spanish home. Everything is unpacked and arranged. All the urgent DIY jobs are done and you have a clear day ahead to start on your new garden.

The first essential steps are the same, whether you have a small town- house patio, an acre or two of level or terraced land, an area of pine forest or a rocky perch on a mountainside.

As outlined in chapter 1.1, the opportunities for designing, developing and enjoying your new garden in Spain are many. At the same time, as outlined in chapter 1.2, there are start up and ongoing problems to be faced before finalising your garden design and starting the construction and landscaping work.

We therefore suggest the following initial programme of work. It might take six months if you are retired and resident or a year or two if you are an absentee gardener:

1. Review and finalise your lifestyle needs as well as those of your partner and resident family, if any. Also give some thought to the probable needs and expectations of visiting family members, visiting friends and possibly tenants, if you plan to let for part of the year. Recognise that if you want an open-air life, taking full advantage of the Spanish climate, the garden will be the place where you spend much of your time for most of the year. For us, the house is a place to sleep and a shelter from adverse weather. Chapter 2.1 will help you with this important step.

2. With your lifestyle analysis in mind, start to decide on the features and facilities you would like incorporated into the garden, for instance summer shade, sunny sheltered winter corners, a pool or Jacuzzi, cooking facilities, terraces for eating and relaxing, facilities for children and exercise. If space allows, would you

build a tennis court, table tennis terrace or petanc/boule piste? Would you like to grow organic vegetables or keep some hens? More ideas are listed in chapter 2.1 and section 3. You may end up with a long list, so set priorities for the space you have.

3. Sketch out a site plan on a large sheet of paper. Draw the boundaries, house, drive and pool (if already built) to scale. Don't draw in any more features at this stage. Make a few copies of the outline plan. Then complete the following steps 4, 5, 6 and 7 in parallel. If you have not yet finalised the siting of the house to be built, develop several tentative plans before making a final decision.

4. If you are a keen gardener, go over your plot systematically. Make notes of the following and think about whether they offer opportunities or constraints for a creative garden design:

a. The direction of the prevailing winds.

b. The existing natural features, such as mature or seedling trees, large rocks, terrace walls, hollows, slopes, clumps of herbs, bulbs and other natural plants that are worth preserving.

c. Views to be protected and enhanced.

d. Views to be blotted out if possible.

e. The depth and quality of the soil. Dig holes at several points around the garden to test for variations. See chapter 6.1.

f. The location of large surface or buried rocks. If you suspect they exist, knock a metal rod into the ground to locate them and their size. We failed to do this sufficiently. As a result, some early-planted trees remain stunted.

g. Mark on your plan where weeds grow profusely and where nothing grows wild. The former may be a good place for flowerbeds and the latter areas best covered with paths and terraces.

h. Naturally sheltered corners and the most exposed parts of the plot.

i. Signs of erosion by storm water. You may want to retain or divert natural water flows.

If you are a non-gardener and have already decided that you want nothing more than a minimalist garden, totally terraced, with high walls and no flower beds or trees, then just focus on a, c, d, and h.

5. Start to visualise a few possible garden layouts and sketch them out on a copy of the site plan. Check out their viability against your lifestyle analysis and site survey information. Have vision and be creative. Read through other chapters of the book to stimulate further ideas and enhance the ones you have. Sections 2, 3, 5, 7 and 8 include relevant chapters.

6. The chapters in Section 4 give the details of 350 popular plants. Study them to gain an insight into the plants that are the easiest to grow and the most colourful and perfumed. Especially note the indications of drought and frost resistance, if your garden has a fast drying soil or is exposed to cold winter winds.

7. Wander around your neighbourhood, public gardens in local towns and nearby botanical gardens, if they exist. Make a note of the types of plants and trees that do particularly well and those that look as if they struggle. Note whether the plants are in full sun or shade and protected from winds. Also record the fact that certain plants that you expected to see are conspicuous by their absence. You will now have a feel for the types of plants that do well. Now visit local garden centres to see what they have available – the sizes of trees and typical prices. Find out if they grow and harden off their own plants or if they are mainly imported from hot houses in Holland, France or Italy, for instance. We give guidelines for buying plants in Chapter 6.2.

8. You now have the information at your fingertips to make informed decisions, so review and integrate all your ideas into an initial garden design. We say "initial" because most of us make modifications as we progress. Before finalising the design:

• Review relevant chapters in Sections 2, 3, 4, 6, 7 and 8.

- Ensure you plan sufficient shade and shelter from winds.
- Decide whether the garden is to be formal or informal.
- Consider the colour combinations that would give you greatest pleasure. Reflect on the ideas of chapter 4.18, "Painting with Plants".

9. Now draw up a list of the main things that need to be done during the next year and decide whether the work is for you, a landscape gardener or a regular handyman gardener. We discuss this issue in depth in Chapters 9.1 and 9.2.

10. If you have not been preparing the site parallel with the above tasks, now is the time to start in earnest. Gather up all visible and shallowly buried stones, rocks and rubble and stack them in graded piles. They will all come in handy over the next few months, as indicated in this page.

11. While gathering rocks and rubble start to deal with any weeds. On a small plot, do this by hand using a Spanish tool, preferably a mattock, for less effort. Chapter 9.5 describes the tools to use on Spanish soils.

Start a compost heap in an out-of-the-way corner of the garden.

As an alternative to a compost heap, lay weeds as a thick layer on an area where you plan to have an important flowerbed or to grow vegetables. Add a layer of dampened horse, goat or sheep manure and then cover with an old carpet.

In several months the soil will have been improved with the help of earthworms and will be ready for planting. We discuss this approach in more detail in Chapter 7.4.

If you have a large plot, arrange for the plot to be ploughed or rotovated, except where you plan to construct terraces and paths, which will require a firm base.

12. You can now start laying out the garden in earnest, preferably during the autumn and winter months:

RECYCLING ROCKS, STONES AND RUBBLE

Large rocks:
Dry stonewalls
Rockeries
Pond surrounds
Enhance natural outcrops
Spray painted sculptures
Stand alone features
Weigh down umbrella

Medium sized rocks:
Edging of paths and beds
Cobbled paths/terraces
Building walls
Watering rings around trees
Topping boundary walls
Building a stone seat
Building a barbecue or oven

Small rocks or stones:
Natural surround for cacti
Mosaic designs in paths
Firming stakes and posts
Bottom drainage in pots
Weighting pond plant pots
Mulch over black plastic
Levelling pots and tables

Building rubble:
Terrace/path foundations
Soak aways/surface drains
Shed foundations
Bottom drainage of raised beds
Infill behind walls
Base for a rockery
Firming posts and stakes

a. Plant hedges first, as they will take time to mature.

b. Then plant any large trees that will provide vital summer shade.

c. Proceed to lay out a network of paths and terraces, as discussed in Chapter 2.4.

d. While laying the above, build in conduits for an electrical circuit for lights, and pumps for the pond and fountain, or consider solar alternatives.

e. Plumb in a water system with taps at several convenient places around the garden.

f. Follow with the construction of flowerbeds and special features in the most sensible sequence. Aim to complete the garden section by section, leaving areas that are not an eye-sore until last.

Guidelines for the planting, supporting, watering and feeding of plants are given in Section 6. One important task is to improve the soil in the planting holes for trees and large shrubs and flower beds in general before doing any planting. This is discussed in detail in Chapter 6.1.

13. Aim to have the garden sufficiently developed by the first or second summer, so that you can acclimatise yourself to summer temperatures and humidities, and start to enjoy an outdoor lifestyle.

Our top ten priorities would be as follows:

a. Plant a thick fast growing hedge.

b. Plant or retain trees for shade.

c. Buy a large umbrella or gazebo to use until the trees have grown.

d. Fill the semi-shade of the covered terrace or naya with colourful and cheerful plants to warm it up.

e. Fit awnings if the suns rays come into the naya or shine through unshuttered windows.

f. Make early sheltered areas comfortable. The more cool and tempting you make it, the more likely family members will realise that an afternoon in a Spanish garden does not have to be sweltering.

g. Purchase or build a temporary barbecue. Also purchase a paella ring and pan, so that a variety of dishes can be cooked al fresco.

h. Install a drip irrigation system.

i. Install a mini water feature or fountain for the cooling sound of water.

j. Close-plant your first flowerbeds to give a mass of summer colour rather than the odd dot.

14. Get used to wearing a straw hat when working in the garden.

1.4 RECOVERING AND IMPROVING AN EXISTING GARDEN

When you buy a property, the existing garden might look wonderful but by the time you move in it might have become a jungle, especially if there has been no-one resident or no gardener for some months.

You should recover the existing garden as quickly as possible and prevent further deterioration, though it's advisable to live in the garden for a year before deciding on major changes, unless the garden is a real disaster.

Decide on changes not by reference to gardens you had in northern Europe but by thinking about the new open-air lifestyle you can enjoy in Spain, the new types of plants that are possible to grow here, and the need for summer shade, winter sun and shelter from gales.

If there is a lot to do, decide immediately whether to try to do it all yourself or employ a gardener, whether to do an initial clean up and some construction work, or to garden on a continuous basis. See Chapter 9.2 for possibilities.

If you continue to employ an existing gardener, evaluate his or her efforts over the first six months before deciding whether you need to make a change. Chapter 9.3 provides some guidelines.

The following is a list of issues that you need to consider when taking over an existing garden:

a. The sighting, style and surfaces of terraces.

b. The style and sense behind the network of paths and their safety, including steps.

c. The provision for summer shade and winter sun.

d. The extent of shelter from strong winds.

e. The cleanliness of plants near to the swimming pool.

f. The cleanliness and condition of the swimming pool and its surround.

g. The existence of quiet corners for a read or siesta.

h. The possibilities for outdoor cooking.

i. The quality of hedges.

j. The framing and blocking of the best views.

k. The effectiveness of the watering system.

l. The diversity, age, condition and health of plants and whether you will have year-round colour. You will need to be resident for a year to gain the full picture.

GUIDELINES FOR TAKING OVER AN EXISTING GARDEN

Type/Condition of garden taken over	Suggested first actions
A perfectly maintained garden that at first sight you don't want to change.	a. If it is now midsummer, check that there are no wilting plants. If there are, water them fast. b. If there is a watering system, check that all jets are working and clear if necessary. If there is no watering system, consider installing one as soon as possible. c. From day one keep on top of weekly deadheading, pruning, cutting the lawn and cleaning the pool. See Chapters 3.3 and 6.8. d. Ensure that you carry out a first winter cutback in January and February as described in Chapter 6.9. e. If you do not have the time to do the above or you don't know where to start, employ a gardener. If a gardener exists keep him/her, at least for a time.
A well- maintained garden that is not really your cup of tea but the position and views are marvellous.	a. Live in it for a year and get the feel of it. b. See what flowers during each season. c. Review the garden along the line of Chapter 1.7. Decide on the most attractive features, the horrors and the priorities for change. Some issues that you will need to consider are listed in the "Some Issues to Consider" table below. d. Observe other gardens to get some idea of what plants grow well locally.
A garden that was well- maintained but has been allowed to become untidy.	a. Don't let it get any worse. b. Do a little weeding and tidying up every day. c. If you have to, weed kill gravel drives and paths. d. If there is a lawn, mow it and trim the edges. e. Prune straggly shoots on climbing shrubs and trim other shrubs to shape. f. Keep on top of it for the next year before deciding on any major changes. g. During first year proceed as in c and d in second box above.
The garden is bleak and bare. The previous owner never made much effort.	Treat as a new site and read Chapter 1.3.
The 25 year- old garden of a previously absentee gardener. What shrubs or trees exist are large, mature and possibly dominating.	a. Live in the garden for a few months and see what summer shade and winter sun you have before deciding whether any plants are really overcrowding the garden. b. Recognise that new replacement plants will take years to give the same shade and seasonal colour. Rather than cutting down mature trees, hire a tree surgeon to prune them professionally and check their health c. Decide whether the garden will be manageable. Will you be physically capable of pruning large plants such as prickly cacti, palms and yuccas, bougainvilleas and bignonias covering walls, pergolas and buildings and 20-metre-high trees? d. Review the garden along the lines of the "Some Issues to Consider" table below, and Chapter 1.7. e. Most importantly, decide where you need some extra colour. If the soil is root-bound from old trees and shrubs, it is often best to construct raised beds for planting smaller succulents, bulbs, perennials and shrubs. See Chapter 2.5.

Type/Condition of garden taken over	Suggested first actions
What was a garden is now a wilderness. Plants haven't been pruned for years and are taken over by weeds, stunted or dead due to lack of water. Small plants are smothered by larger ones, and everything is entwined.	a. Have a good breakfast. Get out into the garden with large pruners and a garden saw. b. Start to go through the garden methodically, clearing the path around the house and then follow each path in turn. c. As you progress, concentrate on removing low, overhanging branches, any dangerous spiky and pointed ends and excess branches of cacti, aloes and yuccas, so that you can start to clear areas safely. d. Aim to clear a terrace area or part of an overgrown lawn as soon as possible so that you can occasionally rest awhile in comfort. e. Clear off the cascading weeds from dry stonewalls. f. Start to clean up perennial and shrub beds one by one. Go through them carefully. Remove weeds, prune each plant as you discover it. Search underneath the larger plants for signs of lower growing plants or bulbs. The best time to clean up the flower- beds is from October to March or even May, as you can prepare the beds for new growth in the spring. If you clear the beds during the summer, the sudden change from deep shade to sun and the late heavy pruning will cause much stress to plants and some won't survive the shock. g. As each flowerbed is cleared, give it a good soaking and a liquid feed to encourage new growth. Check and restart the watering system if one exists. If not, install one. If you intend to be an absentee gardener, water sufficiently to keep plants alive. Any more may result in the return of the jungle. h. If you decide to employ someone to help – beware. He or she may come in and chop and clear and, if not an experienced gardener, may not recognize what is worth saving. i. Having rediscovered and cleared the heart of the garden, prune trees to shape and cut out rampant climbers. If cut hard, most will soon rebud and grow. j. If there are large unplanted areas of long grass and weeds, use a strimmer to speed progress. k. Finally, complete the clearing by trimming the outside hedges, possibly a tough job if they haven't been cut for years. l. Now sit back and watch the garden recover through a spring and summer. Decide whether the garden is really what you want and what you need to change in the short and longer term. Refer to "Some Issues to Consider" below, Chapter 1.7 and Section 5 before completing this task.

Some issues to consider

1. The possibility that plants such as bamboo, cacti and aloes have been allowed to grow into unsightly and overpowering clumps and whether they would be best split or cleared out and replanted.

2. The condition of the soil. Is it hard and baked? Is it the same 10cm and 20cm down? Is it root bound? If worried about some areas of plants, dig up one or two and check the extent and health of their root balls.

3. If (2) indicates a problem you can mulch the beds with 10-15cm of good

compost and work into the soil each winter for two years, or dig out each flower bed in rotation and enrich the soil as you would in a new garden. See Chapter 6.1. Recognise that you will probably loose a few plants doing this but you will also be able to consider totally different plantings.

4. The variety, state and health of fruit trees, bushes and plants. See Section 8.

5. Where could a vegetable patch be fitted in? If there is no area of good soil, could a raised bed or two be constructed? See Chapter 7.3.

6. The condition and effectiveness of the irrigation system.

7. The condition of the greenhouse and garden frame if existing.

8. The possible location of features such as a fountain, pond, rockery or vegetable garden.

9. The signs of wildlife in the garden.

Whatever you do, think hard before destroying a good existing garden, and if you do so, at least offer the plants you might otherwise destroy or bury to nearby neighbours. What you don't want may be a goldmine of new varieties to them.

1.5 CHALLENGES FACING ABSENTEE GARDENERS

The main challenge you face as an absentee gardener is the creation of a garden that can survive during long absences and is easy to rejuvenate to its full glory once you are back in Spain.

The first thing you must decide is whether you can maintain such a garden alone, working on it for very limited periods of the year, or whether you will need the help of a gardener.

The table below illustrates the different types of absentee owners as well as our suggestions for the type of gardens they should have, and whether or not they need the help of a gardener.

If you decide to hire a gardener to construct and maintain your garden, we suggest you next read the following chapters:

- Chapters 2.1 and 2.2 to help you decide on the type of garden that would satisfy both yourself and tenants when letting.
- Chapters 9.1, 9.2 and 9.3 to help you decide on the type of gardener you need.
- Chapters 2.16, 2.17 and 6.5, which include ideas for minimising the costs of watering and maintaining the garden.

To help you get to grips with what lies ahead, some important 'Do's and Don'ts are listed below. We suggest you review them and then read the following chapters:

- Chapters 2.1 and 2.2 to help you decide on the type of garden for your planned lifestyle in Spain.
- Chapters 2.16, 2.17 and 6.8, which include ideas for keeping the maintenance and watering requirements of your future garden to a minimum.
- Chapter 2.3 for suggestions related to understanding and cleaning up your site.

In many cases you will want to include time-consuming features in your design but will wisely delay working on them for a few years until you are retired. In the meantime, you can work on the garden framework, leaving spaces for those future features.

If you are resident for 25 weeks each year, you will have rather more time for gardening than when you were working, so do enjoy the challenge and exercise but be sure you find a reliable gardener who can keep your winter-by-winter progress intact during the summer months.

PROPOSED PATTERN OF PERSONAL VISITS	EXTENT OF LETTING PLANNED	TYPE OF LETTING U: Unsophisticated S: Sophisticated		YOUR PERSONAL INTEREST IN GARDENING		SUGGESTED TYPE OF GARDEN	YOUR NEED FOR A GARDENER
		U	S	High	Low		
4 weeks yearly, increasing by 2 weeks yearly for 4 years until full retirement in Spain	None	-	-	●		Develop at own pace zone by zone but keep simple until you have retired.	Low
					●	Have a basic garden laid out during year one	High
4 to 6 weeks in summer. Unlikely to retire to Spain	None	-	-		●	As above	High
4 weeks in summer, 2 at Christmas and Easter, possibly 2 in the autumn. Will probably retire to Spain	None	-	-	●		Develop at own pace zone by zone but keep simple until retired or you decide to sell.	Low
					●	Hire gardener to develop and maintain basic garden	High

PROPOSED PATTERN OF PERSONAL VISITS	EXTENT OF LETTING PLANNED	TYPE OF LETTING U: Unsophisticated S: Sophisticated		YOUR PERSONAL INTEREST IN GARDENING		SUGGESTED TYPE OF GARDEN	YOUR NEED FOR A GARDENER
		U	S	High	Low		
6 to 8 weeks in spring and autumn. No intention of retiring to Spain.	As much as possible in summer.	●		●		Self-develop basic garden as quickly as possible.	Low/ medium
			●	●	●	Have a good but low maintenance garden laid out as soon as possible and self-improve when in Spain, if a keen garde-ner. If not, get gardener to work under your supervision	High
180 days a year from October to April.	Let throughout the summer.	●		●		Work hard during first winter to get all the site neat and good framework of garden established. Progress during each winter visit to achieve the sort of garden you would have if resident.	During autumn and winter low to medium, but high during summer.
					●	Hire a landsca-ping contractor to install ins-tant garden.	High throughout the year to construct & maintain.
			●	●		As above	As above
					●	As above	As above

PROPOSED PATTERN OF PERSONAL VISITS	EXTENT OF LETTING PLANNED	TYPE OF LETTING U: Unsophisticated S: Sophisticated		YOUR PERSONAL INTEREST IN GARDENING		SUGGESTED TYPE OF GARDEN	YOUR NEED FOR A GARDENER
		U	S	High	Low		
1 or 2 weeks only. Property bought as an investment.	As much as possible year-round.	•		•	•	Hire a contractor to establish a minimal garden as soon as possible.	High
			•	•	•	Hire a contractor to establish a more complete garden to support the rental you plan to charge.	High

GETTING STARTED

Prepare a plan that gives first priority to:

a. Stabilising the soil around the house. It can get very muddy if it rains.

b. Creating a temporary terrace in order to sit and eat out (stone chippings over black plastic is the most serviceable).

c. Introducing some early colour from plants in pots at the front door and on the naya or terrace.

d. Providing shade and shelter from the wind. Plant trees on the windward side and where the main siesta terrace will be.

e. Making your garden secure and private. Build high walls/fences with tall gates and plant fast growing hedges.

TEN ESSENTIAL DO'S

1. While you are an absentee gardener, work on the garden only 40-50 % of the time you spend on holiday visits, plus a week dedicated to developing the garden each spring and autumn. Remember that you bought your holiday home in Spain to enjoy the climate and lifestyle, not to work all day in a hot garden during July and August. Work in the early hours before the sun gets up (you won't see many Spaniards in the fields after lunch until the sun is well down).

2. Be realistic about what can be achieved each year when gardening on a part time basis. Decide on a phased development plan for a period of three or five years. Delay the more complex, time-consuming features until you retire. You will then have the time to enjoy the challenges.

3. First decide on those areas of the plot that can be left for the time being as they are not eyesores for instance, the areas of meadow grass that can be strimmed each spring, copses of trees that give shelter and have a good underlay of leaf mould, areas allocated longer term as a vegetable garden, orchard or swimming pool area.

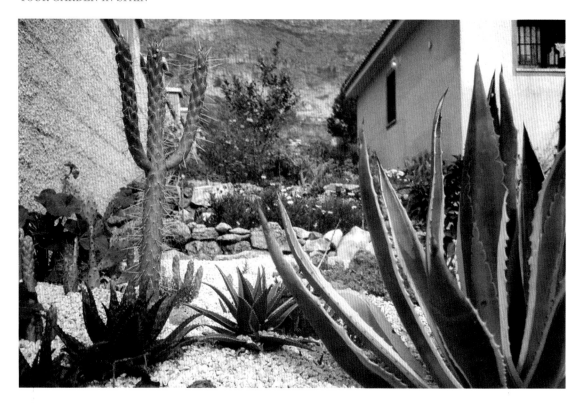

4. Then focus your efforts on the other areas, starting with the areas immediately around the house or those that can be seen from doorways and windows.

5. Recognise that all the other chapters in the book are relevant to you, but that you need to constrain your enthusiasm to have a complete garden for a few years or until you are resident.

6. As in all gardens, focus first on completing those things that make an outdoor lifestyle possible. A practical programme would be as follows.

● Lay a main path around the house, leaving a gap for plants. Cover the soil with stone chippings to avoid splash back.

● Decide where the most important terraces will be and lay them quickly with stone chippings laid over black plastic sheeting with a few drainage holes pierced with a fork – or use a proprietary woven plastic underlay.

● Decide on the joining paths and likewise lay provisionally with stone chippings

over black plastic. Later when you lay the primary paths with a solid surface you can use the chippings as the ballast for your concrete foundations. With (a) and (b) done, you can now move around and eat on pleasantly located terraces and avoid taking dust or mud into the house.

● Buy an umbrella, chairs, table and loungers and you can already enjoy the tidy areas of the garden.

● Construct a temporary barbecue, knowing that a better-designed version will come later, or invest now in a trolley barbecue or Mexican oven. Both are convenient ways of cooking and both can be moved around the garden as it develops, before you decide on their permanent location. Now you can enjoy al fresco eating between your labours.

● Start to dig a trench around the plot for planting a hedge during your first late-autumn, winter or spring visit. Put down a layer of well-rotted manure or bags of an organic compost/fertilizer along the bottom of the trench in preparation.

• Decide where you will plant trees and dig large planting holes in preparation. Use the holes as temporary compost heaps and fill with green kitchen waste. Cover with a layer of soil when full and leave for a year to rot down. Alternatively, buy bags of compost ready for planting. Plant at the same time as the hedge to give shade for next summer.

• Lay out a watering system with a battery-operated, timer switch in readiness to water the hedge and other plants during your absence. Batteries should last about a year.

• Now decide where the first flowerbeds will be, in addition to those around the house. Mark them out and improve the soil ready for your first plantings as outlined in chapter 6.1. Areas for later flowerbeds are best covered with plastic sheeting and chippings at this stage for neatness and to minimise the evaporation of moisture from the plot. Just rake away the chippings and roll back and cut the plastic to shape when you are ready to do the next bed. Edge the beds with small rocks to keep the chipping off the soil.

• Select drought-resistant, low-maintenance plants and plant as per hedges and trees to ensure that good root systems are developed to survive during the first hot, dry summer and early autumn.

• Recognise that an attractive, typically Spanish garden can be achieved using just palms, an olive tree, cacti, aloes, succulents, aromatic herbs, bougainvilleas, orange bignonia, plumbago, oleanders, lilies, agapanthus and lantanas. As an absentee gardener, buy young climbing plants with big root balls to give them the best chance of establishing themselves. Once you start to plant daisy-like margaritas, etc., your maintenance needs will start to go up, as they need regular deadheading and trimming to prevent them from becoming leggy.

7. Mulch around all plants with stones, compost or bark chippings laid over woven plastic to help keep roots cool and minimise evaporation and the weeds that grow during your absence.

8. For some instant colour, buy a few

attractive containers that will fit in with your vision of the finished garden and plant them up with trailing geraniums and annuals. Treat the annuals as expendable and replace on the first day of each visit. Put the geraniums on a low volume drip on the irrigation system.

9. Above all keep the garden simple while you are an absentee gardener to ensure that the maintenance required during the first week of each visit is low and the preparations for leaving at the end of each visit are minimal. Just remember before you leave to ensure that the watering system is working and set it on, say, five minutes a day.

10. Year by year, review whether you are still happy to persevere without a gardener to help you with the construction of paths, terraces, rockeries etc., or do some maintenance work between your visits. Consider the progress you are making and the time and effort that you are putting into it. If you are still having fun, enjoying the exercise and seeing satisfying results, stick will your solo efforts.

10 ESSENTIAL DON'TS

1. Don't waste time on laying a lawn. It will be impossible to give it the early care and attention required as well as the regular cutting and weed control afterwards, unless you retain a

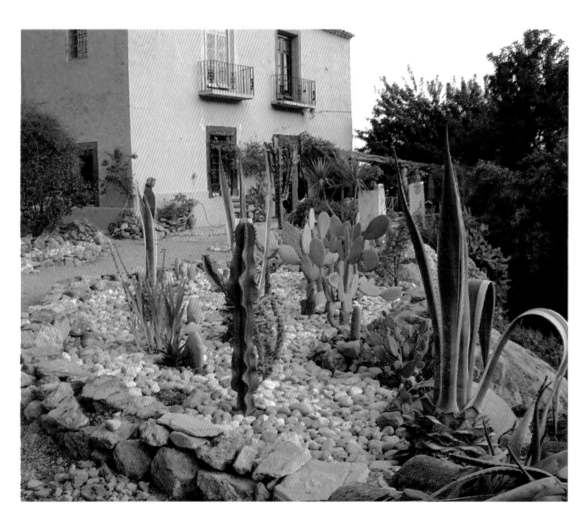

gardener. Lawns are thirsty! They need regular watering.

2. Don't plant thirsty plants and expect them to be there when you come back. The tables in Section 4 indicate which plants are most drought-resistant and vice versa.

3. Don't lay loose crazy paving or slabs without concrete foundations to create instant paths. They won't stay level after a couple of storms and the gaps between will soon be home to weeds.

4. Don't start a vegetable plot until you have the time to do it properly, but once you have enriched the soil in all flowerbed areas, you can mark out the area and start to improve the soil in anticipation of your retirement. See Chapters 6.1 and 7.2.

5. Just because you see plants growing alongside motorways and on hillsides, don't assume that Spanish plants don't need watering. They do. Even drought-resistant plants need watering until they have established deep-tap roots.

6. Don't despair if a few plants die. It's part of the learning process. They may have done so even if you had been a resident gardener.

7. Don't forget that the more you plant the more maintenance work you create. Most shrubs and perennials need to be trimmed or cut back during the winter to secure good spring and summer colour, so don't plant very vigorous climbers that will create jungles in your absence. See chapter 6.9.

8. Don't plant plants that are too tender for your area. Avoid them if you know that frost is possible on even one night a year.

9. Don't forget to provide for summer shade and shelter from cool winter breezes for the non-gardening members of the family.

10. Don't assume that your garden will be as colourful as the garden of your neighbour, a fulltime resident and keen gardener who is in the garden every day.

The above guidelines should enable you to make a quick start and steady progress visit by visit. If they come as a shock, then reconsider your decision to go it alone and employ a good gardener to assist you or a landscape gardener to do it all. But don't forget that landscape gardens still require aftercare.

1.6 TYPICAL APARTMENT AND PENTHOUSE CHALLENGES

In theory there is no reason why most apartment and penthouse terraces should not be green and colourful, at least for part of the year, even producing a few organic peppers and tomatoes. After all, the areas are small, the time required to design, construct and maintain a mini garden is rather less than a typical small villa, and water is readily at hand.

In addition, the horticultural industry is geared up to help. The manufacturers of pots and containers now offer a wide range suitable for apartment terraces. Some hang on terrace balustrades, on end and inner walls and from the ceiling like hanging baskets. Others are regular pots that stand on end sideboards or on the floor. Many now incorporate a self-watering reservoir to minimise the frequency of watering and water absorbing gels can be mixed into the potting compost to make things even easier.

Furniture designers and manufacturers are giving special attention to improving the style and durability of furniture, not only seats, chairs and sideboards for terraces, but also pergolas, trelliswork, planters etc., for penthouse roofs.

We were therefore somewhat saddened when we carried out a survey of some two hundred apartments in early July in a well established development on the Costa Blanca where the occupancies are approximately 40% permanent, 30% absentee owners who generally reside for the summer months, and 30 % holiday lets. Less than 10% had good displays of flowering or evergreen plants, less than 1% grew tomatoes or peppers, less than 10% had attractive displays of ornaments or artefacts, 15% had empty window boxes, troughs or pots, and 15% only displayed a clothes horse. Few looked like a 'home' in the sun, yet the best display could not be bettered. The situation with penthouses was very similar.

The opportunity is waiting for you. You could in one go:

- Improve the attractiveness of your outdoor living space.
- Improve the appearance of the total apartment block.
- Enhance the neighbourhood.
- Start an enjoyable small scale terrace garden or a spectacular penthouse roof garden from which to enjoy 360 degrees views.

Yes, there are a few problems such as the strong winds and salt spray on front line blocks, plus carrying all materials and plants up several floors – but the furniture arrived safely!

Where there's a will there's a way. We have seen some wonderful terraces, not only on the seafront but inland, with geraniums surviving winter snows because the heat loss through terrace doors established a sufficiently cosy winter microclimate.

Chapters 5.4 and 5.5 present practical ideas for transforming your terrace. A list of plants suitable for terraces facing east, south, west and north is included in Chapter 5.4.

1.7 IMPROVING YOUR GARDEN ANNUALLY

Most gardeners are never totally satisfied with their gardens, for a number of reasons. As the various areas of the garden mature, they look different to when first planted out. New ideas are inspired by travels, reading and visits to garden centres.

New gardeners are not fully aware of the outdoor lifestyle that the Spanish climate offers and the need for additional terraces,

facilities and internal mini-gardens becomes apparent later on.

After a couple of years, we all realise that some plants do well in our individual microclimates while others struggle or die. And the scenery can change. Unexpected new construction work can obstruct a favourite view or nearby woods can be felled.

Such internal and external changes inevitably inspire ideas for a series of improvements that year by year take us nearer to our visions of the ideal garden in Spain. Rather than initiate ad hoc changes, we suggest you carry out a thorough review of your garden once a year in order to decide which of the many possibilities will be most beneficial. The best time for a total audit is late summer or early autumn. Major changes can then be made during the cooler autumn and winter months.

Unless your garden is simply a small patio or an apartment terrace, we suggest you assess the pluses and minuses of your garden area by area.

Divide the garden up into manageable, self-contained chunks – for instance, the front garden, the back garden, the side gardens, the pool area, the naya, upstairs terraces, the cooking and eating terraces, the orchard and vegetable gardens.

Reflect on each area in turn, preferably with your partner and other living-in family members. Involve your gardener, too, if you have one. Then ask yourself the following basic questions:

a. What have been the greatest successes in the garden, season by season, during the past year?

b. How can similar effects be achieved in other parts of the garden?

c. What have been the real disappointments and failures in the garden during the past year?

d. What changes should be made now?

Sometimes it helps to look at any photographs you might have taken of the garden area you are reviewing. It also helps to use a checklist of questions (such as the one below) to ensure that nothing is left unturned.

a. Have we been totally satisfied with the overall result achieved season by season (autumn, winter, spring and recent summer)?

b. Was the development and maintenance work involved worthwhile?

c. Did we have a continuous display of colour from last September until now?

d. Are we likely to have a colourful garden this autumn and for Christmas?

e. Has there been perfume in the air when we worked, strolled, rested or ate in the area?

f. Have there been sufficient contrasts or harmony between the various colours, textures, shapes and heights of the various varieties of plants and trees and the colours of paths, terraces, walls and garden furniture etc?

g. Have we made sensible use of planted or empty pots, ornaments and sculptures to enhance the area? Could we do more or have we over done it?

h. Do we have adequate shade and are the shady areas as colourful, restful and interesting as the sunny areas of the garden?

i. Do we have shelter for sitting out in the winter sun when cool breezes blow?

j. Are all the plants and trees healthy and in good condition?

k. Are all constructed features – terraces, paths, steps, walls, etc., – attractive, in good condition and safe?

l. If annuals were planted during the past year, were they worth the effort of deadheading and the cost of watering? Should we replace them with perennial plantings?

m. What are the main focal points of the garden? Is this part of the garden one of them or is the garden too focussed on the swimming pool, for instance?

n. Do we attract a good assortment of wildlife such as butterflies, birds and lizards to the garden? When we wander round the garden, does each area/mini garden link with the next in an attractive or creative manner?

o. Do we have colourful, stimulating and entrancing views from overlooking windows and doorways, seats, etc?

p. Was the vegetable area productive? Should we extend it?

q. Did fruit trees crop well? Should we plant more or replace some with other trees or shrubs?

r. What were the watering needs? Were individual specimen plants and the overall effect worth the cost?

s. How many hours a week were spent on maintaining this area of the garden? Was it worthwhile or should we redesign the area to reduce the maintenance required? (Chapter 2.17 may give some relevant ideas).

t. Last but not least in importance, does this area enhance our enjoyment of the garden and support our planned lifestyle?

Having completed the audit area by area, ask yourself the following questions:

- What do we need to change?
- What do we need to add?
- What do we need to take out/away?
- Do we need different plantings or colour schemes?
- How can we best reduce the amount of maintenance work required now, or as we grow older?
- How can we reduce the cost of watering the garden?
- How can we make more parts of the garden eye-catching for next year?

Inevitably, you will come up with ideas for improving each area, but it might take too much effort and cost too much money to complete them all this autumn and winter. In this case, review the list, set priorities, decide when to make the changes and whether to do them yourself or seek outside help. Finally, start some of the changes now. It's amazing how the gardening year soon passes.

PLANNING YOUR SPANISH GARDEN

2.1 DESIGN THE GARDEN TO MATCH YOUR LIFESTYLE

MOST FOREIGNERS buy property in Spain with a very different lifestyle in mind to the one they knew in their previous country. This new lifestyle has more to do with the open air – in a climate that on average is warm, dry and healthy. Good gardens are an extension of the house. Many families spend more time in the garden than in the house for most months of the year, retreating inside only to sleep and avoid the occasional storm.

Such changes in lifestyle are only successful if your garden is properly designed and constructed from day one. You should provide shade for hot summer days and sheltered sun for cooler winter days, and maintain a sensible balance between terraces, paths and flowerbeds, planted with plants that require the minimum of maintenance and the minimum of watering. You should also give careful consideration to outdoor cooking facilities and to planning a pool if you decide to have one. And in making decisions it is important to keep in mind whether you are gardeners or non-gardeners, resident or non-resident owners.

We regard an early analysis of your planned lifestyle, short and longer term, as the important first step in designing your garden. With an outdoor lifestyle, what your garden and surrounding vistas look like from within the garden is more important than what the garden looks like from within the house. The latter, of course, is also important, but less so than in northern and central Europe where the garden is normally seen more from inside the house, and most of the time in the garden was spent cutting the lawn and weeding – when it wasn't raining.

So how do you want to spend your time? What proportion of the typical day do you yourself, family members and visiting friends wish to spend in the garden in good weather? What facilities will be desirable? And so on. The questionnaire that follows is designed to help you clarify your preferred lifestyle, so that the garden you end up with, whether it's just a few square metres or a hectare, is both practical and a pleasure.

A GARDEN LIFESTYLE QUESTIONAIRE

YOUR DEDICATION TO GARDENING

1 Am I a dedicated gardener interested in making gardening my number one or two hobby? Does my partner have similar interests so that the design, construction and maintenance of the garden will be a team effort?

2. For how many hours a week will other hobbies and commitments allow us to garden?

3. For how many years are we likely to be able to cope with doing everything ourselves?

4. Are we likely to take on a gardener in the short or longer term? If so, will we want to simplify the design to minimise the cost of the gardener?

EATING AND COOKING PLANS

1 How frequently would we want to eat out in the garden at breakfast, lunch and dinner (not forgetting tapas and sun downer) time?

2. Would we want to do the above on the naya, a terrace close to the house or on cosy, interesting, colourful and perfumed terraces spread around the garden?

3. How many people will be eating in the garden on a normal day, and how frequently are we likely to entertain guests? What is the maximum number we need to cater for when designing terraces and cooking facilities?

4. Do we want to cook in the open air, using a barbecue, Mexican oven or paella stand, for instance?

RESTING PLACES

1 Would we prefer to read, rest and take siestas in beautiful corners of the garden in both the winter and summer – or prefer the haven of the centrally heated and air-conditioned house?

2. Do we need a number of quiet corners or just one area to accommodate the entire family? Are we happier if everything happens on one big terrace around the pool?

3. Will we want to hang hammocks or sky chairs between or from trees?

A GARDEN LIFESTYLE QUESTIONAIRE

ACTIVITY SPACE

1. What leisure activities – for instance, quiet card or board games, painting, table tennis or basketball, petanc/boule – do we need to provide for?
2. Do we want to grow fruit and/or organic vegetables?
3. How often will children be resident? Do we need to provide for a dedicated children's corner along the lines of Chapter 3.6?
4. Do we plan to have a pool? If so, how large?
5. What open-air activities are we likely to give up and take up as we grow older?

OPPORTUNITY FOR ONGOING GARDENING CREATIVITY

1. Do I, my partner or other family members want an instant garden or a garden that will give opportunities for creative construction projects for a number of years (such as constructing ponds and waterfalls, introducing fountains and rockeries, building up collections of plants on raised beds, or building an oven)?
2. Do we need a greenhouse, cold frame and potting table? Do we need an area for compost heaps in order to recycle kitchen and garden waste?

PROVISION FOR ANIMALS

1. Do we need to provide a kennel and run for a dog or dogs?
2. Are we likely to keep poultry, rabbits or any other animals?

GENERAL AMBIENCE

1. Do we need to make the garden safe for elderly, impaired or infirm persons?
2. Do we want to feel enclosed and totally private or open to the surrounding countryside?
3. Do we want to hear the dawn chorus, evening crickets and frogs, or the constant sound of water from fountains?
4. Do we want to maximise the possibilities for colour and perfume throughout the year?
5. Do we want a formal, tidy garden or a more romantic, rustic and natural garden?
6. To what extent do we want a gardener to be around when we are in residence?

The vision and needs of your future garden are developing. Meanwhile, to stimulate an outdoor lifestyle, construct something early on that draws you into the garden on a regular basis. It could be a terrace under a tree or, initially, a large umbrella, a seat in a sheltered corner to enjoy the winter sun, a temporary barbecue until you have time to decide on your final cooking facilities – or anything that helps you to start enjoying the freedom of the garden and to adapt to the Spanish climate.

2.2 WHAT TYPES STYLES OF GARDEN ARE POSSIBLE?

The next step is to clarify your vision of the type and style of garden that you wish to develop. It is important to do this before finalising the features that it is to include.

Fourteen general possibilities are described below. Review them and choose one that would match your life style, personality and ambitions. If you already have a clear idea of what you want, use the list to test whether there might be other options worth considering seriously. One option is a garden comprising a series of connected mini gardens, each having the same or contrasting styles:

1. THE URBAN GARDEN – Straight pathways, square or oblong terraces and pool or lawn, with plants only around the boundary and in pots. Perhaps a reminder of a garden left behind, or the easiest option.

2. THE NATURAL GARDEN – A plant oriented garden aiming to recreate or even improve on nature. At the extreme, a mini botanical garden including a large range of plants with the emphasis on blending colour, perfume and textures. Perhaps meandering paths between a series of mini gardens on either side of the house.

3. THE COURTYARD OR PATIO GARDEN – Aiming to create a magical and cool inner garden with the emphasis on an attractive terrace surface, plants cascading from pots on the walls, climbers going upwards and with flowering evergreen plants around a cooling fountain.

4. THE CONTEMPORY GARDEN – Replacing and purposely challenging/changing nature. Old dry stone walls faced with painted concrete and large pebbles in wire cages as substitutes for plants.

5. THE MYSTICAL GARDEN – Using the concepts of Chinese and Japanese gardens. Raked gravel or a large pond as the sea of life, with rocks as islands and large stepping-stones to an afterlife, and carefully trained trees as the haunted forest.

6. THE OASIS GARDEN – Based on a collection of palms and yuccas around a central swimming pool or pond.

7. THE POOL RESORT – One large terrace, perhaps up to the boundary with no room for planting a hedge. An elegantly tiled swimming pool, loungers, umbrellas, and dining table and chairs providing all the necessary colour. A corner flowerbed and a few geraniums in pots.

8. THE NATURE GARDEN – Semi wild, semi tamed. Maximum of wild plants, many of which are wind-blown or introduced by birds and spring up naturally. Maximum effort to attract and preserve wildlife. Could be on a terraced hillside or in a woodland setting – an old meadow or a rocky hillside.

9. THE FINCA – The priorities being growing vegetables and fruit, keeping poultry and rabbits and a small cottage garden by the front and back door. Perhaps a bougainvillea or grapevine over an arbour for shade outside the south facing door.

10. THE MINIMALIST GARDEN – The garden for the non-gardener who wants none of the mess of plants. Interest created through the textures and colours of walls, the surface of a wall-to-wall terrace, choice of terrace furniture, ornaments and groups of unplanted pots. Perhaps a sculpture or two. Could be very stylish or very bare.

11. THE MODERNISTIC GARDEN – A simple but very effective garden around a pure white cubic-designed house. White unplanted boundary walls. A line of well-clipped citruses with whitewashed trunks set in a perfect sward of green grass, white marble chippings or grey green tinted cobbles or sets. Sophisticated and without the mess of shrubs or potted plants. Could have a pristine pool set in a white terrace surround. Every line straight and geometrical, matching the design of the house.

12. THE WOODLAND GARDEN – Created within a copse or corner of a forest. Soft natural leaf mould pathways between glades that serve as terraces with full and semi shade. Planted with shade-loving plants in keeping with the setting.

13. THE COLOURFUL DOG RUN – A bare earth yard to house the dog or dogs. The walls or high fences festooned and overgrown with thick and colourful perfumed climbers. A quick sweep up and it's all cosy and attractive for an evening barbecue.

14. THE WATER GARDEN – Set around a number of ponds, fountains and brooks. Perhaps fed from a natural spring. The sound of music, colourful flowers, flowing water and bog plants being the main ingredients for success.

Each of the concepts is very different and not all will be to everyone's taste, but each can be made very attractive with a little creativity and dedication. Be individualistic in deciding on the garden that will suit you best. There is no right answer, no right design for the 21st century but, for long-term enjoyment, do choose a garden that is compatible with your lifestyle and your house.

2.3 MAKE THE BEST USE OF NATURAL FEATURES

Whether you have just purchased a plot to build on, a new house on a bare plot or an existing unsatisfactory garden, decide at an early stage whether there are any natural features worth retaining and enhancing as focal points of your final garden. If your house is not yet built, or only partly built, persuade your builder to protect these features. They have a habit of disappearing when plots are bulldozed prior to starting construction or they can get buried under piles of building materials or rubble during construction.

The following features might be gardening treasures:

1. Dry stone terraces, perhaps a millennium or more old. Retain them to create an interesting multilevel garden, and plant the holes in the walls and above as a natural rockery.

2. Walls of old buildings that can be cleaned up and stabilised as features covered with climbers and as useful windbreaks.

3. An old crumbling building or pigeon house that could be restored as a garden shed or hen house.

4. A spring that could become the centrepiece of a water garden or the source of water for a naturally constructed swimming pool.

5. A small ravine or barranca that could have a path up the middle, surrounded by a Mediterranean rock garden.

6. A dried up streambed that could be enhanced with waterfalls to create a magical effect during infrequent flash floods. Either bank could be planted with drought resistant plants and, if the bed is wide, it could be raked as the heart of a Japanese style garden.

7. An ancient gnarled tree that could be topped and trained to grow sideways as a natural sunshade.

8. A self- or bird-seeded flowering tree.

9. A copse of pine or oak trees, which, if in good condition, can be developed as a woodland garden with vital summer shade.

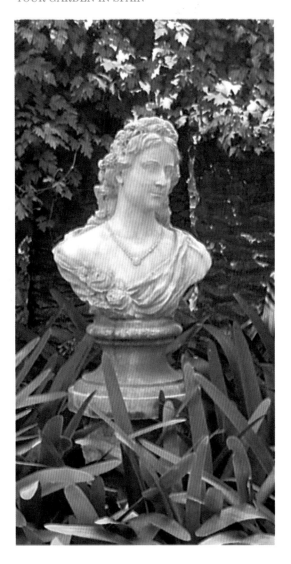

10. A rocky outcrop that could be left natural or developed into a rockery.

11. A natural slope that could be terraced into a more interesting, plant covered hillside garden.

12. A number of large rocks that could be bulldozed or craned into an interesting group.

13. An old well head, drinking trough or wash place. Each can be made the centrepiece of a terrace of potted plants, especially if in the semi shade of an old tree.

14. A natural hollow just right for a sun-

ken, sheltered terrace and a circular bowl rockery.

15. Old water channels used previously for transporting irrigation water. You may be able to tap into an un-chlorinated, agricultural water supply as an inexpensive source of water for the garden, or use as the basis of a water garden or a way of collecting rain water to feed a storage tank.

16. An area of old stone terracing that will look much more attractive than a new crazy-paved stone terrace.

2.4 ESTABLISH A FRAMEWORK OF TERRACES AND PATHS

If your garden is to be designed for an outdoor lifestyle, then terraces need to be carefully sited and constructed as pleasant places for a host of outdoor activities, and surfaced paths with interesting routes need to join up the terraces and the doorways of the house.

TERRACES

Terraces are essential features of Spanish gardens and need to be given much thought before laying a first slab or area of stone chippings. Using a systematic approach and taking initial decisions on the following points will help you achieve the best result:

● What you will need terrace areas for and when you will use them most. Recognise that it is often more practical and interesting to have a number of terraces spread around the garden rather than one large one.

● Where each terrace would be best situated. Near or away from the house? With good internal or external views? In the sun or shade? Some in full view and others quietly tucked away?

● How to fit in terrace areas for different activities. Ensure you allow space for fiesta days when you may have a large group of visitors.

• What shapes would be most interesting and practical – square, oblong, round, oval, hexagonal, or irregular.

• Where they would be best located for convenience in relation to the kitchen door, garage, drive, pool, front door, etc.

Once you have made these tentative decisions, prepare a summary along the lines of the box below, indicating the purpose of the terrace, its minimum size and preferred location.

SUMMARY OF REQUIREMENTS FOR GARDEN TERRACES

TERRACE REQUIRED FOR:	MINIMUM SIZE IN SQ. METRES	PREFERRED LOCATION	ON PATH TO
Breakfasts in sunny sheltered spot for two	15	With a good view	Not important
Winter lunches and summer dinners in sunny spots for 4 to 14	60	Near pond for sound of fountain	Kitchen
Summer lunches in shade for 4 to 14	60	Under large tree	Kitchen
Quiet winter siestas	15	Quiet sunny spot	Unimportant
Quiet summer siestas	15	Quiet shady spot	Unimportant
Cooking with barbeque, paella pan or oven	20	Sun for winter, semi shade for summer	Adjacent to eating areas
As surround to pool	130	At side of house so as not to dominate garden	Naya, covered terrace
Carport for two cars	40	Alongside drive	Front door
Greenhouse, potting table, compost heap and sink	20	In semi shade for half the day	Garage where tools are kept
Mini table tennis	30	Away from siesta areas	Not important
Setting for fountain	10	At an attractive location within network	Not important
Rotary clothes drier	10	Near utility room	To utility room

MIX OF TERRACES, PATHS AND FLOWERBEDS

TYPE OF GARDEN	% TERRACES AND POOL	% PATHS	% FLOWER BEDS NO TERRACES
MINIMALIST	90 - 100	In terraces	0 - 10
AVERAGE with pool	60 - 80	5 - 10	20 - 30
KEEN GARDENER no pool	30 - 40	10 - 20	45 - 50

Aim towards the mix of terraces, paths and flowerbeds you would like to have, with the help of the box above.

The above percentages do not include areas of larger gardens allocated to a dedicated orchard, vegetable plot, tennis court or a large mown or wild area of grass. Small formal lawns within the flower garden area are regarded as lawned terraces.

Now draw a largish site plan, marking:
- House, boundaries and gates
- Direction of the prevailing winds
- Areas that get the morning, midday and evening sun
- Location of natural features you have decided to retain
- Possible location of special features you are considering fitting into your garden design
- A strip around the boundary for hedges and boundary shrub/tree beds. (Allow a metre in small gardens and up to three to six in large gardens)
- Direction of the best external views from the garden

Cut out pieces of cardboard to represent each of your planned terraces to scale and start to lay them out on the site plan. Work out a tentative layout and sketch in a possible network of paths connecting the terraces.

Then cut out full-size pieces of black plastic to represent all but the larger terraces and lay them out according to your plan on the soil, weighing them down with rocks or piles of sand. Mark the larger terraces with a line of sand. Adjust the layouts by trial and error until you are satisfied. Now mark out the sides of pathways between terraces with lines of pebbles or sand.

Walk through your network of terraces and paths. Sit on a chair in each area where you anticipate you will be eating or resting and take in the views. If it feels right, start to lay the paths and terraces, if not, adjust the draft plan by sliding the plastic terraces around, and change the shapes and sizes of the large layouts by adjusting stone or sand lines until you achieve what you want.

PATHS
Before rushing out to buy materials or asking the builder to construct a simple concrete path around the house, it is important to first do some basic design work. Start by asking yourself the following questions: Why do we need paths and how wide should they be? Would they look best straight or curved and what surface would look most attractive and interesting? Am I capable of doing a good job or should I find someone to construct them for me?

WHY PATHS?
Here are some reasons for establishing a network of paths around the garden:
1. To enable persons of all ages to move around the garden easily and safely in any weather, whether or not they are healthy and fit.
2. To move trays of food or drinks, wheelbarrows, gas bottles, garden machinery and furniture around the garden without fear of tripping or unnecessary strain.

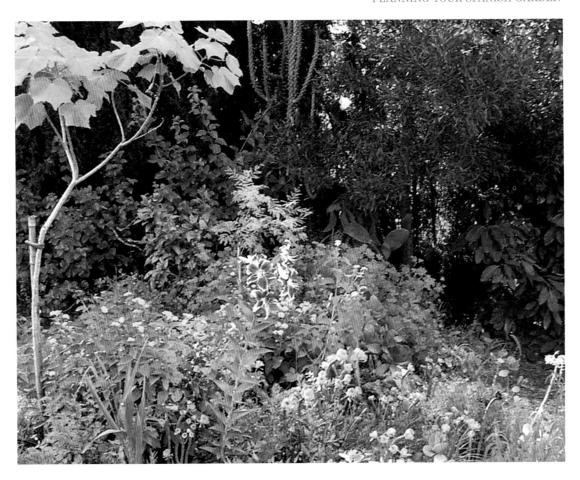

3. To link the different areas, mini gardens and features in an interesting way.

4. To create and approach views within and beyond the garden that are interesting and even spectacular.

5. To reduce garden maintenance and water use by lowering the percentage of the garden planted as flower beds, vegetables or lawn.

6. To shelter and provide a moisture reservoir for the roots of plants lining the paths.

7. To make the garden look longer or wider by designing paths which become narrower from the beginning to the end.

8. To establish the style and aesthetics of the garden.

Most garden paths are straight, even when alternatives would be more interesting and practical. The reasons for this are various. Straight paths are easier to envisage, design and construct than ones that are curved. Paving stones are usually square or oblong, and the laying of curved paths with natural stone slabs as crazy paving is seen as time consuming and expensive.

But here in Spain the reasons are no longer relevant for most gardeners. Many now have the time to spend on laying out an ideal garden, stone slabs are often relatively inexpensive, stone chipping even less so, and good cheap labour is often available. So consider the possibilities of curved, twisting, zigzagging and narrowing paths to add interest and depth. For instance, use stones to lay out a path with parallel sides then change the design so that the near end is widened and the far end narrowed. You will find that an optical illusion makes the narrowing path look longer than the previous one with straight sides. You can enhance the effect by placing a large pot or rock at the beginning of the path and a half size one at the other end.

Many paths are constructed against the wall of a house or outside walls and fences. What a pity that no space is left to plant interesting climbers, shrubs and other plants that can prevent the splash back of dripping rain just as effectively as a path and is much more attractive. However, if an old property has questionable foundations it is wise to concrete up to the walls and avoid close plantings. In all cases, plants with thick trunks and penetrating roots are to be avoided.

Keep slopes very gentle. All surfaces can become slippery with rain or frost. If you need to lose height, use steps or a wheelchair type slope with railings. If possible, use slopes of paths and terraces to channel rainwater to where it is most needed.

Main paths should be 90 to 120cm wide (150 if for persons with wheel chairs or walking frames). Secondary paths should be 50 to 70cm wide, and tertiary paths 30 to 40cm.

For safe steps risers should be 15 to 17cm (10 to 12cm for shallow steps, to create a special effect or to make it easier for infirm persons). The depth of steps is typically 30 to 50cm but a metre or more can be used on long, gentle gradients.

SURFACE MATERIALS
FOR TERRACES AND PATHS

Here are some suggestions for terrace and path surfaces (consider using a number of different surfaces for interest):

1. Light coloured stone chippings laid over plastic are the fastest way of constructing interesting terrace areas and paths on level surfaces or on gentle slopes. We favour the pink tinted and 15-20mm graded chippings, as they look attractive, keep clean and soon bed down to give a firm surface. A fortnightly rake or sweep will keep them looking tidy and torrential rain will soon soak away. On steeper slopes you may need channelling to run off surface water and prevent erosion.

2. Dark coloured chippings create a contrast, but they can look drab in large areas and become more heated by the sun than lighter colours.

3. Square or oblong stone slabs or blocks are excellent in both formal and informal situations, however they can be expensive and very time consuming if you are chipping or cutting the rocks to size yourself. A variety of colours are available. Lay them on a well-prepared concrete foundation to get the levels right to ensure they do not become uneven when heavy rains make the ground underneath soggy. Prepared natural stone can be expensive, so it may be appropriate to consider less expensive concrete slabs that now come in a variety of colours and a range of surface designs.

4. Crazy paving is a less expensive rock slab solution. In most situations, don't be tempted to lay them directly on the soil or on loose sand as they will soon become uneven after storms and the gaps between slabs are more likely to become home for deep rooted weeds than low growing herbs and succulents.

5. Cobbles constructed from well-rounded river pebbles and stones can be very attractive, especially if different sized and coloured pebbles are used to create interesting patterns in the surface. Look out for design ideas next time you visit an old monastery or cobbled village. Work on a square metre at a time to ensure that you get the levels correct.

6. Old bricks laid in a variety of patterns create charming effects and are hard wearing. The traditional herringbone design can be especially pleasing to the eye. Coloured concrete patterned surfa-

ces are a modern alternative, but normally are not as attractive, although some contractors now offer more than twenty designs and can lay many square metres in a day.

7. Grey concrete paths and terraces are uninteresting, so consider using them as the base for a more interesting alternative. Luckily there are now hard wearing polyurethane paints that can be used to paint existing concrete areas. Tints can, of course, be mixed into new concrete and can be very useful in brightening up and adding interest to an economy minimalist garden. Asphalt is also available in a range of colours but tends to look a little urban.

8. Bark chippings can be used to good effect in woodland settings or between raised beds in the vegetable garden.

9. Grass paths can be attractive, especially in the orchard and vegetable areas, but they tend to be scorched or untidy, depending on the weather, unless a regular watering, cutting and edge cutting programme is kept to. For many who do not have a gardener, this will be unnecessarily time consuming.

10. Stone or round concrete stepping-stones can be used for little-used paths across flowerbeds or lawns and large terracotta tiles are another alternative to consider. Choose the rougher finished variety for effect. They are also less slippery when wet than the smooth surfaced tiles, but both tend to gather moss in shady situations. Contractors now advertise non-slip treatments. Shiny-surfaced interior tiles are easier to sweep and wash down, but are not safe or aesthetically pleasing.

11. Railway sleepers have been used to create paths and steps in many informal gardens, but the sale of railway sleepers is now officially banned within the European Community, as the chemicals used to treat the wood are regarded as unsafe.

12. Low-growing herbs such as creeping thyme, camomile and dichondra repens can be used, but are more practical in semi-shaded areas. They will need regular watering and are unlikely to be very hard wearing if used for a main terrace or thoroughfare.

13. Wooden slatted paths and terraces can look very attractive in both formal and informal settings. Although very hot to walk on barefooted during the summer, they can be very useful in boggy or sandy areas.

14. The pea shingle, often used in the UK, is not normally available along the Costas, and builders use graded crushed rock as an alternative in concrete mixes.

15. Broken-up building rubble can obviously be used to create temporary paths in hidden parts of the orchard and vegetable plot or around the potting shed, but is not an attractive long-term solution.

16. Deep compost and well-rotted manure can be used to create weed inhibiting and moisture saving paths between rows of vegetables. In dry weather they are fine but rubber boots will be required for a few days after storms.

17. Bare earth is practical in very dry areas where weeds and heavy rainfalls are not major problems.

EDGINGS

Edgings are useful to contain stone chippings and also to add interest and a formal finish to both paths and terraces. Pebbles, small rocks, natural or glazed terracotta edging tiles or white painted concrete humps can all be used to good effect. Paths are softened when edged with ground cover plants or low clipped box or herb hedges.

MAINTENANCE

Sweep or vacuum paths and terraces regularly and repair any cracks or loose slabs as they occur. If in the shade, remove moss build-ups once or twice a year to prevent them becoming slippery when it rains. Washing up liquid and a stiff brush will remove most. If a tougher build-up has been allowed, use a pressure hose or a proprietary moss remover.

FURNISHING

Treat terraces as outside rooms and furnish tastefully, according to their use and situation.

2.5 DESIGN MANAGEABLE FLOWER BEDS

The number, location, type and style of flowerbeds are important decisions in all gardens. A number of practical possibilities are described below to help you decide on the most attractive and appropriate for your garden. The table summarises some typical situations, shapes and plantings. Recognise that the number, size and complexity of plantings will be the main determinants of the hours of garden maintenance work you or a gardener will need to do each week and the extra work involved in the annual winter cut-back. If you plan to be an absentee gardener, without a gardener during your long absences, minimise the number of flowerbeds and keep plantings simple.

TYPES OF FLOWERBEDS

In each situation a number of types of bed are possible, including:
- Beds level with the surrounding areas.
- Banked beds – for instance, round a raised pool or as dividers between different levels.
- Raised beds to add height and reduce bending. The practical height is between 30 and 90cm. The width should be 75cm (or 1.5 metres if you are able to work from both sides).
- Beds for planting directly, or beds in which to sink planted pots.
- Sunken beds which allow you to flood thirsty plants.
- Rockeries, as detailed in Chapter 3.1.

EDGINGS

The edge of beds can be the edge of paving or the lawn, or they can be edged with small rocks, large pebbles or terracotta pieces. Raised edgings are essential if they are located within areas of stone chippings.

SURFACES

The surface of planted beds can be mulched or left as bare earth. With mulched beds fewer weeds grow, less water evaporates, and stone or wood chippings can be attractive in their own right.

CHOICE OF PLANTINGS

Your choice of plants and trees will need to take into account the colour schemes you wish to create, your need for a single height or banks of progressively taller plants, the desirability of flowers 365 days a year, the need for perfume and your local micro climate.

Full details of some 350 popular plants and trees for a wide range of garden situations are included in Section Four. Read the details regarding eventual heights, widths, and drought and frost resistance carefully before making your final choice.

Wander round your neighbourhood and visit local municipal or botanical gardens to gain an idea of how large mature plants can become. You will have a few surprises!

Decide on whether you want dedicated or mixed beds, a subtropical or Mediterranean garden, and what tropical plants, if any, will have a good chance of surviving your worst winter weather.

Where possible, plant closely for maximum impact, to create shade for the roots of plants and to hide irrigation pipes. Also, weeds have difficulty growing if they receive no direct sunlight. Plant some sacrificial plants, recognising that as they grow they will need to be thinned to avoid overcrowding. Annuals can be used in this way in early years.

Decide on whether you prefer single or multi-coloured beds, harmony or vivid contrasts between areas of the garden, and whether you wish to create some cool beds, using whites, blues and greys or hot beds using vivid reds, oranges and yellows.

FLOWERBEDS – SOME TYPICAL LOCATIONS, SHAPES AND PLANTINGS

WHERE	POSSIBLE SHAPES	POSSIBLE PLANTINGS
Around the border of the garden for hedges	Long oblong strip	Just the hedge or with a perennial or shrub bed in front.
	Long oblong strip with oval front edge.	As above with low growing ground cover or annuals at the front.
	Long oblong strip with wavy edge.	As above, with bulbs mixed in.
	Wider corner beds.	As mini copses of trees or a major shrubbery.
Along the drive	Long strip following edge of drive.	A low or high hedge depending on the length of the drive. Roses, cacti, irises etc.
	A series of small round or square beds set in an area of stone chipping or grass.	A single variety or mix of flowering or evergreen trees, or shrubs. Collections of cacti or succulents. Annuals if in the cooler north.
Between the house walls and surrounding paths or terraces	Long oblong, minimum 50 cms wide.	Climbers up the walls or medium height shrubs to protect walls from splash back from rainwater running off the roof.
	Square or oblong in corner recesses or with a curved edge.	As above or a mini shrubbery, rockery or plant a specimen tree
Around terraces	Narrow or wide following contour of terrace.	In principal, anything of any height, including climbers on trellis.
In the centre of terraces	Square, oblong, round, oval, hexagonal or irregular.	In principal, anything including a tree or trees to give shade. Plant plants that enjoy the semi shade under the tree as it spreads.
Around the drip line of mature trees	Circular or special shape to match situation.	Whatever creates an attractive transition from the shade under the tree to the open garden and brightens up the shady area as a place to have a siesta or eat out of the sun.
Around the trunks of trees	Square or round.	Plants that will survive well in the shade of a tree with dense foliage or the semi shade of a more open tree.
Around the pond	Generally best to follow contour of pond or have a square or oblong bed with pond set in centre.	Low growing perennials and ground cover plants that will ensure a clear view of the flowers of pond plants and any fish. If the planned view is from one side only, plant taller plants on the far side as a backcloth.
Within the open space of the garden	Any shape with a flat surface.	In principal anything, taking into account the size of your garden and the internal vistas you want to develop.
	Circular or square with a domed surface to show off plants.	Use for a special display of annuals, bulbs, herbs or low growing perennials or shrubs.
Alongside paths	Strip beds following contour of path	Low hedges of clipped herbs, shrubs or box, annuals, perennials, roses, shrubs, or bulbs.
	Wide beds on either side with path through middle.	Plant, shrub beds or copses.

FLOWERBEDS – SOME TYPICAL LOCATIONS, SHAPES AND PLANTINGS

WHERE	POSSIBLE SHAPES	POSSIBLE PLANTINGS
Around the pool terrace.	Follow the contour using the outer shape that looks most pleasing.	Plants that have a low flower and leaf fall to minimise the chance of debris being blown into the pool. Plant other plants further back using the idea of concentric plantings described in Chapter 3.3.
In the face of a dry stone wall.	Aim to cover the wall with cascading plants planted in the holes between rocks.	Drought resistant succulents and herbs.
On the vertical walls of the house or patio. *On balconies, terrace walls or railings.*	Window boxes or rows of pots.	Geraniums, petunias, and succulents are the most traditional. Refer to Chapters 3.10 and 5.10 for ideas.

See chapter 4.17 Painting with Plants.

Take into account the colour and texture of leaves and the architectural form of plants, not just the colour of the flowers.

If you plant isolated specimen trees or shrubs for their individual beauty, don't spoil their effect by using competing under plant-ings. The planting and care of plants is covered fully in the chapters of Section Six, and the selections of plants for a wide variety of geographic locations within Spain are listed within the chapters of Section Four.

At each autumn garden review, decide on the successes and failures of your various flowerbeds and change accordingly for the following year. Achieving a wonderful long-term garden is always an repetitive process.

There are many plants that survive in Spanish gardens without ever showing their best, so do ensure that you improve the soil in all flowerbeds before you start to put in plants. You will need to dig well-rotted compost and manure into some, and others will need improved drainage by working in coarse sand or grit. See chapter 6.1

2.6 IS A LAWN FOR YOU?

Lawns are not as popular in Spanish gardens as in Northern Europe, for a number of good reasons.

A well-kept lawn needs much water and, except in some mountainous regions, rain is infrequent. Water is also in short supply and expensive in some areas, especially in the hot summer months.

Many lawns look their best in the winter and spring, not during the summer. Even with a watering system, growth will be uneven and the lawn will look untidy, unless a perfectly balanced spray irrigation system is achieved.

Wild lush meadows are not natural except in the north and northwest of Spain and creating a lawn is therefore often fighting with nature. The work involved in the preparation, planting and aftercare of a good lawn is extensive, onerous and costly. Mowing it can be time consuming and regular edge trimming can be a chore. Wind-blown or machine-distributed cuttings and seed can self-seed in adjacent flower-beds, and be carried by feet into the swimming- pool.

For many gardeners, especially those with small and moderate gardens, the effort and expenditure is better spent on terraces, areas of interesting, coloured stone chippings, special features and flowerbeds.

A weedy, patchy lawn is a nightmare for the proud gardener. There are alternatives that look good, require less upkeep and use less water.

A lawn does have its advantages, of course, and many new gardeners in Spain are willing to take up the challenge. A green lawn can be a reminder of home in northern Europe. It can create a cool look in the summer, and a contrast to a surrounding dry landscape. It can also be a wonderful way to blend a garden into the surrounding hills and woods if you are living in a higher-than-average-rainfall mountain area.

Grass is cooler to walk on than stone slabs in the summer, provides somewhere soft for the children and the dog to play as well as a handy surface for practicing your golf putting.

A lawn gives a feeling of tranquillity without the stimulus of seasonal flowers or colour changes and, if immaculate, can be a joy.

DO IT PROFESSIONALLY

If you do decide to include a lawn in your garden layout, make sure that you do it professionally, whether you do it yourself or use an outside contractor. A good lawn requires even more care here than in northern Europe. Success can depend on the factors shown in the box below.

A good horticultural shop will be able to offer you a wide range of practical seed mixes and help in selecting the one most suitable for your: location and conditions, such as a sunny area, shady or semi-shaded position, near the sea with salt spray, in an inland valley, your average local rainfall season by season, minimum and maximum temperatures and type of use.

SOWING

The best sowing time is early spring or autumn. Sow seed evenly over the surface by hand or using a push seeder. Sow first around the edge and then from end to end and finally from side to side to achieve as even a coverage as possible. Rake the seed lightly into the top of the soil and roll. Then water in well with a fine sprinkler. Avoid causing build-ups of water and the development of rivulets. If possible keep some seed back for later repairs.

THOROUGH PREPARATION OF THE SEED BED

1. Clear the area well, digging out all rubble and rocks down to around 30cm or the depth of a fork.
2. Rotovate and harrow the chosen area, working in well rotted chicken manure and compost from an eco park.
3. If you cannot obtain the manure, dislike the smell or have a soil depth of less than 20cm, import some rich soil to top up to that depth.
4. Decide how you are going to water the lawn. A convenient method is to sink a network of water pipes and pop-up spray heads into the soil at this stage. Install the system so that it can be used as soon as the seed is sown – and you will not have to cut channels later in the established lawn.
5. Rake to a fine tilth, and level. Roll and check levels. Remove high spots and fill in hollows. Repeat until totally level on the flat or across your chosen slope.

THE RIGHT TYPE OF GRASS

When your lawn area is thoroughly prepared, you need to select the appropriate seed, plantlets or turfs you are going to use, taking into consideration the type of grass you want and its watering and maintenance needs. For some practical options, see the box on the next page.

PLANTING

The best time for planting gramma plantlets is the autumn. Plant them 8 – 10cm apart and then sow normal grass seed between. The idea is that the grass seed will cover the bare areas in spring until the gramma grass gets going. In mid summer the grass dies off and the gramma takes over.

SELECTION OF AN APPROPRIATE SEED, PLANTLETS OR TURFS

TYPE OF LAWN AND PLANTS	NORMALLY PLANTED AS	WHEN TO PLANT	WATERING NEEDS	BEST SITUATIONS	MAINTENANCE NEEDS
Course e.g. Gramma	Seeds or plantlets	Spring/ Autumn	Moderate	Any, including high rough use, when left five cms long	Medium. Cutting in proportion to watering
Semi course e.g. Rye	Seeds	Spring/ Autumn	High	Well-used areas	Medium
Fine -e.g. Bermuda grass	Seeds	Spring/ Autumn	High	Little- used areas	Very High
Fine/semi coursemix	Seeds, or turf	Spring/ Autumn	High	High or moderate use areas	High
A herb alternative e.g. Dichondra repens or Thymus serpyllum	Seeds	Spring/ Autumn	Moderate	Low usage in semi-shade and shade	Low, rarely need to trim and doesn´t need mowing

WATERING

Keep the sown area damp with a fine spray until the roots are well established and it is ready for its first cut. Then water to keep the grass green but not overly lush. This will maximise the time the lawn will look at its best, minimise the frequency of mowing and control your water bill. A deep watering down to the lowest roots twice a week in mid summer will be more effective than a surface sprinkle twice a day. If you are unsure about the effectiveness of your watering, dig out two 20cm square turfs – one before and one after watering – to examine the soil/root conditions. Replace the turfs and firm, and then give them a good soaking and a second firming.

AN APPROPRIATE CUTTING CYCLE AND LENGTH

The frequency of cutting will depend on the fertility of the soil, top-up fertilising, the extent of rainfall and watering, the wear and tear of the lawn – and your standards of tidiness and perfection. A short cut will dry out and burn quicker but kill off any weed seedlings as they occur. A long cut will dry out more slowly, be more hardwearing but will allow weeds to become established. If you want an area of meadow rather than a civilised lawn, just let the grass grow and make hay twice, in the spring and late summer.

SEASONAL MULCHING

All lawns benefit from an annual spring scarification – to remove dead grass and moss – and a light mulching with a sand/ compost or sand/peat substitute mix. Sprinkle the mulch evenly over the grass after scarification and then brush into the grass. If it does not rain within a week, water it in.

FEEDING

Lawns are hungry. Give the lawn a dressing of a balanced lawn fertiliser each spring and autumn. Don't over feed, and ensure that it is washed down into the soil as soon as applied with a copious watering to avoid burning the lawn.

REGULAR WEED CONTROL

Remove deep-rooted perennial weeds by hand and weed kill with selective weed killer each spring. If you have decided to treat your grass area as a pasture with wild flowers, just let the weeds grow.

CONTROL OF USE

The intended use of the lawn would have determined the type of grass sown or planted. If you want a perfect lawn, ensure that no hard wearing activities are allowed.

REPAIRS

If patches develop, dig up the area to a depth of 10cm, rake to a fine tilth, firm and re-sow the patch with the same seed as used originally.

Over a period of time visible and annoying bumps, hollows and broken edges may develop. Make an 'X' cut through the turf over each bump. Roll back the turf from the centre of the 'X' and then scrape out the excess soil. Roll back the turf one or two times and take out more soil until you are happy that all is level. Put the turf back, firm and water well. Hollows are easier. Just fill them with a sand/compost/soil mix, and firm.

To remake the curved or straight edge of the lawn, cut out the offending area and turn the turf round. Cut to shape. Fit odd pieces into the interior gap. Fill any holes with a sand/compost/soil mix and finally firm and water well.

SOME PRACTICAL ALTERNATIVES TO A LAWN

If you don't want the bother and expense of a lawn, there are plenty of alternatives to choose from.

1. A swimming pool and terrace.
2. An orchard with or without an underlay of wild grass and flowering wild flowers, allowed to grow naturally with a once or twice-a-year cut/strim.
3. Large terraces surrounded by mature trees for summer shade.
4. Areas of attractively coloured stone chippings. Larger areas can be broken up with flower-beds surrounded by rocks, a rockery, specimen palms, cacti and succulents. They can also be laid with contrasting areas of differently tinted chippings, or even raked into designs as in Japanese gardens.
5. A simulated dry riverbed.

6. A copse of evergreen or flowering deciduous trees with paths of stone or wood chippings meandering through.
7. A simulated oasis with a central swimming pool or water lily pond surrounded and shaded by a circle of palms.
8. An organic vegetable plot.
9. Just more of a colourful Spanish garden.
10. If you have a very large garden to provide privacy, or as investment with the intention of selling off one or two building plots, fence unused areas off and leave them wild.

2.7 LARGE AREAS OF STONE CHIPPINGS

Many gardeners have laid large areas of stone chippings as paths, formal terraces, patios, courtyards and as a general cover for bare sun-baked soil or sticky mud after torrential rains. The benefits, problems and ways of livening them up are outlined below.

THE BENEFITS

1. You can quickly produce a clean tidy surface, which is especially important if you are an absentee gardener.
2. Chippings laid with the minimum thickness of 10cm over black plastic will suppress weeds.
3. Chippings serve as a good mulch for shrubs and trees planted through plastic into the earth below.
4. A reservoir of moisture builds up under the plastic if holes are made in the plastic sheeting, or woven plastic material is used. This is very beneficial when plants are planted through the chippings/plastic or alongside in an adjacent flower-bed.
5. The surface can soon be swept or vacuumed, even under trees.
6. A large circle, square or oblong of chippings can be a good substitute for a lawn. Less preparation and maintenance is required and in many cases, chippings

frame or set off plants better than the green of a lawn. Also, most importantly, your watering bill will be very much lower.

7. A good contrast to the dominant green of the rest of the garden.

8. Shows off central features well.

9. Chippings are relatively inexpensive.

10. Easy to lay and rake flat.

11. Can be used on gentle slopes or as a series of low terraces behind low dry stone walls.

12. A minimalist garden can be quickly established as a permanent garden or as a base from which to develop a full garden. At each stage the chippings can be raked back and the plastic rolled back to expose the soil for preparing the next flowerbed, vegetable garden, pond, etc.

13. Flooding from heavy rains quickly drains away, and chippings provide a mud-free environment.

COLOUR AND SIZE

Our favourite is a 1 1/2 or 2cm graded light-coloured chipping because it looks bright, clean and does not absorb and reflect the heat as much as the darker colours. However, there are a wide range of sizes, colours and tints available from quarries by lorry load and in smaller quantities from garden centres.

PROBLEMS

1. The need to sweep or rake to give a per-

fect finish for special occasions – but it doesn't take long.

2. The need to sweep, rake or vacuum leaves, especially under trees – but you don't have to cut the lawn.

3. The building up of humus in chippings under trees if they are not cleaned frequently.

HOW TO LIVEN UP LARGE AREAS

1. Surround the area of chippings with flower or shrub beds.

2. Plant specimens – such as palms, cordylines, flowering trees, aloes or a mini orchard – through the chippings.

3. Create a cartwheel herb bed, perhaps with a bay in the centre – surrounded by four segments of rosemary, sage, lavender and rue between the spokes and with an outer tyre of variegated thyme.

4. Make a raised bed, in the centre or offset, to house a collection of succulents, cacti or bulbs.

5. A bed of yellow lantanas surrounded by purple ground cover lantanas.

6. A fountain or pond.

7. An aviary.

8. A seat in the sun or under a tree.

9. A raised bed vegetable garden.

10. A pattern of square beds planted with herbs and perhaps edged by a low box hedge, as sometimes seen in monastery gardens.

2.8 PROVIDE FOR SHADE

Why shade? One could well ask the question when one sees developers bulldoze mature trees or copses to create clear building sites; or expatriates who buy a traditional Spanish property with a shady garden and chop down most of the trees in order to build a larger terrace around the pool, enlarge the lawn for sunbathing, or do away with the bother of sweeping or raking up leaves.

Such actions are a great shame as shade has always been an essential ingredient of successful gardens in Spain. It provides

personal protection from the burning sun. The cool deep shade of an ancient tree is a wonderful place to hang a hammock or sky chair for a restful siesta, or to lay out a table for a midsummer luncheon party.

Shade or semi-shade is the natural haven for many naturalised Spanish garden plants that originated in the jungles of the South and Central Americas and Asia – and many seedlings and young propagated plants develop best in dappled shade.

There are several ways to provide for shade, some are natural and others are special constructions that have become popular over the years.

SHADE FOR PERSONS AND PLANTS

1. Large, spreading, mature specimen trees or groups of younger or smaller trees.

2. The natural shade along the north side of the house, and tall hedges along the southern boundary.

3. The natural shade of enclosed patios, especially with a centrally planted tree.

4. A deep naya – an important feature of many old Spanish properties and now luckily incorporated in the design of many new houses.

5. Wooden or metal pergolas draped with vigorous climbing plants.

6. Shady passage ways filled with shade-loving plants as often seen in villages in the Alpujarras.

7. A grape vine trained along a metal frame. The traditional front or back porch in many Spanish villages.

8. Pergolas covered with canvas, canes or tiles.

9. Large umbrellas. The range of shapes and colours now available ensure that one can find something to fit in with any garden setting.

10. The traditional swing chair with a canopy.

11. The increasingly popular open tent-like gazebos now available in a variety of sizes cloths and colours.

increasingly popular, although restricted by urbanisation regulations and local bylaws in some areas.

Their benefits are as follows:

1. The provision of privacy from neighbours, passing pedestrians, lorries and, of course, builders if you are living on an expanding urbanisation. Privacy allows all parts of the garden to be used unseen.

2. A windbreak from hot summer winds and cold winter winds. In many situations it will be impossible to grow tender sub-tropical and tropical plants without such year-round shelter.

3. Shade on the north side for summer terraces and plants that are best out of direct sunlight.

4. A continuous outer wall of green from a hedge or climbers trained up walls, panels or a wire mesh fence. Some are in flower for many months of the year.

5. A natural transition from your garden to external vistas.

6. A contribution to personal security if combined with high gates, but do select gates that enhance the appearance of your house and the neighbourhood.

7. Reduction of the noise transmitted to or from adjacent properties.

8. Encourage wildlife, especially birds that roost or nest.

INTERNAL DIVIDING HEDGES

Hedges or fences of various heights can be useful within the garden for the following reasons:

1. To help divide the garden up into a number of zones or mini gardens.

2. To provide internal screens and windbreaks, for instance around the pool, the Jacuzzi, an eating terrace, cosy corners, a seat for winter days, the tennis court, carport, orchard, the children's garden or the vegetable garden.

3. To line the drive. A long curved drive lined with a well-clipped hedge can be an impressive entrance to a larger property.

4. To add interest and intrigue as one wanders from one part of the garden to

12. A traditional Spanish outdoor kitchen with room for a dining table.

13. Awnings and blinds outside nayas or doorways – especially useful for apartment and upstairs terraces and balconies.

With such a choice, no garden should be without shade. Personally, we believe nothing beats the shade under the natural umbrella of a spreading tree. Carobs, oaks, figs, olives, tall varieties of citrus, avocados, palms, pines, acacias and many other flowering trees can provide useful shade.

2.9 HEDGES, WALLS, FENCES AND GATES

EXTERNAL BOUNDARIES

High hedges, fences and walls around the entire perimeter of the garden are becoming another, passing under green arches and through verdant – perhaps perfumed – passage ways.

5. To provide the basis of a maze in a large garden.

6. To surround formal flower-beds. Rose, hibiscus and perennial beds can be well presented in this way.

7. To edge pathways or around a lawn.

8. To give shelter for wildlife such as birds, lizards, insects, etc.

SOME POSSIBLE HEDGING PLANTS

There are many plants available for different types of hedges, including the following:

1. **For thick high boundary hedges** – cypress, thuja, oleander, pittosporum, privet, gandula, bay, berberis, lantana, and hibiscus. A three- metre high prickly pear cactus hedge will really keep people and animals out.

2. **Colourful climbers for fences** – bignonias, bougainvilla, jasmine, plumbago, honeysuckle, Brazilian flame vine, solanum, morning glory, and ivies.

3. **For medium height internal hedges/screens** – box, bottlebrush, euonymus, pittosporum, lantana, teucrium and hibiscus.

4. **For low internal hedges** – box, lavender, rosemary, euonymus and rue.

SHAPING HEDGES

Hedges need to be regularly trimmed to stimulate dense foliage. Once dense, some of the hedging plants listed lend themselves to topiary and can be clipped into interesting shapes – sloping sides, curving tops, arches, balls, birds sitting on the hedge, etc. Hedges flower less if kept tightly clipped.

GATES

The choice of gate has a major impact on the appearance of a property from the road and also on the style of garden inside the gate. The choices include the following:

1. **Stylish** – traditional cast and wrought iron gate in a whole range of simple or artistic designs.

2. **Urban** – the solid sheet metal gates now in fashion. They can be constructed from a single sheet – or eight smaller interwoven bowed sheets – to create a pseudo woven effect. Some single sheet gates have raised designs that add interest and style.

3. **Wooden** – the four- or five-barred gate most suitable for natural surroundings, or an elegant solid wood gate set in an archway. Normally they have a small inset pedestrian door. Traditionally varnished, they can add style, security and the image of entering a large townhouse or country estate.

Choose what goes best with your property and the style of garden.

2.10 CREATE WINDBREAKS AGAINST STRONG WINDS

Many Spanish gardens are in exposed positions and windbreaks are required to cope with regular strong gusty winds that can spoil your enjoyment of an otherwise attractive garden by making it chilly to sit out in the winter or on a summer evening after a scorching day on the beach.

Winds can quickly dry out the garden soil and flowerpots and evaporate water off the surface of a pond or pool, make it difficult to control the barbecue, roll pots over and cause damage to plants – even uprooting or snapping off, mature trees.

Strong winds can make it impossible, or at least very difficult, to grow more tender plants, so think about the need for windbreaks at an early stage in your garden design.

POSSIBILITIES

Here are 15 suggestions for both natural and constructed windbreaks:

1. Build boundary walls rather than installing wire mesh fences, and make sure

they are strong enough to withstand the buffeting of gales.

2. If the builder has provided wire mesh fences, cover them with shrub, cane, wood or plastic slat fencing panels or strong closely woven cloth. This creates an instant windbreak while climbers on the fence – or a hedge in front – are growing.

3. Site the eating and resting terraces on the down-wind side of the house.

4. Retain any existing trees. Trim the tops and train them to grow sideways. If one or two windswept trees survive, consider keeping them as attractive features even though they give little shelter. Their shape may add atmosphere to the future garden and a reminder of why the estate is called windy ridge.

5. If a small copse of holm oak or pines has survived, keep them as a valuable windbreak. If you consider felling trees on the perimeter to create space, or in the centre of the garden to create a woodland glade, recognise that you might be changing the aerofoil characteristics of the copse and even creating a chimney effect in the centre. Both may cause trees to fall in a strong gale especially if the soil is soft after heavy rains. The shape and leaning of natural trees in the vicinity of your house will give an idea of the severity of past gales.

6. If you have a large garden with no natural windbreak, consider planting a two, three or even four rows of trees along the windward boundaries. Plant either evergreens alone or evergreens with deciduous flowering or fruit trees on the down wind side of the evergreens. Ensure that all trees are well staked and guyed from day one. If they are in a very exposed position, re-guy as they grow.

7. Construct Dutch-style reinforced glass windbreaks at strategic points in the garden that you can sit behind and still enjoy the best garden views. Plant some aromatic and colourful plants downwind of the screen.

8. Similarly, glaze in nayas on the windy

sides of the house so that you can sit in the sun and enjoy views on the windiest of days.

9. Plant internal hedges to give shelter to terraces, other plants and the swimming-pool.

10. Build internal screen walls as alternatives to hedges.

11. Build a garden naya or an outdoor kitchen (much loved by Spaniards).

12. If you have a pool or Jacuzzi, invest in a strongly constructed cover to conserve the heat and reduce water evaporation. If you can afford an all-weather swimming cover, you can also try to grow some semitropical plants inside.

13. Low growing plants can be protected by a semicircle of rocks. One sees ancient vineyards and melons protected in this way around the Mediterranean costas and islands.

14. Protect young plants with cloches. Five or seven litre-capacity water bottles with the bottom cut out and held down by canes in the middle and around the outside are an inexpensive solution.

15. If totally demoralised, move to a more sheltered situation! Gardening should be a joy as well as a challenge, and some challenges can eat up retirement years rather than enhance them.

2.11 ENHANCE VISTAS BEYOND THE GARDEN

If you are lucky you will have one or more good views of the sea, a lake, mountains, rolling countryside, forests, a distant village, a castle or across a picturesque valley – or your best view might only be of interestingly shaped and coloured roofs. Whatever they are, ensure that you make the best of them when designing and constructing the garden. Here are a few suggestions:

1. Lop or remove trees that block the view if you are certain the middle view will not be spoilt soon by high-rise building.

2. Offer to pay for the felling of a tree or two on adjacent land if they block out what could be your best view.

3. Plant and trim boundary hedges and trees to create a frame that draws one to the best views.

4. Site regularly-used terraces and garden seats where you will be able to enjoy the views for many hours each day, throughout the year, and from both sunny and shaded situations.

5. Plant the garden so that the internal vistas become harmonious foregrounds for the distant views.

6. If the land falls away beyond your property and nothing sticks up from below to mar the view, plant nothing. Perhaps even make one edge of your pool the effective link between your garden and the sea, valley or seascape beyond.

7. Don't forget that the view from the pool is important. If you cannot look into un-built territories, then plant the surrounding hedge or shrubs so that they block out surrounding buildings but enable tree or mountaintops to be seen.

8. Do what you can to persuade later developers or owners to site new houses and keep rooflines low, so as to not destroy or seriously spoil your best views, especially if you have enjoyed them for many years.

Yes, it can be difficult, but with a little thought we have managed to improve two views and keep one. Unfortunately, a new house now blocks out the forth and the western sunsets that we enjoyed for 15 years. However, a fast growing acacia soon blocked out most of the house.

2.12 CHOOSE COMPATIBLE AND COMFORTABLE GARDEN FURNITURE

Chairs, seats, tables, drinks trolleys, sun loungers, hammocks, sky chairs, umbrellas, lights and drying frames are all essential features of a garden and penthouse terrace designed for outside living. Buy the best that you can afford, recognising that the quality, style and colour of garden furniture can enhance or mar the aesthetics of a wonderful garden. Ask yourself the following questions:

Does the furniture we brought with us really look good in the garden or do we need to think about replacing all or part of it? What style, material and colour of furniture would best suit the part of the garden where it is required? Within your budget what would be the most comfortable, last the longest, weather the least and require minimum maintenance?

Visit a few garden centres and furniture stores that specialise in selling Spanish and imported ranges of furniture. Look at wood, metal, wicker, rattan and plastic chairs, seats, tables, etc. Recognise that:

- Alloy furniture needs less maintenance than that constructed from steel tubing. Some are designed to look like traditional cast iron work.

- White wicker furniture might look elegant by the pool but clash with the more informal areas of the garden.

- Winter-weathered plastic can soon be cleaned but teak takes longer to sandpaper and re-oil. Cane and wicker are least resistant to damp conditions. Paints are now available for plastic and wooden furniture in the shade of green that blends in best with your garden.

- Surfaces of plastic tables can be plain or designed. The surfaces of wooden or metal tables can be tiled, of marble, mosaic, stone or glass.

- A table for six can easily be expanded to one for 10,12 or even 14 by cutting out an oval shaped tabletop from plywood or chipboard. Split in half, it is easier to transport around the garden and store in the garage.

- Hammocks and sky chairs for hanging between or in trees can be of cotton or synthetic material. A double hammock is generally more comfortable for single use than a single hammock.

• Garden umbrellas now come in a wide range of sizes, with metal or wooden posts. Some have a winding mechanism for raising and lowering the umbrella.

• Shade can be provided not only by large umbrellas but also by awnings, roofed wood- or metal-framed gazebos, and roofed or thickly plant-covered pergolas.

• Garden seats in cosy corners can be easily constructed from natural rock with a comfortable seat.

• A softly upholstered swing seat may be more useful than a rigid, harder seat.

• A seat round the trunk of a tree can be more useful and look better than a raised flowerbed, which would be difficult to keep colourful in the deep shade.

• Elegant iron-framed pavilions found in old majestic Spanish gardens are again becoming popular, especially where a wonderful coastal or mountain vista can be seen from a vantage point in the garden.

• The colour of the cushions for chairs and seats, the covers of pavilions, gazebos, umbrellas and table clothes are seen more than the frames – so take as much care over the colour scheme in your garden as you would over your lounge.

• The most expensive is not always the best to look at or the most comfortable. It is most important to test the comfort of all chairs and seats in the shop before buying.

• Lastly, the washing line! An umbrella frame takes up the least room and can be easily removed and stored during party days.

2.13 USE POTS AND CONTAINERS CREATIVELY

Pots and containers can add much to the ambiance and completeness of a Spanish garden and are, of course, the basis of gardening on apartment and penthouse terraces, in enclosed patios and in minimalist gardens designed to have few or no plants.

Luckily, a wide choice is available with different materials, colours, designs, glazing, and sizes – some for hanging on walls or from ceilings, others for standing firmly on the ground, from tiny pots to terracotta wine and water storage jars standing several metres high. Self-watering pots with a built-in water reservoir are now widely available.

Pots and containers can look attractive, either filled with plants or empty, strategically placed as individual pots or in interesting groups.

There are, however, some general do's and don'ts as summarized below:

SOME DO'S

Before you go out to buy the first pot or container, decide why and where you need them, which will be used for plants and which will be used empty, what varieties of plants you plan to use and whether you prefer internally or externally glazed pots. The latter when filled with plants will dry out less quickly than traditional, basic, terracotta pots.

You should then size the pots you need and know the numbers of each size required. Consider whether you want to put a single plant in each pot or create a more dramatic display by planting several similar plants or a mix of compatible plants in a single container.

Before buying, visit a garden centre to check on the sizes of pots your chosen plants will be in. Be sure your new pots are large enough to give the roots of the plants room for growth when transplanted.

Then visit one or two pot shops and consider what colours, finishes and shapes would best blend in with the rest of the garden in their planned positions, which pot finishes will reflect sunlight and surrounding colours and which will be non-reflective and show their pure colours. Then consider whether a single design would look best or whether you should try and mix the heights, widths, shapes, surface designs, etc.

If the display of pots you are selecting from is at a garden centre, place some plants in them before making your final decision. If you are buying in a pot shop, take a few plants with you to try out there..

Consider the question of seasonal or permanent plantings. Both may well have a place in your garden. Seasonal plantings include:

Autumn – pansies, kalanchoas and carnations.
Winter – poinsettias, azaleas, bulbs or cyclamen
Spring – primulas, begonias and bulbs.
Summer – petunias, portulacas, begonias.

Permanent plantings embrace a wide range of plants that do well in pots, provided they are placed appropriately. Our favourites include the following:

In the sun, for instance on a terrace or low wall – zonal and ivy leaved pelargoniums/geraniums, succulents, argyranthemums, herbs.
In the semi shade, for instance in the naya or on a north facing front step – fuchsias, aechemia, begonia rex, streptocarpus, gardenias, camellias, azaleas and hydrangeas.
In the shade – ficus, philodendron, plectranthus, pothos, hostas, spider plants and calathea.

Make sure you fill pots and containers with a compost that is water retaining but well draining. It is a good idea to add a little water absorbing gel into the bottom third of the compost before planting up.

Don't forget that planted pots will need regular watering – once or twice a day if placed in the sun during the summer. A typical compost can absorb its own weight of water but lose it within 24 hours by evaporation from an unglazed terracotta pot. They are therefore not suitable for absentee gardeners unless planted up with drought resistant plants, such as succulents and cacti, or replanted on the first day of each visit.

Obviously, there is no problem if an absentee gardener is prepared to run a drip irrigation watering system to each pot. There is only a limited amount of natural food in potting compost, so feed potted plants once a month in the winter and once a week in the summer.

It's a good idea to place empty pots in groups to create artistic features. Such groupings can look especially attractive on penthouse roofs, around the pool, on large areas of stone chippings, on walls, in corners or niches of patios or on the elegant tiled courtyard of a minimalist garden. Be sure to weigh them down to stop them from blowing over in strong winds. Consider making a water feature out of an urn or pitcher on a terrace or flowing into a pond.

Plant pots don't have to stand vertically. They can look very attractive when laid on their side – with a plant coming out of the mouth – on a terrace, a flowerbed or rockery.

SOME DON'TS

Most plants in pots need regular watering. If this will be a chore or something you are liable to forget, then control the number of pots or select larger glazed pots that will dry out less quickly than unglazed terracotta pots. Other don'ts include:

Don't create clashes between adjacent plastic, terracotta, and glazed pots. Why not place plastic pots inside other more attractive pots, making sure they have drainage holes? Your display will look better and the pots will not dry out as quickly.

Don't leave annuals in pots in the full sun. They will survive better in dappled shade, and brighten up such areas at the same time.

Don't forget that the heat reflected off terraces can dry the underneath of the leaves of plants at the same time that the heat from the sun dries the tops – especially when pots are placed on dark coloured terraces.

Don't place pots of bulbs in deep shade as they will go leggy and grow weak.

Start them off in a totally dark cellar and then bring them out into semi-shade.

Don't forget to drill holes in pots that will be left empty to prevent them filling with rainwater that can go sour and attract mosquitoes.

Don't forget to give all pots a spring clean.

Don't allow plants to become root bound in pots. Check them annually and pot on when roots reach the inner sides of the pots and are growing out of the bottom.

Don't leave diseased plants in pots, especially when near others. Remove them to a nursery area if you think that they can be saved, or put them in a plastic bag in the rubbish bin (not on the compost heap).

Don't leave plants to die in pots or containers visible from the road when you leave the house for long periods. It is an obvious sign of an absent owner.

2.14 CHOOSE ORNAMENTS CAREFULLY

Carefully chosen and placed ornaments add interest and charm to many gardens, enhancing the natural beauty of plants or even replacing them in minimalist absentee non-gardener gardens. However, tasteless ornaments can turn an otherwise charming garden into an eyesore.

An amazing range of sculptures and concrete figures are on sale at garden centres and pottery shops. It is obvious that tastes and the skill of the sculptors, mould makers and painters vary widely. No doubt ornaments turn up in gardens as presents, instant holiday buys, arm twisting by children or additions to an addictive collection.

Our advice is to try and select ornaments that do something for you – and be sure to place them in situations where they truly add to the overall charm, mystique and aesthetics of your garden and, most importantly, enhance rather than overpower nature.

2.15 PROVIDE FOR THE ELDERLY, IMFIRM AND IMPAIRED

Many foreigners retire to Spain and take up gardening as an active hobby – hoping to tend their gardens into their eighties or even nineties. But as each decade passes, many find it harder do all the propagation and maintenance work unaided and need the help of a gardener.

Even so, they can still continue to potter, if only to care for a special plant collection in the garden or greenhouse and, with less time spent physically working in the garden, there is at last more time to just wander around and sit in the garden and enjoy the results of many years of dedicated labour.

It could be your partner is unable to garden for one reason or another. He or she – as well as a family member or visitor – has impaired sight or movement but would love to enjoy the perfumes, beauty and feel of the garden as much as possible. Keep this in mind when designing your garden, and incorporate special features to make it amenable to the elderly and impaired – or construct the garden in a way that would allow such features to be added at a later date without having to totally redesign it.

Consider the following actions and features:

To enable safe movement around the garden:

* Ensure that the surface and slopes of all paths are safe.

- Make paths wide enough for wheel-chairs, walking frames and two persons walking side-by-side.
- Add edges to paths to help sight impaired walk with a stick.
- Construct shallow riser steps or gentle slopes.
- Fit handrails to both sides of slopes and steps, around the most colourful and perfumed flowerbeds, and the fishpond.
- Repair any looseness or cracks as soon as they occur.
- Remove any prickly or spiky plants well away from paths and terraces, or preferably have none.
- Cut back all branches of bushes and trees that could cause eye injuries or catch on clothing.
- Remove trees and posts in or alongside paths or terraces to prevent collisions.
- Position hose reels away from the main thoroughfares, and always leave coiled up.
- Position flower pots off the edge of terraces so they cannot be tripped over.
- Sweep up fallen leaves and fruit daily. They can be slippery even in dry weather.
- Ensure that garden tools and children's playthings are not left around.
- Have the garden electricity circuits checked to ensure that they are safe and the wire cannot be grabbed onto and pulled loose.

To enjoy smells and textures:
- Plant perfumed and aromatic plants that sight-impaired persons would especially enjoy.
- Include jasmine, lemon, rosemary, thyme, curry, alliums, lavender, mint, scented lilies, but avoid poisonous plants such as datura.

To enjoy sounds:
- Install fountains and bird tables, baths and boxes that attract birdsong and add interest to all gardens, especially for persons who have the time to sit and listen. Visually impaired persons often have especially sensitive hearing.

- Hang wind chimes that make pleasing sounds in a gentle breeze, but be sure to test the sounds in the shop before buying!
- Install loudspeakers on a cosy terrace or in the greenhouse so that favourite tunes can be played and the sound adjusted by the listener.

To enjoy the best vistas:
- Construct or place safe, non-tipping, heavily-constructed seats at various vantage points around the garden – preferably in the shade for hot days and in un-shaded spots for overcast days.
- Provide sturdy tables for drinking and eating, reading, writing, and doing hobbies.
- Install a two-way walky talky system from the house so that beverages can be requested, messages passed on or assistance called for.

To be able to continue doing some gardening:
- Recognise that even gentle gardening helps keep one physically and mentally fit – but equally that one needs to keep fit for gardening. Take regular walks within your limitations and do some stretching exercises before commencing to garden.
- Purchase lightweight, ergonomically designed tools.
- Build raised beds in the garden and in the greenhouse at a height that will enable work to be done while sitting down. Make the tops of the sidewalls easy to sit on. Even consider building beds as a raised table with room for legs beneath, with a potting table the same height alongside or a raised bed in the shape of a horse shoe that allows the entire surface to be worked by turning on a seat or in a wheel chair.
- Stock the garden with small - and medium - height plants that can be tended without undue stretching.
- Move to a smaller property or apartment and start to specialise in container and window box gardening – or have the gardener maintain the garden and enjoy

your personal container/window box area.

• Increase the area of terraces and reduce the number of large shrubs.

• Revert to small - scale vegetable growing and don't attempt to work a large vegetable plot.

2.16 PROVIDE FOR COLLECTING AND CHANNELLING RAINWATER

Gardeners in Spain are very glad when the rain comes. Plants in the garden immediately look refreshed, potted plants on the naya can be moved out into the rain for a cleansing shower, and the hours spent on watering is reduced for a time.

However, unless the garden is designed to collect and channel rain water to where it is most needed, much water is wasted when there is a heavy downpour, especially during the autumn and spring gota frias. Precious water seeps down to the water table, runs out through the gate and pipes in the garden wall or over a boundary terrace. This is a great loss as plants are better when watered with rainwater than with chlorinated domestic water, and rainwater is free.

To save rainwater, you can do the following:

1. Fix guttering on at least part of the roof and run the water to a storage tank or a large water butt.

2. Slope paths and terraces to channel water to flower beds, the vegetable plot and pond.

3. If necessary, build a raised edge along paths to improve the channelling.

4. Edge receiving flower-beds with small rocks so as to distribute the water evenly, rather than allowing a torrent to make a channel and cause erosion.

5. Edge the entire garden area with at least a 30cm wall to keep excess water on your plot and avoid overflowing into the neighbour's plot or the street. Yes, it will flood a little, but this will soon soak down into the soil when the rain stops, providing you take the following precautions:

• Construct some paths and terraces with stone chippings laid on porous plastic sheeting. The water will soak away quicker than through sun-baked, hard earth.

• Mulch shrub beds and around trees.

• Keep bare soil loose by hoeing. This will allow the earth to take up rain-water more quickly and reduce the evaporation during the dry spells.

• Plant closely to reduce the areas of earth that is baked by direct sun light.

6. If the land slopes, construct a network of channels and pipes to move rainwater to where it is most needed.

7. If you plan to have a long, hard-surface drive, consider designing it to channel water to a storage tank. Slope the drive from either end to the middle and sideways so that water runs down the middle – or into a channel along one side – first into a settling tank and then into a storage tank. From there you can irrigate the garden by gravity or by using a pump.

2.17 AVOID UNNECESSARY MAINTENANCE WORK

Maintenance is largely self-imposed. It is directly related to the complexity of your garden design and the extent of your interest in gardening. What a dedicated gardener will accept as a reasonable amount of work in return for a colourful and perfumed garden will be regarded as an unacceptable amount of work by a non-gardener.

It is important to consider the maintenance work you are creating for yourself at an early stage in the design and development of your garden – as well as at the time of your annual garden audit – as even dedicated gardeners will be looking to reduce the amount of work required as they grow older

How maintenance intense is your current or future garden and how might you reduce the maintenance work required? Complete the following questionnaire and take note of the general observations given for various scores. Reflect on the garden that you are designing – or already have – and go back to the questionnaire to confirm or decide on the top 10 areas for reducing the amount

of ongoing maintenance work. Finally, decide how you could achieve that by redesigning some aspects of the garden.

To assess the extent of the maintenance work in your garden, add up the number of times that you have answered 'yes' and multiply by two. Add this score to your number of 'partially' answers. Finally compare your scores with the statements on the next page.

Remember that there always needs to be sensible balance between the colour, perfume and beauty of your garden and the work required to achieve it if you are to enjoy life in Spain to the full.

25 MOST TIME-CONSUMING MAINTENANCE TASKS

The 25 most time-consuming maintenance tasks	Is this required in your garden?			Tick your top 10 areas for reducing maintenance work
	Yes	Partially	No	
1. Cutting and caring for lawns.				
2. Weekly sweeping up pine needles.				
3. Regular deadheading daisy-like flowers.				
4. Cleaning up fallen carob beans and olives.				
5. Pruning and spraying fruit trees and cleaning up fallen fruit.				
6. Cleaning weeds from cracks in unsealed crazy paving and poorly laid chippings.				
7. Trimming hedges.				
8. Cleaning large terraces around swimming pools, especially if surrounded by dirty plants.				
9. Weeding a large organic vegetable plot.				
10. Annual clean up of an intensely planted garden.				
11. Cutting back spring/summer flowering perennials.				
12. Daily watering summer annuals.				
13. Caring for a large number of plants in pots.				
14. Painting walls not covered by plants.				
16. Hand watering with a watering can or hose.				
17. Weeding rockeries.				
18. Trimming herbs after flowering.				
19. Growing plants from seed.				
20. Propogating from cuttings				
21. Weeding sparsely planted and un-mulched flower beds.				
22. Keeping on top of the compost heap.				
23. Weeding driveways, paths and chippings.				
24. Cutting fronds off palm trees.				
25. Heavy pruning of fast growing trees like acacias.				
NUMBER OF TICKS IN COLUMN.				

2.18 ECO GARDENING

There is one further decision to be made before you lay out the garden, prepare the soil or add the first plants, and that is – to what extent will you manage your new garden along ecological/organic lines?

major way, the natural food chain balance will be disturbed, which could result in:

- Fewer bees in the garden to pollinate flowers.
- Fewer butterflies.
- Fewer beneficial insects that normally feed off other insects.
- Fewer frogs and toads that feed off

FINAL SCORE	OBSERVATIONS FOR ABSENTEE GARDENERS	OBSERVATIONS FOR RESIDENT GARDENERS
37 - 50	Take on a good gardener fast!	Probably the garden of a dedicated gardener. If you are not one, find a good gardener fast.
25 - 36	Decide what can be delayed until you retire or take on a reliable jobbing gardener.	Probably a balanced garden for you if you like gardening, and not too onerous for most employed gardeners.
13 - 24	Probably a manageable and satisfying garden.	Probably a very manageable but basic garden.
1 - 10	An ideal garden for a non-gardener but perhaps unexciting.	An ideal garden for a non-gardener but perhaps unexciting.

In Chapter 7.8 we summarise the levels of eco gardening and provide a basis for evaluating the extent of your practices in the vegetable garden where the benefits are most apparent. However, the principles of eco/organic gardening have equal benefits in the flower garden and orchard – and an increasing number of organic-based insecticides, pesticides, fungicides and fertilizer products are seen alongside inorganic chemical products in horticultural shops, garden centres and some agricultural co-operatives.

The choice is now there, but if you decide to go down the inorganic, chemical route you should be aware that you will destroy beneficial insects and micro organisms as well as those that cause problems. There is evidence that once you start to use chemicals in a

slugs and insects in the garden pond and rockery.

- Fewer birds that keep down unwanted insects in the flowerbeds and hedges, visit the garden to forage for food or nest in the shrubs or hedges.
- Fewer worms in the soil to work in fallen vegetable material, manure and compost.

So decide now, in principle, whether or not your garden will be a chemical free zone. Will pests and diseases be normally treated with ecological/organic solutions? Will wildlife be actively attracted to the garden? Will excess land be allowed to develop as a natural area?

Fortunately, every year more and more products are available for the gardener who decides to go the eco/organic route.

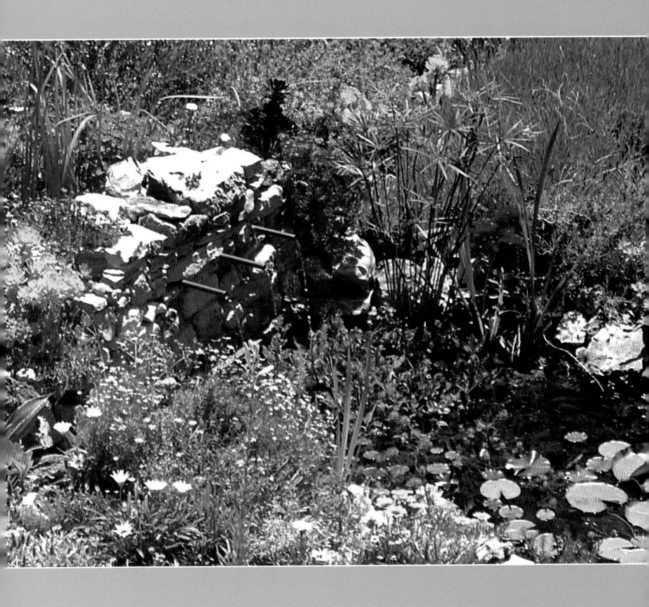

SECTION THREE
ADDING INTERESTING FEATURES

3.1 A COLOURFUL ROCKERY

A ROCKERY *(un jardincito rocoso)*, a popular feature of many Spanish gardens, is a sloping or flat mini-garden constructed of rocks and earth and with plants planted between the rocks. The rocks retain moisture and provide shade for the roots of the plants.

A rockery can be interesting and colourful throughout the year as a wide range of flowering and foliage plants grow well in the microclimate of a rockery, whether by the seashore or high up on a mountainside, though naturally some of the plants will change.

It is a good way to use the existing rocks of an area of a natural hillside, an old dry stone terrace wall or the rocks churned up by the builder. Of course, if you have no free rocks on site a lorry load can be easily purchased. A rockery is also a good way to hide a pile of inherited builders rubble.

If you have a split-level garden, a rockery can provide a natural transition from one level to the other and, when well constructed and planted, a rockery requires relatively little watering, weeding and no feeding.

Types of rockery

Rockeries can range from a mini-rockery in a stone basin to a large-scale rockery in a mountainside garden. The following are possible and all can be attractive:

1. A planted front of a dry stonewall. If the wall already exists, push earth and succulents that are drought resistant into the holes. If you are building a new dry stonewall, plant up between rocks while building. In this case you can ensure a bed of soil for each plant within the wall.

2. A rockery on top of a dry stonewall. Plant the front as above.

3. An interesting sloping surround for a raised up swimming-pool.

4. A clean surround for the swimming pool terrace – as most rockery plants do not drop leaves and flowers that could blow into the pool.

5. Either side of steps or a zigzagging path if you have a major difference in levels at some point in the garden.

6. A natural outcrop of rock.

7. A rock garden that you can walk around or even over. This would be a good way of covering over a large heap of builder's rubble. In such cases, start by covering the rubble with 10cm of soil and then watering well to work soil into the spaces within the pile of rubble. Then add a further 25cm of soil before starting construction.

8. A covering for the natural slope of the garden – not only for attractiveness and colour but also to use natural features, control rain water run off, and as an alternative to less interesting terrace walls.

9. The easiest treatment for a wild rock strewn-mountain slope that may also be covered with natural herbs, alpines, bulbs and shrubs.

10. A natural surround for a pond, particularly one with a cascade or waterfall.

11. A rockery spiral or snail that offers a greater depth of soil at the centre – and the north side will provide a degree of shade for the roots of plants.

12. A miniature rockery built up in a stone trough or sink as an interesting stand-alone feature on a terrace.

Success factors

Decide where a rockery will have most impact and interest in relation to the rest of the garden. Will it be a stand-alone feature, a mini- garden, or a transition between one part of the garden and another. Decide on the width and vertical fall to be built up or used if on an existing slope.

• Have a clear vision of the style of

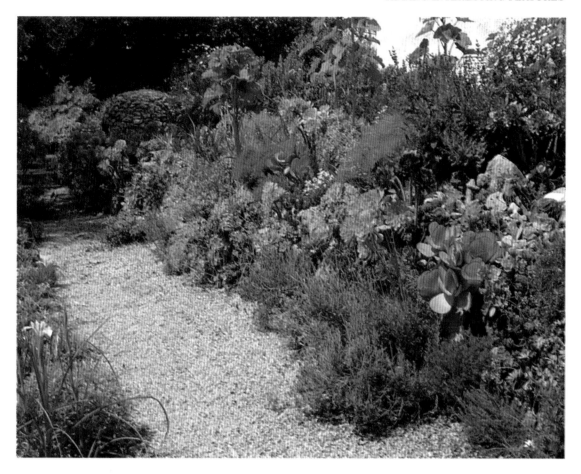

rockery you intend to build before you start construction, whether you intend to create a terraced effect with lines of rocks, have a wild mountainside-effect with randomly placed rocks, enhance a rocky outcrop or construct a combination of compatible styles.

• Weed the area thoroughly before you start, otherwise the weeds will thrive in the microclimate of the finished rockery. Construct with natural-looking rocks. In general, weathered rocks look more natural than clean virgin rocks just blown out of the rock face of a quarry. Try and obtain a mix of sizes. Check that you can move the largest safely or obtain help.

• Build up the rockery from the bottom. Work the base of each rock into the earth until it looks natural as an individual

rock and in relation to adjacent rocks. Ensure that each rock is stable and then level the earth between rocks.

• Add or remove soil until you achieve the best effect. If you have a heavy clay soil, mix sand and compost into the soil as you progress. Most rockery plants thrive in a moist but well-draining soil and are often reasonably drought resistant.

• Aim to plant appropriate plants in every gap between rocks. Plant as you go, in order to place the end of roots or cuttings under rocks or when the construction work is complete or a combination of both.

• Stand back every so often and consider the rockery as a whole. Ask yourself, "Does it already begin to look good? Does it look like a miniature natural landscape?

Am I making the best of the lie of the land and enhancing natural or built features such as steps, a pond or waterfall? What will it look like when the plants start to spread and mature?"

Answer these questions yourself and adjust accordingly. The fine-tuning of your rockery will inevitably be a process of trial and error.

Cover the earth around plants with a mulch of fine stone chippings or volcanic ash. Many rockery plants can rot if waterlogged around the stem and surface roots.

Be prepared to be ruthless with plants every few years, especially on small and medium- sized rockeries.

What plants are appropriate?

A wide range of plants, as shown in the box below:

Would you like to achieve broad sweeps of colour, using one variety of plant, or a kaleidoscope effect by mixing a large number of types of plants? Do you want your plants to smother the rocks or remain in the spaces between? Do you want to develop a collection of one type of plant, for example succulents or cacti.

Whatever your choice, aim for a range of interesting forms, colours, flowers and textures of leaves.

Maintenance required

As with the rest of your garden, a rockery needs regular care. Below is a maintenace list:

1. Seasonal deadheading and cutting back of dying flowered stems.

2. An annual cut back or trim of plants that are starting to outgrow their allotted

Typical types of plant	Low level rockery (below 400 metres)	High level rockery (above 400 metres)
Short and limited spread.	Succulents, oregano, thyme and gazanias.	Frost resistant succulents and herbs
Short and spreading.	Creeping thyme, verbena and lotus	Purple and white trailing lantana.
Medium height and limited spread.	Cacti, sage, succulents and ajania.	Frost resistant cacti and common sage
Medium height and spreading.	Some rock roses, arctotis, cascading rosemary, chamomile, santolina, freesias and cacti.	Dwarf junipers, azaleas, Heathers and rock roses
Taller but limited spread.	Some rock roses, irises sage, aeoniums, rue, and alliums.	Dwarf conifers.
Taller but spreading.	Lavender, lantanas and pelargonium graveolens.	Agave and brooms.

Decide on the type and size of rockery you want. Do you prefer a level, mixed or graded from front-to-back height of foliage (for example, low succulents at the front and taller cacti or herbs at the back)? Do you want a semi-wild or neat rockery?

space or remove/reposition one or two rocks to give the most attractive plants space to spread. Ensure that you use cuttings to propagate new plants.

3. Removal of plants that have just become too large and dominate or upset

the balance of the rockery.

4. Weeding, but relatively little if you have used plenty of rocks and close planting. Remove weeds while small. It will be more difficult if their roots are allowed to become established under rocks or between the roots of established plants.

5. A twice-a-year clear out of any accumulated debris – dead leaves, twigs, etc. – from between the plants and rocks. Add to the compost heap.

6. Remove and replace any dead plants.

7. Top up the rock or volcanic chippings still visible around plants.

8. Take cuttings to propagate new plants to use as in-fills, replacements, to use on a new rockery area or to swap with a friend for a rockery plant that you do not have. There are an enormous number of interesting succulents and herbs.

9. Watering during prolonged dry spells.

3.2 PONDS, FOUNTAINS AND SPRINGS

Ponds, fountains and springs can add a special dimension to all gardens in Spain – from the smallest terrace or patio to the large landscaped garden. They are relatively simple to install, have a number of benefits that no other features can offer and can be fascinating features throughout the year.

They create an interesting focal point, one that draws your attention – especially if situated in a quiet area or set against a pleasing backdrop. The sight and sound of running and splashing water has a calming and cooling effect, and watching wildlife such as fish, frogs, toads, damsel flies, dragonflies and visiting birds can be very stimulating to all ages. There is also the added satisfaction of breeding fish and terrapins, although the latter are voracious vegetarians and pond plants can disappear overnight.

The creation of a humid area gives you the opportunity to grow water plants, some of them very beautiful and spectacular, and with care and a little luck many can be grown from seeds in the Spanish spring and summer climate. In some gardens ferns will grow in shady situations.

WHERE TO PLACE THEM

They can provide very effective centrepieces for a terrace, a mini garden, an inner patio, or a total garden. They have immediate visual and mental impact, especially when the water is playing or running.

For maximum impact and benefit site them:

- Where they can be seen from the spot where you regularly eat, rest, read, take a siesta or work – especially from the kitchen or study.
- In less visible places where they will add interest to a stroll around the garden – perhaps within an enclosed mini garden or patio.
- Alongside or within a secret haven within the garden.

If you are lucky enough to have a natural spring flowing for part or the whole of the year, make this the centrepiece of a special mini water garden.

FORMAL OR INFORMAL DESIGNS

Chose a design that matches or compliments the style of your house, garden and overall environment. A design in this context, whether simple or complex, includes shape, size, colour of rock and other materials, a natural or manufactured look.

We have a well head with an internal fountain and a pond – with three spout fountains coming out of dry stone walls at either end of the pond – as the eye-catching centre piece of the main part of our garden. Each is built and surrounded by natural stone from the local mountain. The designs are natural and rustic, stimulated by traditional artisan constructions seen in rural Spanish villages.

Nearby neighbours have just the opposite. Being absentee non- gardeners, their garden is wisely Spartan – with large areas of stone terraces and raked stone chippings that match the light cream colour of the house. There are no climbing plants around the house because the pathways constructed by the builders have left no gap for planting. A formal, simple, no-fuss, cast-simulated stone fountain set in the centre of a terrace adds interest to an otherwise boring front garden. Anything fussy would look out of place. Around the corner, a carved marble fountain looks equally at ease in a more heavily-planted garden with mature conifers and shrubs.

A hillside finca that we recently visited was lucky enough to have a natural spring dripping out of the mountainside. This was channelled into an old earthenware pipe that fed a large pool and then overflowed into a natural rock channel feeding a bog garden – very simple, natural and effective.

Another house, 600 metres up in the hills, had a large shady terrace under large palm and rubber plants. In the centre, a weathered, imitation, animal drinking trough, with a continuous trickle of water from a spout at one end, looked perfect set in a sea of healthy ferns in pots.

Many garden centres are well stocked with a very wide range of fountains, prefabricated ponds and cascades and self-contained water features for the garden, small terrace or patio. Study them carefully and consider what you could construct yourself before making a purchase. In either case, construct or buy what will fit naturally and harmoniously into your garden.

SPRINGS

An imitation spring can be constructed with water coming out of a bank, a dry stonewall or a patio wall. The water can either fall into a catchment tray, a channel or stony stream bed that then runs through part of the garden or into a pond from where a submersed pump recycles the water.

PONDS

Attractive ponds can range from a small, one-square-metre pool in the flowerbed of a small garden to a mini lake in a 3000-square-metre garden.

The three most popular ways of constructing a pond are as follows:

a. Buy a moulded glass-fibre or pressed plastic pond that can be sunk into the ground or be built up around. This is easy and speedy to install. The drawbacks are the limited range of shapes, sizes, and depths available. Also, the imitation rock effects of some of the surrounds and inbuilt or matching cascades are not very aesthetic.

b. Dig out a hole of any size, depth and shape and line with a sheet of butyl pond liner laid over a sand base to stop any jagged stones in the earth from puncturing the liner when it is filled with water. The drawbacks are the folds that develop in the sheet in irregular shaped ponds and the life expectancy of the liner, typically quoted as ten to fifteen years.

c. Construct a reinforced concrete pond. This is the most expensive and time-consuming method and most gardeners would want to contract the work. Cracks and leaks can develop if the concrete shell is insufficiently thick, waterproofed and reinforced – especially around curves.

Each type of construction needs to be edged with terrace slabs for a formal finish, wooden duckboards for a semiformal finish or large rocks and a rockery to give a natural effect.

CASCADES AND WATERFALLS

The sight and sound of a sheet or spout of water dropping down from one pond to ano-

ther can add special magic and interest. Single or multi drop falls can be constructed, with the water landing directly onto the surface of a lower pond or onto weathered stones at the bottom of the falls.

FOUNTAINS

The following are three popular designs for fountains:

d. Horizontal fountains with one or more spouts coming out of a wall into a catchment tank or the surface of a pond.

e. Vertical fountains out of the surface of ponds. Pump sets normally come with a range of jet heads to create a variety of spray shapes.

f. Traditional stand-alone fountains. Prefabricated single or multiple tier designs are readily available.

MINI WATER FEATURES

In recent years an amazing array of mini water features have become available for gardens, patios, apartment or penthouse terraces with the pump and water sump normally integral.

Solar powered pumps are becoming more available. Some operate only when the sun is out, while others have integral batteries that power the fountain and attractive lights for several hours after dark. Prices seem to be coming down and they are safer than mains electricity around the garden.

PLANTS FOR SPECIAL MICROCLIMATES

You need to use different plants for different microclimates. For instance, ferns and irises are suitable for a humid microclimate beside a spring and in the shade, while the following variety of plants are essential to a well-balanced, healthy pond.

- Oxygenating plants, some of which have flowers.
- Floating plants that give colour, shade and have long trailing roots that harbour insects on which fish can feed.
- Plants with deep roots that put up broad leaves and spectacular flowers.

- Perimeter plants grown in pots or in on a marshy shelf.

Fountains can look attractive with no surrounding clutter, but equally they can be enhanced by the careful placing of pots of geraniums if the fountain is in the sun or by ferns if in the shade.

FISH

A good aquarium shop or water-garden centre should be able to supply you with healthy goldfish, koi carp and pond sturgeon.

MAINTENANCE

Regular maintenance is important if you want to keep your water feature attractive and healthy. Below are some guidelines:

a. Keep trays and pond bottom clear of leaves and dead flowers.

b. Clean off algae in spring or leave natural according to situation.

c. Top up water level regularly and keep jets and filters clean.

d. Clean pump filters regularly.

e. Thin out heavy weed growth in summer to leave room for fish to be seen and fed.

f. Thin out plants and prune roots if vigorous during the winter clean up.

g. Add a little Eco Bio Algicide or a small bundle of fresh straw if the water goes green. Once ponds are a balanced eco system you should have little problem with the condition of the water and any residual mud stirred up should soon settle. If you empty and refill a pond you will be back to square one, as most ponds develop algae during their first few months.

h. Add a little pond disinfectant every couple of months as per instructions to maintain health of fish.

i. Don't overcrowd the pond. Too many fish will stunt their growth and cause health problems.

j. Don't overfeed, as uneaten food will rot on the bottom. Three times a week in summer and once a week in winter should suffice.

k. Remove dead leaves and flowers to reduce the build up of decaying matter on the bottom of the pond. Net out decaying matter from the bottom of the pond during winter clean up.

l. Don't use the special fertiliser blocks sold for water lilies in small ponds. If you do, new leaves and roots will smother the pond.

m. Don't worry about mosquitoes and gnats, as the fish quickly devour any larvae.

3.3 SWIMMING - POOL OR JACUZZI

This chapter is not about the technical design of a pool but about the options and decisions required before you decide and start to construct.

A permanent swimming-pool can be, in theory, any shape, depth and size. It's just a matter of budget and size of your garden. In practice, pools are normally oblong from 2x8 metres upwards to Olympic size.

Where should you site your swimming-pool? The choices include the following:

1. In or above the ground, or half-sunken, surrounded by a banked herb bed, shrubs or a rockery.

2. As a main feature of the garden within a terrace attached to the house or very visibly central to the total garden.

3. As a secondary feature tucked away from the main daily view from the house, perhaps surrounded by a hedge as a separate mini garden.

4. If your land slopes away below your boundaries, with no buildings beyond, a pool up to the boundary can create a wonderful scenic effect.

5. If a narrow pool, to one side of the house or one side of a patio.

6. In the middle of a lawn, but be warned that grass cuttings could be carried into the water.

7. In the centre of a large non-slip terra-

ce, preferably in a light colour as dark colours absorb, retain and reflect the most heat.

Before you finalise the site, recognize that if a pool is the main focal point of a garden it can become boring after a year or two, will need to be kept meticulously clean all the year round and will seriously constrain the overall layout of the garden. A Jacuzzi or childrens' pool are less obtrusive eco options, especially for smaller gardens.

SIZING THE TERRACE AROUND THE POOL

Ensure that you provide sufficient space for the greatest number of visitors you expect. Allow for sunbathing and resting under umbrellas. Remember, the wider the terrace the less chance there is of dead flowers and leaves being blown into the pool.

You can avoid leaves being blown into the pool by designing the garden in a series of three concentric circles or oblongs around the pool, depending on the shape of the pool and garden – the inner area being the pool terrace.

If you want plants on the terrace around the pool have them only in pots and exclude any plants which drop leaves or dead flowers on a regular basis. It is best to restrict yourself to interesting succulents.

In the next area, outside the pool area, have a densely planted bed of interesting, colourful and perfumed plants that have minimum leaf and flower falls, for instance succulents; herbs such as rosemary, sage, thyme and lavender; daisy-like plants which, although they need dead heading, do not drop their flower heads (Argyranthemum/marguerite, dimorphotheca, euryops and felicia.); and summer lilies of various sorts.

If you want shade around the pool, there are very few trees that do not drop leaves, flowers or fruit. The cleanest and most attractive are Canary Island palm and washingtonia fan palms.

Surround the flowered area with a dense internal hedge, either a metre-high hedge as a dividing filter between the clean plants listed above and less clean plants in an area beyond, or a two-metre hedge – perhaps lavender, pittosporum, teucrium fruticans, or cupressus leylandii – separating the pool garden from the other areas.

In the outer area, plant your favourites such as lantana, hibiscus, bignonias and bougainvilleas that do drop flowers and leaves that blow around.

MAINTAINING THE SWIMMING POOL

Here are some basic seasonal guidelines for maintaining the pool:

Summer maintenance

Check and adjust the ph and chlorine or salt level regularly – daily if the pool is being used by many children covered in sun tan lotion. Install a continuous scrubbing system or vacuum the entire pool twice a week. Always backwash afterwards. Remove floating insects and leaves with a pool net and clean out the skimmer at least twice a week. Maintain water level above the skimmers to prevent air from entering the pump. Reduce oil build up on tiles by showering before entering. If the pool starts to look murky beware! Check your readings immediately. It can go green in hours and if it does, add liquid chlorine and run the pump continuously, backwashing every four hours until clear. If you get muddy rain, let the fine particles settle to the bottom of the pool and then vacuum to waste to clear. Use a flocculent if the mud stays in suspension.

Autumn preparation for winter

If you do not use your pool during the winter months it is still preferable to keep it clean to maintain its good appearance and hygiene, to avoid mosquitoes and to avoid the cost of emptying and refilling the pool in the spring. It is not wise to leave pools empty all winter.

A practical way of keeping the water clean is to place copper sulphate crystals in the skimmer pot, then run the pump until the crystals are dissolved and distributed around the pool. Another solution is to seal the pool under a thick heavy black plastic sheet or wide insulating cover, ensuring that no light enters.

Winter maintenance

If the water has been kept clean with copper sulphate, ensure that the pool is clear of leaves etc. If the pool has been tightly covered, nothing need be done at this time.

Spring preparation for use

If the pool has been sealed all winter, just give it an extra special clean, including hosing down the surrounding terrace.

If you have used copper sulphate, it should now be used up, so give the pool a good brushing, allow the dirt to settle for a day and vacuum to waste. Add chlorine to bring the level up to around 1.0 ppm and acid to bring your pH readings up to 7.2 to 7.6.

Swim as soon as the water is at a tempting temperature!

3.4 FACILITIES FOR *AL FRESCO* COOKING

Cooking and eating outdoors is possible for most months of the year. It is one of the real delights of living in Spain, particularly if one has a delightful garden. For variety and a good diet think beyond just a fixed or portable barbecue.

The following are easy to provide for in your garden design and offer the possibility of al fresco cooking and eating in different parts of the garden according to your mood or season.

- An easily built or purchased wood fired oven to prepare roast meats and vegetables, pizzas and home baked bread.
- An earthenware Mexican oven that

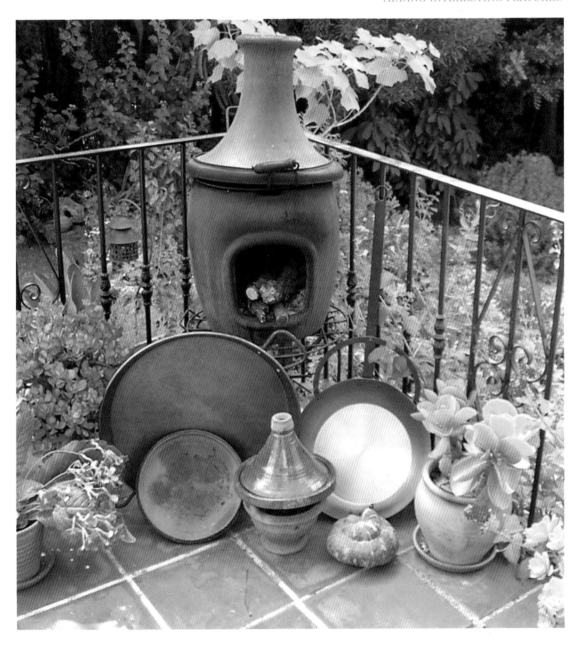

doubles up as a barbecue and oven is especially useful for roasting meat, fish and vegetables in foil.

• A pair of Moroccan tagine dishes for the slow cooking of spicy North African recipes over charcoal.

• A paella pan and gas ring on legs for cooking traditional paellas and fideuas.

• An earthenware cooking plate for cooking pita bread on a barbecue or tagine burner.

• A traditional migas pan for cooking chilly flavoured migas and spicy sausages Andalusian style.

• A fondue, raclette or hot stone meat cooker.

• A solar cooking box or grill.

The ultimate, of course, is a Spanish style

outside kitchen incorporating a barbecue including a spit for roast lamb and suckling pig, an oven, paella ring, sink and worktops.

3.5 A HERB GARDEN

There is a wide range of herb plants that are native to Spain and add perfume, flowers, colour and texture to formal or informal areas and in general, enhance the overall garden.

A good herb garden should display a collection of herbs in an interesting manner, making good use of the various heights, colours, leaf textures, flowers and seed heads. It should also make harvesting herbs easy, provide space for adding new herbs that you come across and allow spreading herbs to be controlled.

The following practical designs are suggested:

1. Plant between the spokes of an old wagon wheel or a similar bed constructed with terracotta tiles forming the dividing spoke.
2. A square or oblong dedicated garden with an outer bed and a number of inner mini beds. Additional interest can be achieved by constructing raised outer or inner beds.
3. As an herb border alongside or around the vegetable plot.
4. As a raised spiral or snail shell bed – the different depths of soil and sunny and shady side being planted according to the preferred habitat of different herbs.
5. As a border to a path near the kitchen
6. As a collection of pots and containers, either all the same size or more interestingly of different sizes and heights. This could be fitted in at the end of an apartment terrace.
7. A middle ages knot garden with interesting shapes achieved by growing and trimming herb plants into a variety of interweaving low hedges and infills.
8. As internal clipped hedges. Rosemary

and lavender are especially useful in this respect.
9. As an informal collection of herbs worked into a rockery or flowerbeds.
10. As a lawn of creeping thyme or dichondra in a semi-shaded area. These herbs could also be used for the pathways within a formal herb garden.
11. A long raised bed with a handrail at the front as an interesting bed for persons with impaired sight who can gain pleasure from smelling the variously perfumed leaves.

WHAT TO PLANT

What you plant will depend on how you intend to use herb plants in the garden and after being harvested. They can add perfume to the garden. Strong-smelling herbs include rosemary, lavender, thyme and the curry plant. Herbs such as marjoram, mint and lemon verbena have more subtle smells. Separately and in combination they can create a pleasing aromatherapy effect while you are working, eating or resting in the garden.

Herbs, especially lavender, rosemary and thyme, attract butterflies and can be arranged attractively in pot-pourri bowls for the terrace and house.

They also, of course, can be used in cooking to flavour all kinds of dishes, to make refreshing and healthy infusions as an alternative to tea and coffee as well as a base for distilling essential oils.

Several herbs are also very useful on the vegetable plot in producing ecological feeds and insect deterrents, and as beneficial companion plants.

PROPOGATING FROM CUTTINGS

Many herbs, including sages, thymes and mints, can be multiplied by taking root cuttings and planting them directly in the garden or growing them first in pots to achieve a strong root ball before planting. Rosemary, sage, rue, lavender and others can be propagated from stem cuttings.

GROWING FROM SEED

We find that April and May sowings of herbs are the most successful. We sow sun loving herbs that can withstand a degree of dryness directly into the garden where required. These include dill, coriander, aniseed, fennel, dandelion and borage. We grow herbs such as parsley and basil, which need to be kept constantly damp, in pots or trays before planting seedlings into larger pots to be kept in the semi-shade.

To ensure your herb garden will be successful, do the following:

1. Plant in water-retentive but well-draining, fairly rich, gritty soil. Herbs generally dislike heavy, clayey, waterlogged soils.

2. Keep all new plants damp until deep tap roots have been put down. This may take one or two years. Once established, most perennial herbs need little watering except during prolonged very dry spells.

3. Purchase and plant small or medium sized plants in preference to large ones, especially if planting in the late spring or summer rather than in the autumn or winter. It is important that the root ball is large enough to support the sometimes-forced top growth.

4. Herbs in the ground need little if any feeding, however, annual herbs in pots can benefit from a weak feed every so often.

5. Keep herbs tidy by trimming between harvests. Trimmings can be immediately used, dried or used as cuttings for propagation.

HARVESTING LEAVES, ROOTS AND SEEDS

Harvest daily as required or cut and dry for later use. Dry in the sun or a cool oven before storing in airtight containers. Herbs for cooking can be conveniently stored in ice cubes in the freezer.

3.6 A CHILDREN'S CORNER

A children's garden can provide much to interest and absorb children. They should have a large enough area to plant a mix of plants that they can later on:

- **Pick and dissect** – for example, margaritas, marigolds, sunflowers, portulacas, petunias, nasturtiums and zinnias.
- **Smell** – sweet peas, jasmine, San Diego, and herbs such as rosemary, thyme and curry.
- **Make an infusion from** – peppermint and lemon verbena.
- **Eat with a meal** – radishes, courgettes, tomatoes, lettuces, carrots, spinach and melons.
- **Eat when they like** – wild strawberries, peas, perpetual lettuce and rocket.
- **Have a competition with** – pumpkins for weight and sunflowers for height.
- **Dry and paint** – gourds.
- **Care for a few years** – seedling trees such as oak from acorns, avocado from the stone of a ripe fruit, olive from a fallen olive and citrus from orange or lemon pips. Allocate them an area of easily worked soil in the semi shade. Perhaps help them lay it out as a wagon wheel so that they can plant different seeds between the spokes or a raised snail bed.

Provide them with a garden hose or mini irrigation system, plant pots, potting compost, mini tools and some of your seedlings. Give them some pocket money to buy their own small plants when you visit a garden centre. Let them do what they like. Just let them know that plants die if they are not watered and then give just enough support to ensure a few successes.

If you help children start a garden, you should also take them around the garden and explain which plants can be poisonous and which are dangerous because of the prickles and spikes. Poisonous plants include anemones, arum lily, box, cyclamen, datura, iris, ivy, lantana, lilies, morning glory, daffodils, oleander, poinsettia, solanum, tobacco plant and wisteria.

In an age where children spend much time indoors on the computer, doing homework, watching television or on a mobile telephone, it makes sense to encourage outdoor activities with interest and challenge.

3.7 ATTRACTORS FOR BENEFICIAL WILD LIFE

Wildlife in the garden is beneficial for a number of reasons. Their movement, colours, noises and breeding cycles add interest. Their pollinating activities help fruit trees and flower plants to pollinate. Seeds in the droppings of recently migrated birds may germinate interesting and unusual plants. Their foraging for food loosens the surface soil, which in turn lessens water evaporation. They devour many unwanted insects and slugs. Worms in high humus soils cultivate the soil effortlessly hour after hour.

The wildlife that can be attracted includes butterflies, birds, crickets, lizards, frogs, toads, bats, worms, and hedgehogs. Do so consciously. Develop your garden as a haven from the polluted modern urban environment, for wildlife as much as for yourselves.

Wildlife is under constant threat with the continual cutting down of mature trees and copses, the filling in of ponds and *barancas* (gulleys), the clearing of natural mountainsides and heath lands, the construction of wind generators, the drying up of ponds due to changes in the water table and the removal of top soil.

All this is being done to enable the construction boom to continue, including the residential estates in which most expatriates and Spaniards live. Outside urban environments, the ever-increasing threats of plastic horticultural land and the use of concentrated pesticides, herbicides and fertilizers don't help. However, there are many practical things that can be done, all of them bringing almost immediate benefit to your garden. When developing a new garden or improving an existing one, consider the following ways to attract and retain wildlife:

1. Plant thick hedges and shrub beds that will attract sheltering and nesting birds.

3. Replace trees cut down by builders or felled because they were unsightly, unsafe, dead or diseased.

3. Put up nesting boxes for birds in trees or on high walls. Fix them in situations that are difficult for cats to reach. If possible, put up a number of boxes with different size entry holes for different species. Many garden centres now stock a wide range of boxes.

4. Leave a pile of straw and twigs in an out-of-the-way corner of the garden as handy nest-building material.. A totally tidy garden presents little of interest to birds and they will soon move on.

5. Preserve or build dry stone walls. Plant some holes between the stones and leave the others as homes for lizards and insects.

6. Put up a bat box under the eves. When bats move in you have nightly eaters of mosquitoes and gnats.

7. Hang up a bunch or two of herbs high up on the naya wall to give shelter for geckos, those lizards with suction feet that allow them to walk across ceilings and do such a good job of catching any mosquitoes, gnats, flies and moths that settle.

8. Install a birdbath in a quiet part of the garden, preferably where you can see it from your favourite eating or resting places. You will be surprised by the variety of birds it will attract. If possible, top up the birdbath with unchlorinated rain water from a butt or with water from a local fountain or spring.

9. Set up a self-standing or hanging bird table. We prefer a hanging one out of the way of marauding cats. Stock it with a variety of seeds and nuts, preferably not dry chunks of bred as these can swell up in their stomachs and can be especially harmful to fledglings.

10. Hang up half coconuts and peanut/seed feeders from the boughs of trees where cats will not be able to jump up or down onto feeding birds.

11. Construct a pond, where frogs, toads, dragon and damsel flies, and birds will soon add to the continuous interest of the fish in the pond.

12. If you have a water butt, add some oxygenating pond weed and a couple of gold fish to eat any mosquito and gnat larvae that might hatch.

13. Construct a compost heap that will attract worms and other insects beneficial to the composting process as well as providing food for blackbirds that love to peck around the base of the heaps. Use the compost to plant and mulch around trees, shrubs and vegetables. This will attract breeding worms as well as shelter roots from the sun, preserving moisture and providing essential nutrients.

14. If you have a lawn, leave one corner to grow long, preferably allowing a few wild flowers to develop. Butterflies need such an area for laying eggs, and other insects will also be attracted. A controlled clump of nettles is also beneficial.

15. If you have room, go a stage further and allow a natural wilderness corner to develop. Encourage natural grasses, herbs and wild annuals and perennials to take over. If starting with a clear area or previously rotovated corner of the orchard, accelerate the process by planting a mix of wild plant seeds. Poppies, fennel, scabious, marigolds, dandelion, wild garlic, wild chichory, clover, lupins, buttercups, valerium, irises, san diego, decorative thistles and lavatera would all be good starters. Among shrubs, add brooms, buddlias, thyme, rosemary, and rock roses.

Before you sow seeds or plant plants, take a spring drive through rural areas and observe what is growing and flowering wild alongside motorways. Some of the totally natural wind-blown, bird- dropped flower displays are amazing by any standards. The challenge is to do as well as nature in your own nurtured patch. It won't be easy but patience will be rewarded.

16. Stop using chemical pesticides, insecticides and herbicides in the garden. Seek out natural ecological products and solutions.

17. Plant some sunflower seeds or plants. The open flowers will attract pollinators and the seed heads can be hung up to attract seed-eating birds in the winter.

18. Make a point of including plants that are especially attractive to butterflies, which we refer to as the "flying flowers" of Spanish gardens for the beauty they add. Without appropriate plants only the odd butterfly will pass by – but with the right plants a garden can team with hatches of butterflies of all colours and hues.

The right plants provide a continuous supply of easily accessible nectar as well as stems and leaves on which the butterflies can lay eggs and the hatching caterpillars can feed.

The best nectar supplying plants are those with bright coloured, fragrant open flowers. Their favourite flowers include bougainvilleas, lantanas, margaritas, marigolds, purple buddleia (our yellow one just doesn't work), ice plants, rosemary, lavender and thyme.

If you do not have a wild area and if fields or mountainsides that used to surround your garden are now under concrete and bitumen, plant up a few pots of tall wild grass, thistles and nettles. A few decorative cabbages in pots or a flowerbed will also provide food for some varieties of caterpillars.

19. The humming bird hawk moth is also an interesting summer visitor to watch. It feeds by sticking its long proboscis into deep necked flowers such as nicotiana (tobacco plant), honeysuckle, stephanotis and devils tongue (caesalpinia).

20. Grow evergreen climbers up fences, into trees and over sheds to give winter shelter for the chrysalises of butterflies.

21. When you do the winter cleanup, leave a metre cube of leaves, twigs and dried weeds in a quiet rarely visited corner of the garden. With luck you will attract a hedgehog that feeds on slugs and a variety of nuisance insects.

Action on even only a few of the above ideas will add interest to your garden and arrest the disappearance of species from your neighbourhood.

3.8 A NATURAL AREA

A wild, naturalised area has a number of benefits if you have a large plot or a site set on a wild moorland, mountainside or in woodlands. Retaining its wild beauty may be the best garden for your location.

There are several practical benefits to retaining or developing a naturalised area or garden:

1. The preservation of a diversity of wild plants that may be disappearing fast from your area of Spain due to new roads, urbanisations and the wide use of weed killers.

2. Preserving the continuity from your natural garden to unspoilt surrounding heathland, mountainside or woodlands.

3. A low-maintenance, maximum-interest area of the garden, orchard or otherwise unused part of the site. Increasingly, 15,000 square metre sites are being sold in rural areas to enable a house to be legally built. Few new owners, especially if retiring to Spain, will have the motivation, energy or budget to turn the whole site into a cultivated garden, and there is a limit to how much fruit can be usefully harvested from an orchard.

4. An appropriate wilderness or naturalised area will require little, if any, irrigation once established. Any established plants have already survived the rigours of being parched in the summer and perhaps waterlogged and frozen in the winter.

5. Many wild plants thrive in poor shallow soils and flower profusely in the spring before many cultivated annuals, perennials and shrubs come into flower or are at their best. However, many die off in the summer.

6. A small-scale wilderness area can be an attractive way of dealing with a very impoverished or rocky corner of a smaller garden, covering a large heap of builder's rubble, an unploughed, uncut area of an orchard or a rough bank around the flower or vegetable garden.

7. A truly natural area will require little maintenance, as by definition it is an area that will be left to grow naturally, only thinning out the wilderness when the balance between grasses, flowering plants and shrubs looks wrong or if it becomes an uncomfortable fire risk.

8. In time a naturalised garden will become a haven, a small but important nature reserve for a whole host of birds, butterflies, insects, reptiles, small mammals and even larger ones such as rabbits, wild boar and deer.

The area you have that is suitable for a naturalised garden could be one of four

typical sites: a rocky heath land or mountainside, a flowering bank, a mound of
builder's rubble or a wild meadow.

A ROCKY HEATH LAND
OR MOUNTAINSIDE

With this type of site you can either leave it
as it is, if you want it to be totally wild, or
you can clean up the area to discover what
plants you have and make the best of them.
Even if you wish to leave it totally wild, we
suggest that you clean up part of the area
as follows:

a. Decide which mature trees, strong
saplings or stunted but attractively shaped trees you want to keep. If necessary,
prune them to pleasing natural shapes,
cutting out dead wood and retaining any
windblown effects. The trees may be
oaks, junipers, pines, carobs, olives,
almonds, birches, pomegranates etc.

b. Cut back overgrown evasive shrubs
such as gorse, broom, holly oaks, mountain palms, etc. Decide which are in
good situations and cut the others back
to the ground and treat the stumps
with acid applied on a paint brush to
avoid harming other plants or the soil
structure.

c. The spaces between rocks are probably
rich in flora but not all of interest. So,
space by space, clear all the grass and
low-priority plants such as dandelions
and wild chicory. Also cut back the dead
stems of bulbous plants.

d. Trim large rockroses, thistles, euphorbias, rosemary and lavenders, thymes,
etc., to shape and to stimulate new
flowering side shoots.

e. Now do nothing more until the spring, when you can really see what plants will flower, especially bulbous plants that appear from nowhere. You may be pleasantly surprised by the natural collection of wild narcissi, grape hyacinths, tulips, gladioli, orchids, irises, lilies etc that you have inherited. You will also discover the extent and colours of naturally occurring flowering plants, of which there can be many. We suggest you purchase a book of Mediterranean/mountain wildflowers to identify them all.

f. Once you know what you have, decide where you need to have infills by planting seeds, transplanting, taking cuttings or purchases. The best source of wild plant seeds is probably Semillas Silvestres S.L., based in Córdoba *(informacion@semillassilvestres.com)*.

g. Choose the best route for paths. The choices are bare earth or stone chippings laid over plastic to keep them clear of weeds. Meander the paths between widely spaced rocks and past some of the best clumps of plants.

A FLOWERING BANK

The aim is to create a mass of colour that matches the best you have ever seen driving along motorways or country lanes in the spring. And that's some challenge. Try the following for a good chance of success:

a. Choose a semi-shaded bank or one that is in full sun for half the day.

b. A plant-covered bank will have had years of natural soil improvement. Each year worms and ants will have been working dead vegetation into the soil, enriching it and improving its moisture retaining properties. Check that the soil is reasonably friable and well draining. A solid bank of clay is unlikely to be successful but if that is what you have, mix compost, sand and some fine stone chippings into the top 10 to 15cm of earth.

c. In the autumn and spring, plant a mixture of seeds of plants that can thrive on banks, such as marigolds, wild sweet peas, broom, poppies, lupines, antirrhinums, stocks, fennel, wild garlic, borage, valerian, decorative thistles, decorative grasses, holihocks, euphorbias, daisies, lavatera, scabious, etc. Some will be available from the address given above and packets of mixed wildflower seeds will be found in some seed display racks. Wildflower plants should not be dug up and transplanted, but some seeds are easy to collect during the summer.

d. Dampen the bank after planting and keep damp until strong plants are established. Then leave the bank to grow wild.

e. Pull out clumps of grass if they start to take over from the flowering plants.

You should have a self-perpetuating colourful bank of perennials and self-seeded perennials within a couple of years.

A MOUND OF BUILDER'S RUBBLE

Create an interesting shaped heap and then cover with ten centimetres of a rich sandy soil mix. Hose the embryo bank well to wash as much soil as possible down into the spaces in the rubble, then cover with a second ten centimetres of earth and continue as for a flowering bank.

A WILD MEADOW

You can create your own wild meadow by taking the following steps:

a. Stop cutting an area of a lawn, meadow or spare piece of land.

b. Stop using any weed killer or chemical fertilizers on the area.

c. Allow the existing flowering plants and grasses to grow, flower, seed and die back naturally. As the meadow thickens, more birds will be attracted and drop other seeds. Wind-blown seed will also gradually add to the diversity of natural plants. Yes, some will be what you normally call weeds in the flowerbeds, but so were all now-useful herbs and bedding plants before seed men and natural medicine experts discovered they had useful benefits.

d. Plant additional seeds from your

own garden and the roadside as well as seeds from mixed wildflower packets. These will have more chance of taking off if the meadow is semi shaded and naturally damp in the late winter and spring. Obviously, an area near a spring, river and high up on a misty slope is likely to be more successful than one in an arid area. Include the seeds mentioned for banks, together with salvias, clavels, hollyhocks, buttercups and san diego.

e. Before planting new seeds, cut the meadow in September or October and rake off all the cuttings. Then aerate the surface of the soil and spread a centimetre of soil over the surface. Brush the soil into the aeration holes.

f. Then scatter your mix of seeds over the surface in patches or evenly, according to the picture you want to create.

g. Sieve a poor soil and sand mix over the seeds and firm.

h. To achieve the optimum germination conditions it may be worth splitting your seeds into two or three containers and making successive sowings two or three weeks apart in both the autumn and spring. As occurs in nature, some seeds will probably germinate in the autumn and some in the spring.

i. Spray the planted area with water to keep it damp but not waterlogged. This should help achieve a higher germination rate than in nature. You can also raise seedlings in trays or pots for planting out.

j. Then just leave the meadow to grow

and develop naturally.

k. In most areas, cut the meadow in early autumn and remove the cuttings. By not haymaking in the hottest months the grasses will protect the roots of plants from the sun. In the lusher areas of the Pyrenees and the northern coasts of Spain, you can probably cut twice and get two lots of flowers.

l. Don't waste scarce water on the area unless you are planning to produce fodder for animals and need as high a crop as possible.

To encourage wild life, consider placing a bird table and bird bath, a pond with natural surrounds and a small pile of logs within your wild areas.

3.9 AN AVIARY OR POULTRY HOUSE

An area of only four to nine square metres is sufficient for housing a small flock of breeding budgerigars, a pair or two of mini doves, a pair of parrots, two to four egg laying chickens, or a small flock of pedigree bantams for eggs and breeding. A larger aviary/poultry run would allow the keeping of geese, guinea fowl or peacocks, which have the additional benefit of being good watchdogs in country areas. Whatever the size, ensure that part of the structure is roofed to provide sufficient summer shade.

The benefits of having birds in your garden are many. Their chirping and antics interest all ages, the chickens provide fresh eggs and wildlife are attracted by the prospect of a free meal of scattered grain. They eat the outer leaves of brassicas, their manure is a natural fertilizer for the vegetable garden or orchard and it acts as an accelerator for the compost heap. But ensure that you negotiate the keeping of a cockerel with the neighbours if living in the middle of an urbanisation.

3.10 TOPIARY FEATURES

There are many shrubs and trees that can be trimmed and trained into interesting shapes as hedges or freestanding specimens. Training is achieved by attaching a wire frame to the tree, around which to trim or hold a branch in a special shape, or weighing branches down with weights. In many ways topiary for the garden is using the skills of the bonsai specialists on normal- size trees and shrubs. Incidentally, a collection of Bonsais on a north facing terrace, or in the shade of tree, can add considerable interest and be a wonderful hobby for a gardener in later years.

The easiest trees for practicing the art of topiary include box, yew, cypress and bay. The easiet shrubs include pittosporum, euonymus, privet and rosemary.

Standard shrubs are a mild form of topiary and can be effective in many garden layouts. Those available in garden centres include bottle brush, hibiscus, lantana, oleander, plumbago, wisteria, bougainvilleas, roses, polygala and fuchsias.

99

SECTION FOUR
350 POPULAR
SPANISH PLANTS

4.1 AN INTRODUCTION TO 350 USEFUL PLANTS

THIS SECTION PROVIDES a practical guide to some 350 of the most popular plants used in Spanish gardens. They are selected on the basis of being readily available and easy to care for in typical micro climates.

Below is a summary of the main uses, benefits, greatest problems and soil needs of the plants included:

1. ANNUALS

A. USES
Can be grown in containers, large pots, hanging baskets, window boxes and flower beds.

B. BENEFITS
1. Instant colour.
2. Numerous varieties to choose from.
3. Able to create continuous twelve months of colour by sequential planting of seasonal varieties.
4. Most have a long flowering season.
5. Many can be raised from seed.

C. GREATEST PROBLEMS
1. Thirsty plants that need regular watering, once or twice a day on hot days.
2. Need regular deadheading to stimulate continuous flowering.
3. Can be flattened by heavy rains and winds.
4. Can be difficult to maintain a constant temperature for germination and growing on.
5. Most not frost hardy.

D. SOIL NEEDS
Very fertile, rich in humus, water retaining but well draining.

2. PERENNIALS

A. USES
Normally grown in dedicated beds or mixed beds with shrubs.

B. BENEFITS
1. Large number of varieties. Jointly they can give colour all the year round.
2. Many produce cut flowers for the house.
3. Easy to propagate by separation or from root and stem cuttings.
4. Many do well in the inland frost belt.
5. Many can do well in pots.

C. GREATEST PROBLEMS
1. Need regular deadheading to keep neat and stimulate a long flowering period.
2. Major annual cut back required, normally in the winter.
3. Can grow leggy and woody after a few years. Need to maintain a backup of young propagated plants as replacements.
4. Need to be on a drip watering system in the summer to prolong flowering.
5. Some grow into large clumps that need dividing every few years.

D. SOIL NEEDS
Generally fertile, rich in humus, water retaining and free draining

3. HERBS

A. USES
Grow in a dedicated herb garden, pots or containers, around the vegetable plot, on the rockery or in mixed beds.

B. BENEFITS

1. A wide range of varieties grow well in Mediterranean conditions as well as higher up on mountainsides.
2. Many drought and frost resistant.
3. Provide a wide range of flower colours, perfumes, formats and leaf colours and textures.
4. Wide range of culinary, aromatherapy and natural medicinal uses.
5. Mostly perennials that can be propagated from cuttings plus some useful annuals that can be grown from seed.

C. GREATEST PROBLEMS

1. Annuals require regular watering.
2. Annuals grown from seed require continual nurturing.
6. Annuals can go to seed fast in the high Spanish temperatures.
7. Perennials require annual pruning to stop them going leggy and woody.
8. Pots and containers need regular watering. Once herbs go dry they often do not recover.

D. SOIL NEEDS

Fertile, free draining, non clayey and gritty.

4. GROUND COVER

A. USES

1. Carpet planting at front of flower beds, under shrubs and trees, within rockeries and cascading down banks and walls.

B. BENEFITS

1. Rapidly fill up bare spaces with a mass of greenery and flowers.
2. Smother weeds.
3. Reduce surface evaporation.
4. Many are drought resistant.
5. Natural mulch around taller shrubs and trees.

C. GREATEST PROBLEMS

1. Many need deadheading to keep them neat.
2. Need trimming back regularly to stimulate new side shoots and prevent the heart becoming leggy/woody.
3. Can become the home of slugs and snails.
4. The more vigorous need controlling.
5. Can smother less vigorous plants.

D. SOIL NEEDS

Enriched soil, moisture retentive and well draining.

5. FLOWERING SHRUBS

A. USES

The backbone of Spanish gardens as individual specimens and planted as shrubberies, in mixed beds and as hedges.

B. BENEFITS

1. A wide choice of endemic and naturalised plants.
2. Come in all heights from a few centimetres to many metres.
3. Many slow growing so don't outgrow gardens for years.
4. Most grow well in full sun.
5. Some grow well in the shade and semi shade.

C. GREATEST PROBLEMS

1. Need watering until well established.
2. The more vigorous need regular pruning to control their size.
3. Some need dead heading to stimulate follow on flowering.
4. Tropicals and tender sub-tropicals can be wiped out by a single frost.
5. Some can be become very large after ten or fifteen years if they are not pruned hard during each year's winter cut back.

D. SOIL NEEDS

As for perennials, except for acid loving shrubs such as camellias, heathers, blue hydrangeas, rock roses and azaleas.

6. CLIMBING SHRUBS

A. USES

To cover walls, fences, pergolas, dead trees, old buildings and to climb up through trees or cascade down banks.

B. BENEFITS

1. Wide range of flowering varieties that can give year round colour.
2. Can be a mass of flowers for months.
3. Many are pleasantly perfumed.
4. Many are fast growing and trainable.
5. Interesting tropical species will grow in warmer and sheltered situations.

C. GREATEST PROBLEMS

1. Some can get out of control, especially in an absentee garden.
2. Need to regularly check and loosen ties round trunks and branches.
3. Roots of many varieties, especially clematis, need to be shaded to avoid being burnt by the sun.
4. Heavy flower and leaf falls.
5. Many not fully frost resistant.

D. SOIL NEEDS

As perennials.

7. FLOWERING TREES

A. USES

As specimen trees for their flowers, shade, architectural shapes and varying heights. Also as part of boundary hedges to frame the best views and hide the worst.

BENEFITS

1. Attractive seasonal flowerings. Mainly in spring and summer.
2. Mainly deciduous therefore giving good shade in the summer and allowing the sun to shine through in the winter.
3. Grow relatively fast in the right conditions.
4. Once established most are fairly frost and drought resistant.
5. The wide range of leaf, flower, fruit and bark colours and textures brighten up the garden and add interest.

E. GREATEST PROBLEMS

1. Dead flower, leaf and fruit falls need sweeping up. But they are useful on the compost heap.
2. Flowering seasons generally short.
3. Some can become too large for their situation, especially in small gardens, where they may need pruning each winter.
4. Vigorous roots can undermine foundations.
5. Heavy heads can snap off thin trunks unless well staked for some years after planting.

F. SOIL NEEDS

As perennials.

8. EVERGREEN TREES

A. USES

Can be planted as interesting specimen trees, in small groups or copses, as hedges or in containers on terraces, penthouse roofs, patios or the naya. Provide year round shade.

B. BENEFITS

1. Are in leaf all year round and can be trimmed to shape. Some good for topiary and hedges.
2. Give shade all year round.
3. Add architectural form to gardens.
4. Many are suitable for growing in poor soils.
5. Many are frost and drought resistant once established.

C. GREATEST PROBLEMS

1. Many have very spreading vigorous root systems so do not plant near the foundations of buildings.
2. Can be felled by strong winds unless well staked.
3. Generally have shallow root systems searching long distances for moisture so difficult to grow other plants around them.
4. When used as hedges need regular trimming to keep neat and tidy.
5. Some can become very large within ten years and therefore not for small gardens.

D. SOIL NEEDS

Generally as perennials except some prefer a more acid soil.

9. PALMS, YUCCAS AND CORDYLINES

A. USES

Architecturally attractive plants that add interest, form, movement, shade and a tropical touch to any garden.

B. BENEFITS

1. Many varieties available with differing forms of fronds.
2. Generally drought resistant once well established.
3. Large mature palms can be transplanted with care.
4. Rustling fronds create a restful ambiance.
5. Can be grown from seed. Good in a small garden as slow growing.

C. GREATEST PROBLEMS

1. Many have dangerous spikes on the trunk end of the fronds.
2. Can outgrow a small garden within ten years.
3. The trunks of Canary Island palms can break up walls and paths as they expand with age.
4. Pruned fronds cannot be put on the compost heap as they take a long time to rot down.
5. Nor do they readily go through a shredder as they are very stringy.

D. SOIL NEEDS

Rich in nutrients, high in humus, sandy and free draining.

10. BULBOUS PLANTS

A. USES

To brighten mixed flower beds, rockeries, terraces and nayas throughout the year.

B. BENEFITS

1. A wide range with varying flowering seasons available. Some have very spectacular flowers.
2. Can under plant deciduous shrubs with early spring varieties.

3. Many grow into large colourful clumps.

4. Many can be grown successfully in pots and containers.

5. A good source of cut flowers.

C. GREATEST PROBLEMS

1. Shortish flowering seasons.

2. Summer slug damage especially to soft skinned bulbs.

3. Too easy to dig up and damage when dormant if not marked.

4. Can be expensive compared with other plants.

5. When flowering is over the leaves need to be left to die back and can look unsightly.

D. SOIL NEEDS

Generally high in humus and free draining. Best to place a thin layer of grit under bulbs when planting.

11. SUCCULENTS

A. USES

To add interest to rockeries, dry stone walls, the edge of flower beds and paths and nayas and terraces when planted in pots and containers.

B. BENEFITS

1. An amazing number of interesting varieties.

2. Some lovely and interestingly shaped long lasting flowers.

3. Easy to propagate from cuttings.

4. Most are drought resistant.

5. Do well with little care.

C. GREATEST PROBLEMS

1. Some, especially the messems, can go leggy and woody.

2. Need to deadhead those that have flowers on long stems.

3. Thin skinned sappy varieties can be susceptible to frost damage.

4. Spreading varieties can smother small plants.

5. More delicate varieties can rot off if over watered.

D. SOIL NEEDS

Rich in humus, free draining, open, gritty/sandy. Benefit from mulch of chippings or ground volcanic rock to keep stems dry.

12. CACTI, AGAVES AND ALOES

A. USES

To create Mediterranean effects in flower beds, rockeries or in pots on terraces or walls.

B. BENEFITS

1. Drought resistant once established.

2. Can be easily propagated from cuttings or by removing young suckers.

3. Many have spectacular flowers even though some   last for only a day.

4. The majority can be best grown in full sun.

5. A good choice for absentee gardeners.

C. GREATEST PROBLEMS

1. Prickly and spiky. Need careful handling and weeding.

2. Most need light watering until roots are established

3. Some not frost resistant.

4. A 10cm wide aloe can be a metre across within 5 to ten years.

5. Dangerous in gardens with small children.

D. SOIL NEEDS

As succulents.

13. GRASSES AND CANES

A. USES

1. Grasses - To stabilize a bank or sand dune or as an interesting dedicated or wild corner.
2. Canes – As an external hedge or internal screen.

B. BENEFITS

1. Come in a wide range of single and variegated colours. Some have interesting flowering plumes.
2. Short and tall varieties available. Canes from a half to ten metres high.
3. Spread into large clumps within a few years.
4. Clumps can be split for transplanting.
5. When established drought resistant.

C. GREATEST PROBLEMS

1. Canes and pampas can spread rapidly in damp conditions. Once in the garden difficult to get rid of.
2. Spreading cane roots can break into terracotta water pipes.
3. Edge of some grass leaves can cut deeply, especially pampas grass.
4. If allowed to dry out can go brown before maturity.
5. Difficult to grow other plants close to canes.

D. SOIL NEEDS

A high moisture retaining soil. Canes can take off in constantly damp conditions!

14. POND PLANTS

A. USES

To create a balanced, colourful, interesting and healthy water based eco system.

B. BENEFITS

1. Easy to grow.
2. Maintain the oxygen level essential for healthy fish.
3. Some wonderfully exotic flowers.
4. Floating leaves give shade for fish.
5. Little care required.

C. GREATEST PROBLEMS

1. Grow very fast in ideal conditions. Will need thinning and pruning each year.
2. Some die back in winter adding to decaying pond debris.
3. Mostly flower in spring and summer.
4. Clumps of rooted plants can eventually take over a pond if not taken out and split every few years.
5. The clumps can become very heavy and unmanageable.

C. SOIL NEEDS

If in pots fertile and rich in humus.

15. HEDGING PLANTS

A. USES

To create external and internal hedges for privacy, windbreaks, shade and edges for paths and parterres.

B. BENEFITS

1. Wide variety of suitable plants available.
2. Can be pruned to give open or solid screens.
3. Many flower and create colourful boundaries.
4. Many are evergreen.
5. Many can be wired and trimmed into topiary shapes on top of the hedge and arches cut out.

C. GREATEST PROBLEMS

1. Can become straggly and woody if not regularly trimmed.

2. Spreading shallow roots make it difficult to plant other shallow rooted thirsty plants within half a metre.
3. Height and breadth need controlling to minimise work.
4. Generally need a lot of water in the early years.
5. Evergreens can be attacked by fungi.

D. SOIL NEEDS
As shrubs and trees.

16. NAYA PLANTS

A. USES
To brighten up and add interest to semi shaded and shaded nayas, porches and areas under trees.

B. BENEFITS
1. Generally grow best in semi shade and shade.
2. Are evergreen perennials or shrubs.
3. Many flower, some spectacular.
4. Varied range of leaf colours and textures.
5. Some are winter flowering.

C. GREATEST PROBLEMS
1. Fungal diseases if over watered.
2. Pores in waxy leaves can become blocked by dust unless dusted and washed.
3. Can grow out towards light unless occasionally rotated.
4. Some varieties prone to mealy bug.
5. Varied watering needs make watering complex.

E. SOIL NEEDS
A free draining, high in humus, water retaining but gritty compost.

| 4.1 | | | ANNUALS | | | | | | | | |

NAMES *BOTANICAL* English - Spanish	HEIGHT AND SPREAD	TYPICAL FLOWERS COLOURS	When Flowering				WHERE	GHB	GIP/W	PERF	DR	FR
			S	S	A	W						
1 AGERATUM Floss Flower - *Agérato*	L L	Blue	*	*	*		S SS		*		M	L
2. ANTIRRHINUM Snapdragon - *Boca de Dragón*	M M	Many	*	*	*		S SS SH		*		M	L
3. CALENDULA Marigold - *Caléndula*	M M	Orange Yellow	*	*	*	*	S SS		*	*	M	H
4. CATHARANTHUS Periwinkle - *Vinca*	L M	Pink White		*	*		S SS		*		M	L
5. CELOSA Cockscomb - *Celosia*	M L	Red	*	*			S		*	*	L	L
6. ERYSIMUM/CHEIRANTHUS Wallflower - *Alhelí*	M M	Many	*			*	S SS			*	M	H
7. HELIANTHUS Sunflower - *Girasol*	H M	Many		*			S				M	L
8. IBERIS Candytuft - *Iberis*	L/M M	Pink White	*	*			S SS				M	L
9. IMPATIENS Busy Lizzie - Impatiens/*Alegría*	L/M M	Many	*	*	*		SS SH	*	*		L	L
10. LATHYRUS Sweat Pea - *Guisante de Olor*	H M	Many	*	*			S			*	M	H
11 LOBELLA Lobelia - *Lobelia*	L M/H	Blue White Red	*	*			S SS				M	M
12. LOBULARIA Alyssum - *Alisum*	L H	White Yellow Pink	*	*			S SS	*	*	*	M	L
13. MATTHIOLA Stock - *Alhelí*	H M	Many	*	*	*		S SS		*	*	M	M
14. NICOTIANA Tobacco Plant - *Tabaco*	H M	Many		*	*		S SS		*	*	M	L

1. Ageratum
2. Antirrhinum
3. Calendula
4. Catharanthus
5. Celosa
7. Helianthus
9. Impatiens
10. Lathyrus
11. Lobella
12. Lobularia
14. Nicotiana

4.1 ANNUALS

NAMES BOTANICAL English - Spanish	HEIGHT AND SPREAD	TYPICAL FLOWER COLOURS	WHEN FLOWERING				WHERE	GHB	GIP/W	PERF	DR	FR
			S	S	A	W						
15. PAPAVER Poppy - Amapola	M M	Many	*				S				H	M
16. PERICALLIS Cineraria - Cineraria	M M	Many	*	*	*		S SS		*		L	L
17. PETUNIA Petunia - Petunia	M H	Many	*	*	*	*	S SS	*	*	*	L	M
18. PHLOX Phlox - Flox	M M	Many	*	*			S SS		*		M	L
19. PORTULACA Sun Plant - Portulaca	L M	Many	*	*	*		S SS	*	*		M	L
20. SALVIA Annual Sage - Salvia	M L	Red, white, blue and mixed	*	*			S SS		*		M	L
21. SCABIOSA Scabious - Scabiosa	M L	Many		*			S			*	M	L
22. TAGETES PATULA French Marigold - Tagetes	L M	Yellow, orange/ red	*	*	*		S SS		*	*	M	L
23. TROPAEOLUM Nasturtium - Capuchina	M H	Yellow, orange, cream	*	*		*	S SS		*	*	L	L
24. VIOLA Pansy - Pensamiento	L L	Many	*	*	*	*	S SS		*		M	H
25. ZINNIA Zinnia - Zinnia	M L	Many		*	*		S				M	L

COLUMN CODES:
HT = Height: L = low (less than 20cm); M = medium (20 – 40cm); H = high (over 40cm).
SP = Spread: L = little (less than 10cm); M = moderate (10-20cm); H = spreading wide.
WHEN FLOWERING: S = Spring; S = Summer; A = Autumn; W = Winter.
WHERE: S = Likes full sun; SS = Likes semi shade; SH = Likes full shade. GHB = Good in hanging baskets.
GIP/W = Good in pots and window boxes. PERF = indicates that the plant gives out a pleasing smell.
DR = Drought resistance: L = low; M = moderate; H = high. FR = Frost resistance: L = low; M = moderate;
H = high.

15. Papaver
16. Pericallis
17. Petunia
19. Portulaca
20. Salvia
22. Tagetes patula
23. Tropaeolum
24. Viola
25. Zinnia

4.2 PERENNIALS

NAMES BOTANICAL English - Spanish	HEIGHT AND SPREAD	Typical Flower Colours	When Flowering				WHERE	BY SEA	GHB	GIP/W	PER	FOL	EVG	DR	FR
			S	S	A	W									
Daisy like flowers Nos. 1 to 5															
1. ARGYRANTHEMUM Marguerite - Argyranthemum/*Margarita*	H H	Pink, red yellow, white	*	*	*		S			* pots only		*	*	M	M
2. OSTEOPERUM/DIMORPHOTHECA African Daisy - Dimorphothece/*Marguerite*	H H	White, purple, yellow	*	*	*		S	*					*	H	H
3. EURYOPS CHRYSANTHEMOIDES Paris daisy - Euryops/*Marguerite*	H H	Yellow	*	*	*	*	S			* pots only		*	*	H	H
4. CHRYSANTHEMUM Chrysanthemum - *Crisantemos*	H H	Many			*	*	S	*		* pots only	*		*	M	H
5. FELICIA Blue daisy - *Agatea*	M H	Blue	*	*	*		S				*		*	M	M
6. ABUTILON Chinese lantern - *Abutilon*	H H	Many	*	*	*		S SS			* pots only		*	*	L	L
7. AJANIA Ajana - *Ajana*	H H	Yellow			*	*	S					*	*	M	H
8. ARCTOTIS African daisy - *Arctotis*	M H	Many	*	*	*		S	*				*	*	M	M
9. BIDENS FERULIFOLIA Burr marigold/*Bidens ferulifolia*	L M	Yellow		*	*		S SS					*	*	M	M
10. COREOPSIS Tickseed - *Coreopsis*	M H	Yellow	*	*			S SS	*					*	M	H
11. CUPHEA Cuphea - *Cuphea*	H H	Many		*	*		S SS					*	*	M	M
12. DIANTHUS Carnation - *Clavel*	M H	Many	*	*	*		S	*	*	*	*		*	M	H
13. DICLIPTERA SUBERECTA Dicliptera - *Dicliptera*	M M	Orange		*	*		SS			* pots only			*	M	M
14. GAZANIA Gazania - *Gazania*	L M	Many	*	*	*		S	*				*	*	M	M
15. GERANIUMS Cranesbill/*Geranio*	M H	Many	*	*	*		S SS		*	*		*	*	M	L
16. HELIOPSIS Orange sunflower - *Heliopsis*	M H	Mustard, yellow	*	*	*		S	*					*	M	M

1a. Argyranthemum
1b. Argyranthemum
2. Osteoperum
3. Euryops Chrysanthemoides
4. Chrysanthemum
5. Felicia
6. Abutilon
8. Arctotis
9. Bidens Ferulifolia
11. Cuphea
12. Dianthus
13. Dicliptera
16. Heliopsis

4.2 PERENNIALS

NAMES BOTANICAL English - Spanish	HEIGHT AND SPREAD	Typical Flower Colours	When Flowering				WHERE	BY SEA	GHB	GIP/W	PER	FOL	EVG	DR	FR
			S	S	A	W									
17. HELLEBORUS Hellebore – *Heleboro*	M M	White	*			*	SS						*	L	H
18. IBERIS SIEMPERVIVENS Everlasting Candytuft - *Iberis Siempervivens*	M H	White	*	*			S							M	H
19. LEONOTIS Lion's ear - *Leonotis*	H H	Orange		*	*	*	S						*	H	H
20. MALVA Holyhock - *Malva*	H	Many	*	*	*		S	*						H	H
21. PAEONIA CAMBESSEDESII Majorcan Peony/*Paeonia cambessedesii* Pelarganium/*Geranium Nos. 22-25*	H H	Many	*				S				*	*		L	M
22. ZONALE Zonal - *Zonale*	H H	Many	*	*	*		S SS			*		*	*	M	M
23. PELTATUM Ivy leafed trailing - Peltatum/*Murciana*	M H	Many	*	*	*		S SS		*	*		*	*	H	L
24. REGAL Regal - *Regal*	H H	Many	*	*			S		*	*		*		H	M
25. GRAVEOLENS Scented - *Perfumada*	H H	Mauve	*	*	*		S		*	*	*	*	*	H	H
26. PRIMULA Primrose - *Primula*	L M	Many	*			*	SS			*				L	M
27. RUDBEKIA Coneflower/Rudbekia	H H	Many		*	*		S							M	M
28. SENECIO CINERARIA Dusty millar/*Senecio maritime*	M H	Yellow		*	*		S SS	*				*	*	M	H
29. STRELITZIA Bird of Paradise/*Strelitzia*	H H	Orange	*	*			S			*			*	H	L

COLUMN CODES:
HT = Height: L = Low (less than 20cm); M = Medium (20 – 40cm); H = High (over 40cm).
SP = Spread: L = Little (less than 10cm); M = Moderate (10 – 20cm); H = spreading wide.
WHEN FLOWERING: S = Spring; S = Summer; A = Autumn; W = Winter.
WHERE: S = Likes full sun; SS = Likes semi shade; SH = Likes full shade.
BY SEA = Plants suitable for gardens near the sea. GHB = Good in hanging baskets.
GIP/W = Good in pots and window boxes. PERF = Plant has pleasant perfume. FOL = Plant has an attractive foliage. EVG = Plant is evergreen. DR = Drought resistance: L = Low; M = Moderate; H = high. FR = Frost resistance: L = Low; M = Moderate; H = High.

18. Iberis Siempervivens
19. Leonotis
20. Malva
21. Paeonia cambessedesii
22. Pelarganium Zonale
23. Pelarganium Peltatum
24. Pelarganium Regal
25. Pelarganium Graveolens
27. Rudbekia
28. Senecio
29. Strelitzia

4.3 CULINARY AND AROMATIC HERBS

NAMES — BOTANICAL / English – Spanish	USES	WHERE	BY SEA	HT & SP	Leaf	Flower	Seeds	Flow S	Flow S	Flow A	Flow W	Harv S	Harv S	Harv A	Harv W	GIP	PERF	PEREN	ANUAL	DR	FR
1. ALLIUM — Chives/*Cebollino*	C F S	S	*	L M	Green*	Pink		*	*	*		*	*			*		*		M	H
2. ALOYSIA TRIPILLA — Lemon verbena/*Hierba Luisa*	I C S	S	*	H H	Pale Green*	Pale Pink			*	*			*	*			*	*		M	M
3. ANETHUM GRAVEOLENS — Dill/*Eneldo*	C F	S SS		H L	Green*		Seeds*	*					*	*		*			*	L	L
4. ARTEMESIA — Wormwood/*Artemesia*	1	S			Grey*	Small Yellow		*				*	*	*			*	*		H	M
5. BORAGO OFFICINALIS — Borage/*Borraja*	S V	S	*	H H	Green*	Blue, White*		*	*	*		*		*	*			*	*	H	M
6. CHAMAEMELUM NOBILE — Roman chamomile/Camomile/*manzanilla*	1 A	S		M M	Green	White Daisy Like*			*	*			*	*				*		M	H
7. COMFREY — Comfrey/*Consuelda*	1*	S		H H	Green*	Blue			*	*			*	*				*		M	H
8. CORIANDRUM — Coriander/*Cilantro*	C F S V	S SS		H M	Green*	White	*	*	*	*		*	*	*	*		*	*		*	L	M
9. HELICHRYSUM ANGUSTIFOLIUM — Curry plant/*Curi*	F	S		H H	Grey*	Yellow			*	*		*	*	*				*		M	H
10. LAURUS — Bay/*Laurel*	F	S	*	H H	Green*	Cream		*				*	*	*	*			*		M	H
LAVANDULA — Lavender/*Lavanda*																					
11. ANGUSTIFOLIA OFFICINALIS — Lavender/*Lavanda*	A C	S	*	H H	Green Gray	Purple*		*				*					*	*	*	M	H
12. INTERMEDIA — English/*Lavanda Inglesa*	A C	S	*	H H	Green	Spikey Mauve*		*				*					*	*	*	M	H
13. LAVANDA DENTATA — French/*Dentata*	A C	S	*	H H	Green	Soft Mauve/Pink*		*	*	*	*	*					*	*	*	H	H
14. MELISSA OFFICINALIS — Lemon balm/*Melissa*	I F S	S SS		M M	Green*	Pale White, Pink			*	*		*	*	*			*	*	*	M	M

1. Allium
2. Aloysia Tripilla
4. Artemsia
5. Borago officinalis
6. Chamaemelum
7. Comfrey
9. Helichrysum Angustifoliur
10. Laurus
12. Lavandula intermedia
13. Lavanda dentata
15. Mentha

4.3 CULINARY AND AROMATIC HERBS

NAMES / BOTANICAL / English - Spanish	USES	WHERE	BY SEA	HT & SP	Leaf	Flower	Seeds	When Flowering S	S	A	W	Harvesting Season S	S	A	W	GIP	PERF	PEREN	ANUAL	DR	FR
MENTHA Mint/Menta																					
15. PIPERITA — Peppermint/*Hierba Buena*	1 A	S SS		M H	Green*	Mauve				*		*	*	*		*	*	*		M	H
16. SPICATA — Spearmint /*Menta*	F S	S SS		H H	Green*	Mauve				*		*	*	*		*	*	*		M	H
17. OCIUM BASILICUM — Basil/*Albahaca*	A F	S SS		M M	Green Purple*	White			*	*			*	*		*	*		*	M	
18. ORIGANUM — Marjoram - Orégano/*Mejorana*	F	S SS		L M	Green*	Purple, White				*		*	*	*	*		*	*		M	M
19. PETROSELINUM — Parsley/*Perejil*	1 F S	S SS		M M	Green*		*		*	*		*	*	*	*	*	*		*	*	L	H
20. ROSMARINUS — Rosemary/*Romero*	1 A C F	S	*	H H	Green*	Blue		*	*		*	*	*	*	*	*	*	*	*		H	H
21. RUTA — Rue/*Ruda*	1 A	S		H M	Green*	Yellow			*	*	*	*	*	*	*		*	*		M	H
SALVIA Sage/Salvia																					
22. OFFICINALIS — Common sage/*Salvia officinalis*	1 A C F	S		H H	Green Grey*	Purple		*	*	*		*	*	*	*	*	*	*	*		M	H
23. FARANACEA — Mealy cup/*Salvia faranacea*		S		M M	Green	Blue		*	*	*						*	*	*		M	M
24. ELEGANS - RUTILANS — Scarlet pineapple/*Elegans - Rutilans*	1 S	S		H H	Green*	Scarlet*		*	*	*		*	*	*	*	*	*	*	*		M	H
25. SANTOLINA — Cotton lavender/*Santolina*		S	*	H H	Green Grey	Yellow		*	*								*	*		H	H
26. TANACETUM PARTHENIUM — Feverfew/*Tanacetum parthenium*	1	S SS		H H	Yellow /Green*	White daisy like		*	*	*		*	*	*						M	M
27. TARAXACUM OFFICINALE — Dandelion/*Diente de León*	1 S V	S	*	M M	Green*	Blue	Root*	*	*			*	*	*	*				*	M	H
28. THYMUS — Thyme - *Tomillo*	1 A F	S	*	M H	Green Varie-ted*	Mauve, Pink		*	*			*	*	*	*		*	*		M	H
29. VALERIANA OFFICINALIS — Cat's valerian/*Valeriana officinalis*	1	S		H H	Green	Pink	Root*	*	*	*		*	*	*	*				*	H	H

17. Ocium Basilicum
18. Origanum
20. Rosmarinus
21. Ruta
22. Salvia Officinalis
23. Salvia Faranacea
24. Salvia Elegans-rutilans
25. Santolina
26. Tanacetum
28. Thymus
29. Valeriana

COLUMN CODES:
USES – I = Infusion; C = companion planting; A = aromatherapy/cosmetic; F = flavouring. S = Salads; V = Vegetable.
BY SEA = Plants suitable for gardens near the sea. WHERE: S = Likes full sun; SS = Likes semi shade; SH = Likes full shade.
HT = height: L = Low (less than 20cm); M = Medium (20 – 40cm); H = High (over 40cm). SP = Spread: L = Little (less than 10cm);
M = Moderate (10 – 20cm); H = spreading wide. TYPICAL COLOURS AND PARTS USED – Leaf, flower or seeds *.
WHEN FLOWERING: S = Spring; S = Summer; A = Autumn; W = Winter. HARVESTING SEASON: S = Spring; S = Summer;
A = Autumn; W = Winter. GIP = Good in pots. PERF = Plant has pleasant perfume. PERE = Perennial. ANNUAL = Annual.
DR = Drought resistance: L = Low; M = Moderate; H = high. FR = Frost resistance: L = Low; M = Moderate; H = High.

Notes: 1*. Comfrey and dandelion are grown as compost accelerators and liquid fertilisers.

4.4   GROUND COVER PLANTS

NAMES *BOTANICAL* English - Spanish	HEIGHT AND SPREAD	TYPICAL FLOWER OR (LEAF) COLOURS	When Flowering S S A W	WHERE	Ground Cover	ROCKERIES	CASCADING	BYSEA	DR	FR
1 ARCTOTIS African daisy/*Arctotis*	M H	Many	* * *	S	*	*	*	*	M	M
2. ASTERISCUS MARITIME Asteriscus /*Asteriscus*	L H	Yellow	* * *	S SS	*	*		*	M	H
3. CARPOBROTUS Giant pig face/*Carpobrotus*	L H	Purple. Yellow	* * *	S	*		*	*	M	L
4. CHLOROPHYTUM COMOSUM Spider plant/*Cinta*	H H	White (variegated leaf)	* * *	SS SH	*		*		L	L
5. DICHONDRA MICRANTH *(lawn substitute)* Kidney weed/*Dichondra micranth*	L H	Green (dark green)	*	S SS	Lawn				M	H
6. FRAGARIA ALPINA Alpine strawberry/*Fresa alpina*	L H	White, small fruit	*	S SS	*				M	H
7. GAZANIA Gazania/*Gazania*	L H	Many	* * *	S	*	*		*	M	M
8. HEDERA Ivy/*Hedera*	L H	Green, Variegated		S SS	*		*			
9. JUNIPERUS HORIZONTALIS Spreading juniper/*Juniperus horizontalis*	M H	Blue/green		S	*	*		*	M	H
10. LANTANA MONTEVIDENSIS Trailing lantana/*Lantana montevidensis*	M H	Mauve, white, yellow	* * * * *	S	*	*	*	*	M	H
MESSEMBRYANTHEMUM FAMILY										
11. APTENIA Aptenia/*Aptenia*	L H	Pink/red	* *	S	*		*	*	M	L
12. DELOSPERMA Mesem/*Mesem*	L H	Many	* *	S		*	*	*	M	M
13. DROSANTHEMUM CANDENS Rosea ice plant/*Drosanthemum candens*	L H	Many	* *	S	*	*	*		M	M
14. LAMPRANTHUS Ice plant/*lampranthus*	L H	Red, pink, orange, yellow	* *	S	*	*	*	*	M	M
15. LOTUS MACULATES Lotus/*Lotus*	L H	Burnt Gold, Yellow	* * *	S	*	*	*		M	M

2. Asteriscus Maritime
3. Carpobrotus
4. Chlorophytum
5. Dichondra Micranth
7. Gazanias
8. Hedera
9. Juniperus Horizontalis
10. Lantana Montevidensis

4.4 GROUND COVER PLANTS

NAMES — BOTANICAL — English - Spanish	HEIGHT AND SPREAD	TYPICAL FLOWER OR (LEAF) COLOURS	When Flowering S	S	A	W	WHERE	Ground Cover	ROCKERIES	CASCADING	BY SEA	DR	FR
16. ORIGANUM — Marjoram - orégano/Mejorana - orégano	L M	Pink, White	*	*			S	*	*		*	M	H
17. ROSMARINUSUS PROSTRATUS — Ground cover rosemary/Rosmarinus prostratus	M H	Blue	*	*		*	S SS	*	*	*	*	M	H
18. SEDUM RUBROTINCTUM — Christmas cheer/Sedum rubrotitetum	L L	Yellow (succulent leaves go red in dry conditions)	*	*		*	S	*	*		*	H	M
19. THYMUS — Thyme/Tomillo	M M	White, Pink, Mauve	*	*			S	*	*		*	M	H
20. TRADESCANTIA — Spiderwort/Tradescantia	M H	Pink		*			S SS	*		*	*	M	M
21. VERBENA — Verbena/Verbena	M H	Many	*	*	*		S	*	*	*	*	M	H
22. VINCA MAJOR — Greater periwinkle/Vinca major	H H	Violet, Blue	*	*	*		S	*	*		*	H	H
23. VINCA MINOR — Lesser periwinkler/Vinca minor	M H	White, Pink, Blue, Violet	*	*			S	*			*	H	H
24. VIOLA RIVINIANA — Dog violet/Viola riviniana	M H	Blue/Violet	*	*			S SS	*			*	M	H
25. GRASSES (see Chapter 4.16)													

COLUMN CODES:
HT = height: L = Low (less than 20cm); M = Medium (20 – 40cm); H = High (over 40cm).
SP = Spread: L = Little (less than 10cm); M = Moderate (10 – 20cm); H = spreading wide.
WHEN FLOWERING: S = Spring; S = Summer; A = Autumn; W = Winter.
WHERE: S = Likes full sun; SS = Likes semi shade; SH = Likes full shade.
CASCADING – will cascade down over walls and banks.
BY SEA = Plants suitable for gardens near the sea. DR = Drought resistance: L = Low; M = Moderate; H = high.
FR = Frost resistance: L = Low; M = Moderate; H = High.

Other plants that can be used as ground cover include morning glory, nasturtiums and gourds.

11. Aptenia
13. Drosanthemum Canden
14. Lampranthus
15. Lotus Maculates
18. Sedum Rubrotintum
20. Tradescantia
21. Verbena
22. Vinca

4.5 FLOWERING SHRUBS

NAMES — BOTANICAL / English - Spanish	HEIGHT AND SPREAD	TYPICAL FLOWERS COLOURS	S	S	A	W	WHERE	BY SEA	GIP	PERF	HEDGES	EVG	DR	FR
1 BUDDLEJA — Buddleja/*Budleia*	H / H	Mauve, Yellow + Others		*	*	*	S	*		*		*	M	H
2. CALLISTEMON — Bottlebrush/*Calistemo*	H / H	Red, Yellow, White	*	*			S	*			*	*	H	H
3. CAMELLIA — Camellia/*Camelia*	H / H	Many	*	*		*	SS	*	*			*	L	H
4. CEANOTHUS — California Lilac/*Ceanoto*	H / H	Blue, Violet, White	*	*	*		S SS	*	*		*	*	M	H
5. CESTRUM NOCTURNUM — Lady of the night/*Cestro*	H / H	White		*	*		S	*	*	*			M	M
6. CISTUS — Rock rose/*Cistus*	H / H	Pink, White, Yellow	*	*			S	*				*	M	H
7. CORONILLA — Crown vetch/*Coronilla*	H / H	Yellow	*				S	*		*		*	M	H
8. DATURA (Brugmansia) — Angel's trumpet/*Datura*	H / H	Pale Yellow, Pale Pink	*	*	*		S SS	*		*			M	L
9. ECHIUM CANDICANS — Pride of Madeira/*Echium candicans*	H / H	Blue, White	*	*			S SS					*	M	M
10. ERICA — Heather/*Brezo*	M / M	Pink, White	*		*	*	S SS	*	*			*	M	H
11 HEBE — Veronica/*Hebe*	L / L	Many	*	*	*	*	S SS	*				*	M	H
12. HIBISCUS ROSA SINSENSIS — Chinese hibiscus/*Hibisco rosa*	H / H	Many	*	*	*		S	*	*		*	*	M	M
13. HYDRANGEA — Hydrangea/*Hortensia*	H / H	Many	*	*	*		SS	*	*				M	H
14. IOCHROMA — Tube flower/*Iochroma*	H / H	Red, Purple, Blue		*	*		S SS	*	*		*	*	L	L
15. LANTANA CAMARA — Common lantana/*Lantana camara*	H / H	Orange/Red, (Spanish flag)	*	*	*		S	*	*			*	H	M
	H / H	Pink/Yellow White/Yellow White	*	*	*		S	*	*		*		H	M
	M / M	Yellow	*	*	*		S	*	*		*		H	M

2. Callistemon
3. Camellia
4. Ceanothus
5. Cestrum Nocturnum
6. Cistus
7. Coronilla
8. Datura
9. Echium
11. Hebe
12. Hibiscus
13. Hydrangea
15a. Lantana
15b. Lantana Bandera

4.5 FLOWERING SHRUBS

NAMES BOTANICAL English - Spanish	HEIGHT AND SPREAD	TYPICAL FLOWERS COLOURS	S	S	A	W	WHERE	BY SEA	GIP	PERF	HEDGES	EVG	DR	FR
16. *LAVATERA* Lavatera/*La malva real*	H H	Pink, White		*	*		S	*					M	M
17. *MALVAVISCUS* Arboreus Sleepy Malva/*Malvaviscus*	H M	Red, Pink, White	*	*	*		S SS	*					L	L
18. *NERIUM* Oleander/*Adelfa*	H H	Many	*	*	*	*	S	*	*		*	*	H	H
19. *PITTOSPORUM TOBIRA* Japanese mock orange/*Pittosporum*	H H	Cream	*	*			S SS	*		*	*	*	M	H
20. *PHILADELPHUS* Mock orange/*Celinda*	H H	White	*	*			S	*		*		*	M	H
21. *PLUMBAGO* Leadwort/*Plumbago*	H M	Blue, White		*	*	*	S	*	*				H	H
22. *PLUMERIA* Frangipani/*Frangipani*	H H	Cream		*			S			*			M	L
23. *POLYGALA DALMAISIANA* Sweet pea shrub/*Polygala*	H H	Pink	*	*	*	*	S	*	*		*	*	M	H
24. *RETAMA - GENISTA* Broom family/*Retama*	H H	Yellow	*	*			S	*	*	*		*	M	H
25. *ROSA* Rose/*Rosa*	H H	Many	*	*			S	*		*			L	H
26. *RUSSELIA* Coral plant/*Russelia*	H H	Red, Pink, White	*	*	*		S	*				*	M	M
27. *SENNA CORYMBOSA* Cassia/*Cassia*	H H	Yellow	*		*	*	S	*					M	L
28. *STREPTOSOLEN* Marmelade bush/*Streptosolen*	H H	Orange/Yellow	*	*			S SS	*	*			*	M	L
29. *VIBURNUM* Viburnum/*Viburnum*	H H	White	*	*		*	S SS	*			*	*	M	H
30. *ALYOGYNE HUEGELII* Lilac Hibiscus/*Alyogyne*	H H	Lilac, Violet	*	*	*		S	*					M	H

16. Lavaterra
17. Nerium
19. Pittosporum
20. Philadelphus
21. Plumbago
22. Plumeria
23. Polygala
24. Retama
26. Russelia
27. Senna Corymbosa
28. Streptosolen

COLUMN CODES:
HT = height: L = Low (less than 50cm); M = Medium (50 – 100cm); H = High (over 100cm). **SP** = Spread: L = Little (less than 50cm); M = Moderate (50 – 100cm); H = spreading wide. **WHEN FLOWERING:** S = Spring; S = Summer; A = Autumn; W = Winter. **WHERE:** S = Likes full sun; SS = Likes semi shade; SH = Likes full shade. **BY SEA** = Plants suitable for gardens near the sea. **GIP** = Good in pots. **PERF** = Plant has pleasant perfume. **HEDGES** = Suitable for hedging. **EVG** = Plant is evergreen. **DR** = Drought resistance: L = Low; M = Moderate; H = high. **FR** = Frost resistance: L = Low; M = Moderate; H = High.

4.6 CLIMBING SHRUBS

NAMES *BOTANICAL* English - Spanish	HEIGHT AND SPREAD	TYPICAL FLOWER COLOURS	When Flowering				WHERE	FENCES	BY SEA	VIG	GIP	PERF	FOL	EVG	DR	FR
			S	S	A	W										
BIGNONIA FAMILY - *No 1 to 4*																
1 PODRANEA RICASOLIANA Pink trumpet vine/ *Ricasoliana 'Contessa Sara'*	H H	Pink	*	*			S	*	*	H					H	H
2. CAMPSIS GRANDIFLORA Chinese Trumpet creeper - *Campsis grandiflora*	H H	Waxy orange	*	*			S	*	*	H					H	H
3. TECOMARIA CAPENSIS Cape Honeysuckle - *Tecomaria Capensis*	H M	Orange yellow	*	*	*	*	S SS	*	*	H				*	H	M
4. PANDOREA JASMINOIDES Bower vine - *Pandorea Jasminoides*	H M	Pink yellow with dark throats	*	*	*	*	S SS	*	*	H			*	*	H	M
BOUGAINVILLEA Bougainvillea - *Buganvilla* *Popular varieties include Nos 5 to 7*																
5. GLABRA Glabra - *Glabra*	H H M M	Purple White	* *	* *	* *	* *	S S		* 	H M					H M	M L
6. SCARLET O'HARA Scarlet O'Hara - *Scarlet O'Hara*	H H	Red	*	*	*	*	S		*	H					H	M
7. BUTTIANA Buttiana - *Buttiana*	M M	Orange, Gold, Pink	*	*	*	*	S		*	M					H	L
8. CLEMATIS Virgin's bower - *Clematide*	H L	Many	*	*			S SS		*	L					L	M
9. FALLOPIA Mile a minute plant/Russian vine - *Polygonum*	H H	White	*	*			S	*		H			*	*	H	H
10. HEDERA Ivy - *Hiedra*	H H						S	*		H			*	*	H	M
11. IPOMEA Morning Glory - *Ipomea*	H H	Blue, Purple	*	*	*		S	*		H					H	M

1. Podranea
2. Campis Grandiflora
4. Pandorea Jasminoide
5. Glabra
6. Scarlet O´Hara
7. Buttiana
9. Fallopia
10. Hedera
11. Ipomea

4.6 CLIMBING SHRUBS

NAMES BOTANICAL English - Spanish	HEIGHT AND SPREAD	TYPICAL FLOWERS COLOURS	S	S	A	W	WHERE	FENCES	BY SEA	VIG	GIP	PERF	FOL	EVG	DR	FR
JASMINUM Jasmine - *Jazmín* *Popular varieties include Nos 12 to 14*																
12. *OFFICINALE* Common - *Blanco común*	H H	White	*	*	*	*	S	*	*	H		*		*	H	H
13. *POLYANTHUM* Pink - *Polyanthum*	M M	White with pink buds	*	*			S	*	*	H	*	*		*	H	H
14. *NUDIFLORUM* Winter - *Amarillo*	M M	Yellow	*			*	S	*	*	H				*	H	H
15. *LONICERA* Honeysuckle - *Madreselva*	H H	White, Pink	*	*	*		S	*	*	H		*		*	H	H
16. *MANDEVILLA* (Dipladenia) Mandevilla - *Dipladenia*	M L	Many		*	*		SS			M	*				L	L
17. *PASSIFLORA* Pasión flower - *Pasiflora*	H M	Many	*	*			S SS	*	*	M					M	H
18. *PYROSTEGIA VENUSTA* Brazilian flame vine - *Pyrostegia venusta*	M M	Orange	*			*	S	*	*	M					H	L
19. *ROSA* Climbing rose - *Rosal 'trepador'*	M M	Many	*	*	*		S	*	*	L				*	M	H
20. *SOLANDRA* Chalice vine - *Solandra*	H H	Creamy yellow		*	*		S	*	*	M		*			H	L
21. *SOLANUM* Potato vine - *Solano*	H H	White, Blue	*	*	*	*	S	*	*	M		*		*	H	H
22. *STEPHANOTIS* Stephanotis - *Stephanotis*	L L	White		*	*		SS			L	*	*	*	*	L	L
23. *THUNBERGIA - ALATA* Black-eyed Susan - *Tumbergia alata*	H M	Yellow	*	*	*		SS		*	M				*	L	M
24. *VITIS VINIFERA* Grape vine/*Vid*	H H	White	*				S		*	M					H	H
25. *WISTERIA* Wisteria - *Glicinia*	H H	Blue, White, Mauve	*	*			S	*	*	H		*			H	H

12. Jasminum Officinale
13. Jasminum Polyanthum
14. Jasminum Nadiflorum
15. Lonicera
16. Mandevilla
17. Passiflora
18. Pyrostegia
21. Solanum
22. Stephanotis
23. Thunbergia
25. Wisteria

COLUMN CODES:
HT = Height: L = Low (less than 2m); M = Medium (2 – 5m); H = High (over 5m). SP = Spread: L = Little (less than 1m);
M = Moderate (1 – 2m); H = spreading wide. WHEN FLOWERING: S = Spring; S = Summer; A = Autumn; W = Winter.
WHERE: S = Likes full sun; SS = Likes semi shade; SH = Likes full shade. FENCES = Suitable for covering fences.
BY SEA = Plants suitable for gardens near the sea. VIG = Vigorous growth. GIP = Good in pots. PERF = Plant has
pleasant perfume. FOL = Plant has an attractive foliage. EVG = Plant is evergreen. DR = Drought resistance: L = Low;
M = Moderate; H = high. FR = Frost resistance: L = Low; M = Moderate; H = High.

Note: Other plants that can be used as climbers are included in the shrub table (4.6) e.g., plumbago and lantana.

4.7 FLOWERING TREES

NAMES *BOTANICAL* English - Spanish	HEIGHT AND SPREAD	TYPICAL FLOWER AND FRUIT COLOURS	When Flowering S	S	A	W	WHERE	BY SEA	PERF	FOL	EVG	DR	FR
1 ACACIA Wattle/*Acacia*	H W	Yellow	*			*	S	*			*	H	H
2. ALBIZIA JULIIBRISSIN Silk tree/*Albizia*	H W	Pink		*			S	*				L	M
3. ARBUTUS Strawberry tree/*Madroño*	M M	White flower (Strawberry type fruit)		*	*		S		*		*	H	H
4. BAUHINA Orchid tree/*Bauhina*	H H	Pink, Red		*	*		S	*				H	L
5. CAESALPINIA GILLIESII Bird of Paradise Devil's tonque/*Lengua de Diablo*	M M	Yellow		*	*		S	*				M	H
6. CERCIS Judas tree/*Árbol de Amor*	M M	Pink	*				S	*				H	H
7. CHORISIA SPECIOSA Floss-silk tree/*Chorisia*	H H	Salmon, Burgundy		*	*		S	*				M	M
8. CITRUS LIMON Lemon /*Limonero*	M M	White	*	*	*	*	S	*	*	*	*	M	M
9. CITRUS SINENSIS Orange/*Naranjo*	M M	White	*				S	*	*	*	*	M	M
10. EUPHORBIA PULCHERIMMA Mexican flame tree/*Poinsettia*	H H	Red bracts	*			*	S					H	H
11. JACARANDA Jacaranda/*Jacaranda*	H H	Blue		*			S	*				H	M
12. JUSTICIA Justice/*Justicia*	M M	Many		*	*		S		*		*	M	L
13. KOELREUTERIA PANICULATE Golden rain tree/*Koelreuteria*	H H	Yellow		*			S	*			*	M	M
14. LABURNUM Golden chain/*Lluvia de oro*	H H	Yellow	*				S					L	H

1. Acacia
2. Albizia
4. Bauhina
5. Caesalpinia
6. Cercis
7. Chorisia
10. Euphorbia
11. Jacaranda
13. Koelreuteria

4.7   FLOWERING TREES

NAMES *BOTANICAL* English - Spanish	HEIGHT AND SPREAD	TYPICAL FLOWERS AND FRUIT COLOURS	When Flowering S S A W	WHERE	BY SEA	PERF	FOL	EVG	DR	FR
15. LAGERSTROEMIA Crape Myrtle/*Árbol de Júpiter*	M M	Pink, Mauve	* *	S	*				M	M
16. MAGNOLIA Magnolia/*Magnolia*	H H	Many	*	S	*	*			M	H
17. MELIA AZEDARACH Bead tree/*Melia Azedarach*	H H	Lilac (Cream Berries)	* *	S	*	*	*		H	H
18. PARKINSONIA Jerusalem thorn/*Parkinsonia*	H H	Yellow	* *	S	*	*		*	H	H
19. PRUNUS ARMENIACA Apricot/*Albaricoque*	H M	White	*	S					L	H
20. PRUNUS CERASUS Flowering Cherry/*Cerezos de flor*	M M	Pink, Red	*	S					M	H
21. PRUNUS DULCIS Almond/*Almendro*	M M	White, Pink	*	S	*				H	H
22. ROBINIA PSEUDOACACIA False Acacia/*Robina Pseudoacacia*	H H	Pink, White	* *	S	*	*		*	H	H
23. SALÍX BABILÓNICA Weeping willow/*Salix*	H H	Cream	*	S	*		*	*	M	H
24. SCHINUS False pepper/*Falso pimiento*	H H	Cream	* *	S	*			*	H	M
25. SYRINGA Lilac/*Lilo*	M M	Pink	* *	S	*	*			M	H
26. TAMARIX TETRANDRA Tamarix Tetrandra/*Tamarix Tetrandra*	M M	Pink	* *	S	*			*	H	M

COLUMN CODES:
HT = height: L = Low (less than 2m); M = Medium (2 –10m); H = High (over 10m). SP = Spread: L = Little (less than 2m); M = Moderate (2– 5m); H = spreading wide. WHEN FLOWERING: S = Spring; S = Summer;
A = Autumn; W = Winter. WHERE: S = Likes full sun; SS = Likes semi shade; SH = Likes full shade.
BY SEA = Plants suitable for gardens near the sea. PERF = Plant has pleasant perfume.
FOL = Plant has an attractive foliage. EVG = Plant is evergreen.
DR = Drought resistance: L = Low; M = Moderate; H = high. FR = Frost resistance: L = Low; M = Moderate;
H = High

15. Lagerstroemia
16. Magnolia
17. Melia Azedarach
18. Parkinsonia
20. Prunus Cerasus
21. Prunus Dulcis
22. Robinia Pseudoacacia
23. Salix
24. Schinus
25. Syringa
26. Tamarix

Note: There are a number of other deciduous trees such as gingko biloba and white mulberry suitable for the average garden but they have insignificant flowers. There are also many trees in the Prunus family worth considering for their flowers and foliage. A number of fruit trees are included in the above list for the quality of their blossom. They are also included in the list of fruiting trees in Chapter 8.1 along with some other trees that can give good shade in a garden but have less spectacular flowers.

4.8 EVERGREEN TREES

NAMES BOTANICAL English - Spanish	HEIGHT AND SPREAD	Suitability for small and large gardens and rockeries			WHERE	BY SEA	CONTAINERS	HEDGES	SLOW GROW	DR	FR
		Small	Large	Rockeries & smaller beds (dwarf types)							
1 ABIES Fir/Abito	H H		*		S	*			*	M	H
2. ARAUCARIA ARAUCANA Monkey puzzle/Araucaria araucana	H H	*	*		S	*	*		*	M	H
3. CEDRUS Cedar/Cedro	H H		*		S	*			*	M	H
4. CEDRUS LEBANI Lebonon ceder/Cedro lebani	H H		*		S	*			*	M	H
5. CHAMAECYPARIS LAWSONIANA Lawson Cypress/Ciprés lawsoniana	M H	*	*	*	S	*	*	*		M	H
6. CUPRESOCYPARIS LEYLANDII Leyland ciprés/Ciprés leylandii	M M	*	*		S	*	*	*		M	H
7. CUPRESSUS Cipres/Ciprés	M M	*	*		S	*		*		M	M
8. CUPRESSUS SEMPERVIRENS Funeral trees/Cupressus sempervirens	H M		*		S	*			*	M	H
9. EUCALYPTUS GUNNII Cider gum/Eucalipto gunnii	M H		*		S	*				M	M
10. FICUS ELASTICA Indian rubber tree/Ficus elastica	H H	*	*		S SS	*	*		*	M	L
11. JUNIPERUS Juniper/Enebro	M M	*	*	*	S SS	*	*	*	*	M	H
12. PICEA Spruce/Picea	H H	*	*	*	S	*			*	M	H
13. PINUS HALEPENSIS Aleppo pine/Pinus halepensis	H H		*		S	*			*	M	H
14. PINUS NIGRA MARITIME Corsican pine/**Pinus nigra maritime**	H H	*	*		S	*			*	H	H

1. Abies
2. Araucaria
3. Cedrus
6. Cupresocyparis
7. Cupressus
10. Ficus Elástica
11. Juniperus
12. Picea
13. Pinus Halepensis
14. Pinus Nigra Maritime

4.8 EVERGREEN TREES

NAMES BOTANICAL English - Spanish	HEIGHT AND SPREAD	Suitability for small and large gardens and rockeries			WHERE	BY SEA	CONTAINERS	HEDGES	SLOW GROW	DR	FR
		Small	Large	Rockeries & smaller beds (dwarf types)							
15. PINUS PINEA Pine nut pine/Pinus pinea	H H		*		S	*			*	H	H
16. TAXUS Yew/Tejo	H H	*	*	*	S	*	*	*	*	M	H
17. THUJA Thuja/Tuja	M H	*	*	*	S	*	*	*		M	H
18. TSUGA Hemlock/Tsuga	H H	*	*	*	S	*			*	M	H
19. QUERUS ILEX Holm oak/Encina ilex	M M	*	*		S	*			*	H	H
20. QUERUS SUBER Cork oak/Encina suber	H H		*		S	*			*	M	H

COLUMN CODES:
HT = height: L = Low (less than 2m); M = Medium (2 – 10m); H = High (over 10m). SP = Spread: L = Little (less than 2m); M = Moderate (2- 5m); H = spreading wide. SUITABLE FOR GARDENS: Small = up to 1,000 square metres; Large = over a 1,000 square metres.
For rockeries and containers there are slow growing ornamental dwarf varieties.
DR = Drought resistance: L = Low; M = Moderate; H = high. FR = Frost resistance: L = Low; M = Moderate; H = High.

15. Pinus Pinea
16. Taxus
17. Thuja
19. Querus Ilex
20. Querus Suber

4.9   PALMS, YUCCAS, CORDYLINES AND MUSAS

NAMES *BOTANICAL* English - Spanish	HEIGHT AND SPREAD	FORMAT	TYPICAL COLOURS OF a. flowers b. fruit	When flowering S S A W	W H E R E	B Y S E A	P O T S	D R	F R
A. FEATHER PALMS									
1. ARCHONTOPHOENIX Archontophoenix/*Archontophoenix* (fronds fall off naturally leaving smooth ringed trunk)	H H	Single slender Smooth ringed	a. Cream b.Red	*	S SS	*		L	L
2. ARESCASTRUM Coco palm/*Coco*	H M	Single slender Smooth ringed	a. Cream b.Brown/red	*	S SS	*		M	L
3. HOWEA BELMOREANA (Kentia) Sentry palm/*Howea belmoreana* (when grown in pots)	L*/M L*/M	Single slender Smooth ringed	a. Small green b.Brown/red	*	SS	*	*	L	L
4. PHOENIX CANARIENSIS Canary Island date palm/*Phoenix canariensis*	H H	Single up to 1 m wide Rough rippled	a. Small green b. Olive like yellow inedible	*	S	*		M	M
5. PHOENIX DACTYLIFERA Date palm/*Phoenix dactylifera*	H H	Single medium Rough rippled	a. Cream b. Yellow edibled Dates	* *	S	*		M	M
6. PHOENIX RECLINATA Senegal date palm/*Phoenix reclinata*	M/H H	Multiple from base	a. Cream b. Red	* *	S	*		M	L
7. PHOENIX ROEBELENII Dwarf date palm/*Phoenix roebelenii*	L/M L	Single medium rough	a. Cream b. Small black	*	S	*	*	H	M
8. SYAGRUS Syagrus/*Syagrus*	M M	Smooth with rings	a. Cream b. Greeny	*	S SS	*		M	L
B. FAN PALMS									
9. BRAHEA ARMATA Hesper palm/*Brahea armata*	M M	Single with blue/grey stiff fronds	a. Cream b. Yellow	*	S SS	*	*	M	M
10. CHAMAEROPS Mediterranean fan palm/*Palmita* (Indigenous to Spain grows wild on scrublands.)	M M	Multiple Slender Shaggy/ fibrous	a. Male-yellow Female-green c. Orange date like	*	S SS	*		H	H
11. LIVISTONIA CHINENSIS Chinese fan palm/*Livistonia chinensis*	H M	Single medium rough	a. Cream flowers b. Blue fruit	*	S SS	*	*	H	H

1. Archontophoenix
2. Arescastrum
3. Howea Belmoreana
4. Phoenix Canariensis
5. Phoenix Dactylifera
6. Phoenix Reclinata
7. Phoenix Roebelenii
8. Syagrus
9. Brahea Armata
10. Chamaerops
11. Livistonia Chinensis

4.9   PALMS, YUCCAS, CORDYLINES AND MUSAS

NAMES *BOTANICAL* English - Spanish	HEIGHT AND SPREAD	FORMAT	TYPICAL COLOURS OF a. flowers b. fruit	When flowering S S A W	WHERE	BY SEA	POTS	DR	FR
12. TRACHYCARPUS FORTUNEI Windmill palm/*Trachycarpus* Shallow rooted good pot plant	M L	Single medium Fibrous	a. Small yellow b.Dark blue berries	*	S	*	*	M	H
13. WASHINGTONIA FILIFERA Cotton palm/*Washingtonia filifera* *Named because of the cotton like thread between the frond segments*	H M	Single medium rough	a. Small white b.Black berries	*	S	*		H	M
14. WASHINGTONIA ROBUSTA Mexican fan palm/*Washingtonia robusta* *Circular fronds less segmented than filifera.*	H M	Single narrow tapered rough	a. Cream b. Small brown berries	*	S	*		H	M
15. CYCAS REVOLUTA Japanese sago palm/*Cycas revoluta*	L M	Single	Cream	* *	S SS	*		M	L
C. YUCCAS									
16. ALOIFOLIA Spanish dagger/*Aloifolia* (green and variegated varieties)	M M	Branching	a. Cream b. Brown	* *	S	*	*	H	M
17. ELEPHANTIPES Spineless giant yucca/*Elephantipes*	M M	Branching	a. Cream b. Brown	* *	S	*	*	H	M
D. CORDYLINE									
18. CORDYLINE AUSTRALIS New Zealand Cabbage tree/ Cordyline - *Dracena australis*	M M	Branching after flowering	a. After 8 years cream b. Insignificant	*	S SS	*	*	M	H
E. MUSA - BANANA FAMILY									
19. PARADISÍACA (fruiting) Banana-plantain/*Platanero* Variety 'Lady finger' suitable for smaller gardens	H M	New growth each year	a. Pinkish b. Yellow	* *	S SS	*	*	L	L
20. ENSETE (ornamental) Ensete/*Ensete*	M M	As above large wide eliptic leaves	a. Red b. Brownish	* *	S SS	*	*	L	L

12. Trachycarpus Fortunei
13. Washingtonia Filifera
14. Washingtonia Robusta
15. Cycas revoluta
16. Aloifolia
17. Elephantipes
18. Cordyline Australis
19. Paradisiaca
20. Ensete

COLUMN CODES
HT = height; L = Low (less than 2 metres); M = medium (2 – 5 metres); H = High (over 5 metres)
SP = spread: L = Little (less than 2 metres); M = Medium (2 – 5 metres); H = Spreading wide.
BY SEA = Good for gardens near sea; POTS = Suitable for growing in large pots. DR = drought resistance;
L = Low; M = Moderate; H = High. FR = Frost resistance; L = Low; M = Moderate; H = High.

145

4.10 BULBOUS PLANTS

NAMES BOTANICAL English - Spanish	HEIGHT AND SPREAD	TYPICAL FLOWERS COLOURS	When flowering				WHERE	GIP	PERF	FOL	DR	FR
			S	S	A	W						
1 ALLIUM Ornamental alliums/*Allium*	M M	Pink, White	*	*	*		S	*	*		M	H
2. AGAPANTHUS Lily of the Nile/*Agapanto*	M M	Blue, White		*			S	*			H	H
3. ALSTROEMERIA Peruvian Lily/*Alstroemeria*	M H	Many	*	*			SS	*	*		M	L
4. AMARYLLIS Beladonna Lily/*Amarilis*	H M	Many	*	*		*	SS SH	*			M	M
5. ANEMONE Wind flower/**Anemona**	M L	Many	*				SS	*	*		M	M
6. BEGONIA Begonia/*Begonia*	M M	Many	*	*	*		SS	*		*	M	L
7. BERGENIA SCHMIDTII Bergenia /*Bergenia*	H H	Pink	*			*	S SS	*		*	L	M
8. CANNA Canna Lily/*Caña de las Indias*	H H	Many		*	*		S			*	M	M
9. CLIVIA Kaffir Lily/*Clivia*	M M	Orange	*				SS SH	*		*	M	L
10. CROCOSMIA Montbretia/*Crocosmia*	H L	Red, Orange		*			S SS				M	H
11. CROCUS Crocus/*Azafrán*	L L	Many	*		*	*	S SS				M	H
12. CYCLAMEN Cyclamen/*Cyclamen*	M M	Many	*			*	SS SH	*		*	M	H
13. DAHLIA Dahlia/*Dalia*	M M	Many		*			S SS	*			L	M
14. EREMURUS Foxtail Lily/*Eremurus*	H M	Pale white, Yellow, Pink	* *				S SS				M	H
15. FREESIA Freesia/*Fresia*	M M	Many	*			*	S SS	*	*		M	H

2. Agapanthus
3. Alstroemeria
4. Amaryllis
5. Anemone
6. Begonia
7. Bergenia
8. Canna
9. Clivia
10. Crocosmia
12. Cyclamen
14. Eremurus
15. Freesia

4.10 BULBOUS PLANTS

NAMES BOTANICAL English - Spanish	HEIGHT AND SPREAD	TYPICAL FLOWERS COLOURS	When flowering S S A W				WHERE	GIP	PERF	FOL	DR	FR
16. GLADIOLUS Gladiolus/Gladiolo	H L	Many		*			S SS				M	H
17. HEMEROCALLIS Day lily/Hemerocallis	H H	Yellow/Orange		*			S SS	*	*		M	H
18. HYMENOCALLIS FESTALIS Spider Lily/Hymenocallis festalis	H L	White		*			S SS	*	*		L	M
19. HYACINTHUS Hyacinth/Jacinto	M L	Many	*			*	SS	*	*		M	M
IRIS Iris/Iris												
20. IRIS GERMANICA - hybrids Common flag/Iris germánica	H L	Many/single and double	*				S SS				M	H
21. IRIS XIPHIUM Spanish iris/Iris xiphium	H L	Blue, Mauve, White, Yellow	*	*			S SS				M	H
22. IRIS XIPHIUM - tingitana Dutch iris/Iris tingitana	H L	Blue, Mauve	*	*			S SS				M	H
LILIUM Lily/Lirio												
23. LILIUM CANDIDUM Madonna lily/Lirio candidum	H L	White		*			S	*	*		M	H
24. LILIUM LANCIFOLIUM Tigre lily/Lirio lancifolium	H M	Orange		*			S	*	*		M	H
25. LILIUM ASIATIC - hybrids Asiatic lily/Lirio Asiatic	H M	Many		*			S	*	*		M	H
26. MIRABILIS JALAPA Flower of the night/San Diego de noche	H H	Many		*	*		S SS	*	*		M	M
27. MUSCARI Grape hyacinth - Jacinto de panacho	L L	Blue, White	*				S SS		*		M	H
28. RANUNCULUS Buttercup/Ranunculo	M M	Many	*	*			S SS	*			M	H
29. TULBAGHIA Society garlic/Tulbaghia	M M	Mauve		*	*		S	*	*		M	H

We have left tulips and daffodils out the chart as they are well known. However they are best grown in higher wooded areas as in dry areas they tend to be eaten by slugs and other insects searching for moisture.

16. Gladiolus
17. Hemerocallis
18. Hymenocallis
19. Hyacinthus
21. Iris Xiphium
22. Iris Tingitana
23. Lilium Candidum
24. Lilium Lancifolium
25. Lilium Asiatic
26. Mirabilis Jalapa
29. Tulbaghia

COLUMN CODES:
HT = height: L = Low (less than 10 cm); M = Medium (10 - 20 cm); H = High (over 20cm). **SP** = Spread: L = Little (less than 10 cm); M = Moderate (10 - 20 cm); H = spreading wide. **WHEN FLOWERING: S** = Spring; S = Summer; A = Autumn; W = Winter. **WHERE:** S = Likes full sun; SS = Likes semi shade; SH = Likes full shade. **GIP** = Good in pots. **PERF** = Plant has pleasant perfume. FOL = Plant has an attractive foliage. **DR** = **DROUGHT RESISTANCE:** L = Low; M = Moderate; H = high. **FR** = Frost resistance: L = Low; M = Moderate; H = High.

149

4.11 SUCCULENTS

NAMES — BOTANICAL / English - Spanish	HEIGHT AND SPREAD	TYPICAL FLOWER COLOURS	When Flowering S	S	A	W	Leaf Colour	WHERE	BY SEA	GR/COVER	GIP/W	DR	FR
1 AEONIUM — Aeonium/*Aeonium*	H M	Yellow	*			*	Pale green, Burgundy	S	*		*	H	L
2. CARPOBROTUS — Giant pig face/*Carpobrotus*	L H	Purple, Pink,Yellow	*	*	*		Green	S	*	*		H	M
3. CHEIRIDOPSIS — Lobster claws/*Cheiridopsis*	L L	White, Yellow, Pink		*	*		Green	S			*	H	L
4. COTYLEDON — Cotyledon/*Cotyledon*	M M	Orange, Red, Yellow	*				Green	S			*	H	L
5. CRASSULA — Crassula/*Crassula*	M M	Many	*	*			Green	S	*		*	H	L
6. DUDLEYA — Live for ever bluff lettuce/*Dudleya*	L L	Red, White, Yellow		*	*		Green/Grey	S			*	H	L
7. ECHEVERIA — Echeveria/*Echeveria*	M M	Yellow, Orange	*	*		*	Brown/Green	S	*		*	H	M
8. EUPHORBIA — Milkweed Spurge/*Euforbia*	M M	Many	*	*	*	*	Green	S	*		*	H	L
9. GIBBAEUM — Gibbaeum/*Gibbaeum*	L L	White, Pink, Red		*			Green	S			*	H	L
10. GRAPTOPETALUM — Graptopetalum (Echeveria family/ *Graptopetalum*	M M	Pale Pink, White	*	*			Bluish Grey	S	*		*	H	L
11 JOVIBARBA — Jovibarba/*Jovibarba*	L M	Yellow	*	*			Green with brown tips	SS			*	H	H
12. KALANCHOA - (cultivated) — Flaming Katy/*Kalanchoa*	M M	Many	*	*		*	Green	SS			*	M	L
13. KALANCHOA TOMENTOSA — Pussy ears/*Kalanchoa tomentosa*	M M	Rarely flowers					Grey/Green velvety edged, brown spots	S			*	H	L

0. Group of Succulents
1. Aeonium
2. Carpobrotus
3. Cheiridopsis
4. Cotyledon
5. Crassula
7. Echeveria
8. Euphorbia

4.11 SUCCULENTS

NAMES *BOTANICAL* English - Spanish	HEIGHT AND SPREAD	TYPICAL FLOWER COLOURS	When Flowering S S A W	LEAF COLOUR	W H E R E	B Y S E A	G R / C O V E R	G I P / W	D R	F R
MESSEMBRYANTHEMUM FAMILY										
14. APTENIA Aptenia/*Aptenia*	L H	Red	* *	Shiney pale green	S	*	*	*	M	M
15. DELOSPERMA Mesem/*Mesem*	L H	Many	* *	Green fleshy in opposite pairs	S	*	*	*	M	M
16. DROSANTHEMUM CANDENS Rosea ice plant/*Drosanthemum candens*	L/M H	Many (open in sun)	* *	Tiny pale green	S	*	*	*	M	M
17. LAMPRANTHUS Ice plant/*Lampranthus* (More shrubby variety shorter lived)	L H	Red, Pink, Orange, Yellow	* *	Narrow fleshy leaves	S	*	*	*	M	M
18. SEDUM SPECTABILE Ice plant/*Sedum spectabile*	M M	Pink	* *	Green	S SS	*			H	H
19. SEMPERVIVUM Sempervivum/*Semprevivas*	L M	Pink, White, Yellow	*	Green/browny/ Red	S		*	*	H	L
20. SENECIO ARTICULATUS Candle sticks/*Senecio articulatus*	H H	White/ Yellow	*	Blue, Green	S			*	H	M

COLUMN CODES:
HT = height: L = Low (less than 20cm); M = Medium (20 – 40cm); H = High (over 40cm). **SP** = Spread: L = Little (less than 10cm); M = Moderate (10 – 20cm); H = spreading wide. **WHEN FLOWERING:** S = Spring; S = Summer; A = Autumn; W = Winter. **WHERE:** S = Likes full sun; SS = Likes semi shade; SH = Likes full shade. **BY SEA** = Very tolerant of sea spray. **GR/COVER** = Plants suitable for ground cover. **GIP/W** = Good in pots and window boxes. **DR** = Drought resistance: L = Low; M = Moderate; H = high. **FR** = Frost resistance: L = Low; M = Moderate; H = High.

10. Graptopetalum
12. Kalanchoa
13. Kalanchoa Tomentosa
15. Delosperma
17. Lampranthus
18. Sedum Spectabile
19. Sempervivum
20. Senecio Articulatus

4.12 CACTI, AGAVES AND ALOES

NAMES BOTANICAL English - Spanish	HEIGHT AND SPREAD	FORMAT	TYPICAL FLOWER COLOURS	When Flowering S	S	A	W	WHERE	BY SEA	GHB	POTS & WB	DR	FR
1. *ASTROPHYTUM MYRIOSTIGMA* Bishop's cap/*Astrophytum myriostigma*	H M	Spineless, ribbed	Yellow	*				S	*		*	H	M
2. *CARNEGIEA GIGANTEAN* Giant saguaro/**Carnegiea gigantean**	H M	Columnar	Red	*				S	*			H	L
3. *CEREUS* Cereus/*Cereus*	H M	Columnar	White, cream	*				S	*			H	L
4. *CHAMAECEREUS SILVESTRII* Peanutcacti/*Chamaecereus Silvestrii*	L L	Clustering/ floppy	Orange, Red	*				S	*		*	H	L
5. *ECHINOCACTUS* Golden barrel cactus/*Echinocactus*	H H	Round	Yellow, Red, Pink	*				S	*		*	H	M
6. *ECHINOCEREUS* Hedgehog cacti/*Echinocereus*	M M	Globe	Many	*				S	*		*	H	M
7. *ECHIOPSIS* Sea urchin cacti/*Echiopsis*	M M	Columnar, round	Many	*				S	*		*	H	L
8. *EPIPHYLLUM* Orchid cactus/*Epiphyllum*	M M	Pendular	White	*	*			S		*	*	H	L
9. *FEROCACTUS* Barrel cactus	M M	Barrel	Orange, Yellow	*				S			*	H	M
10. *GYMNOCALYCIUM* Chin cacti/*Gymnocalycium*	M M	Round	Yellow, Pink	*				S	*		*	H	M
11. *HAAGEOCEREUS* Haageocereus/*Haageocereus*	H M	Columnar	White (night flowering)	*				S	*			H	L
12. *MAMMILLARIA* Pincushion cacti/*Mammillaria*	M M	Round & columnar clump forming	Many	*				S	*		*	H	L
13. *OPUNTIA FICUS INDICA* Prickly pear/*Opuntia*	H H	Branched joints	Yellow flowers. Red fruit	*	*			S	*			H	M

0. A general Cacti garden
1. Astrophytum Myriostigma
3. Cereus
4. Chamaecereus Silvestrii
5. Echinocactus
9. Ferocactus
10. Gymnocalycium
12. Mammillaria
13. Opuntia Indica

4.12 CACTI, AGAVES AND ALOES

NAMES BOTANICAL English - Spanish	HEIGHT AND SPREAD	FORMAT	TYPICAL FLOWER COLOURS	When Flowering S S A W				WHERE	BY SEA	GHB	POTS & WB	DR	FR
14. OPUNTIA MICRODASYS Bunny ears/Opuntia microdasys	M M	Branched joints	Yellow	*				S	*			H	M
15. OPUNTIA SUBULATA Pole cactus/Opuntia subulata	H M	Columnar joints	Orange	*				S	*			H	M
16. OREOCEREUS Oreocereus/Oreocereus	H M	Hairy Columnar	Red, pink	*				S	*			H	L
17. PARODIA Ball cactus/Parodia	H H	Round	Many	*				S	*		*	H	M
18. REBUTIA Crown cactus/Rebutia	L L	Erect, round & cluster forming	Many	*				S	*		*	H	L
19. SCHLUMBERGERA Christmas cactus/Cactus de Navidad	M M	Drooping flat leaved jointed branches. Indoor or terrace plant	Many	*			*	SS			*	M	L
AGAVES													
20. AGAVE AMERICANA Century plant/Agave Americana	H H	Stiff leaves with sharp edges & tip (variegated)	After 10 years 6m high spike with yellow flowers	*				S	*		*	H	M
21. AGAVE ATTENUATA Agave attenuata/Agave attenuata	H H	Flexible wide pointed. Green leaves	3m arching flower spike yellow flowers when mature	*	*			S	*			H	M
ALOES													
22. ALOE VERA Medicinal aloe/Aloe vera	M M	Low candelabra	Yellow	*				SS	*		*	M	L
23. ALOE ARBORESENS Candelabra - Red hot poker/Aloe arboresens	H H	Tall candelabra	Red	*			*	S SS	*			M	M
24. ALOE MELANOCANTHA Aloe melanocantha/Aloe melanocantha	M H	Clustering	Red, orange	*	*			S SS	*			M	M
25. ALOE SAPONARIA Soap aloe/Aloe de jabón	M H	Clustering	Orange	*				S SS	*			H	M

14. Opuntia Microdasys
15. Opuntia Subulata
17. Parodia
19. Schlumbergera
20. Agave Americana
21. Agave Attenuata
22. Aloe Vera
23. Aloe Arborescens
24. Aloe Melanocantha
25. Aloe Saponaria

COLUMN CODES:
HT = height: L = Low (less than 10cm); M = Medium (10 – 20cm); H = High (over 20cm). SP = Spread: L = Little (less than 10cm); M = Moderate (10 – 20cm); H = spreading wide. WHEN FLOWERING: S = Spring; S = Summer; A = Autumn; W = Winter. WHERE: S = Likes full sun; SS = Likes semi shade; SH = Likes full shade. GHB = Good in hanging baskets. GIP/WB = Good in pots and window boxes. DR = Drought resistance: L = Low; M = Moderate; H = high. FR = Frost resistance: L = Low; M = Moderate; H = High.

4.13 GRASSES AND BAMBOOS

NAMES BOTANICAL English - Spanish	HEIGHT AND SPREAD	SCREEN	VIG	TYPICAL COLOURS (Plumes for grasses) & (leaf for bamboos)	S	S	A	W	WHERE	BY SEA	GR/COVER	FOLIAGE	DR	FR
A. GRASSES														
1 CORTADERIA Pampas grass/Plumero	H H	*		Cream, Pink			*		S	*		*	L	H
2. DASYLIRION Bear grass/Dasylirion	H H			When mature - Creamy/white		*			S SS	*		*	H	M
3. FESTUCA Fescue/Festuca	M M			White		*			S SS	*	*	*	H	H
4. MISCANTHUS Ornamental grass/Miscanthus	M M			Many		*	*		S	*		*	M	H
5. PENNISETUM Fountain grass/Pennisetum	H H			Many		*	*		S	*		*	M	H
6. STIPA Feather grass/Stipa	H			Cream		*	*		S	*	*	*	M	H
B. BAMBOOS														
7. PLEIOBLASTUS AURICOMUS Kamuro - Zasa/Pleioblastus	M M			Variegated		*			S SS	*		*	L	H
8. PLEIOBLASTUS PYGMAEUS Dwarf bamboo/Pleioblastus pygmaeus	L H			Variegated		*			S SS	*	*	*	L	H
9. PHYLLOSTACHYS AUREA Fishpole bamboo/Phyllostachys aurea	H H	*	*	Green		*			S	*		*	M	H
10. PSEUDOSASA JAPONICA Metake/Pseudosasa japonica	H H	*	*	Green		*			S SS	*		*	M	H
11. FARGESIA NITIDA Fountain bamboo/Fargesia nitida	M M	*		Green		*			S SS	*		*	L	M

COLUMN CODES:
HT = Height: L = low (less than 50cm); M = medium (50 – 100cm); H = high (over 100cm). SP = Spread: L = little (less than 50cm); M = moderate (50-100cm); H = spreading wide. SCREEN = Suitable for screening and wind breaks. VIG = Vigorous and can become evasive. WHEN FLOWERING: S = Spring; S = Summer; A = Autumn; W = Winter. WHERE = Likes full sun; SS = Likes semi shade; SH = Likes full shade. BY SEA = Plants suitable for gardens near the sea. GR COVER = Good ground cover. FOLIAGE = indicates that the plant has an unusual and attractive foliage. DR = Drought resistance: L = low; M = moderate; H = high. FR = Frost resistance: L = low; M = moderate; H = high.

1. Cortaderia
2. Dasylirion
3. Festuca
4. Miscanthus
5. Pennisetum
6. Stipa
8. Pleioblastus Pygmaeus
9. Phyllostachys Aurea
10. Pseudosasa japónica
11. Bamboos for sale

4.14 POND PLANTS

NAMES BOTANICAL English - Spanish	HEIGHT AND SPREAD	TYPICAL FLOWER COLOURS	When Flowering S S A W	DEPTH IN WATER	F R
A. MARGINAL PLANTS					
1 ALISMA PLANTAGO AQUATICA Common water plantains/*Alisma aquatica*	H M	White	*	0 - 20cm	M
2. CYPERUS INVOLUCRATUS Umbrella sedge/*Cipero*	H H	Cream	*	10 - 20cm	M
3. IRIS PSEUDACORUS Yellow flag /*Iris pseudacorus*	H H	Yellow	*	0 - 20cm	H
4. IRIS VERISCOLOR Blue flag/*Iris veriscolor*	H H	Blue	* *	0 - 20cm	H
5. MENTHA AQUATICA Marsh mint/*Mentha aquatica*	M H	Lilac	* *	0 - 20cm	H
6. PONTEDERIA CORDATA Pickerel bus/*Pick libelua*	H H	Dark blue	*	20 - 40cm	H
7. RANUNCULUS AQUATILIS Water buttercup/*Ranunculus aquatilis*	L H	Yellow	* *	10 - 20cm	H
8. SCHOENOPLECTUS Zebra rush/*Scripus*	H H	Red brown	*	10 - 20cm	M
9. TYPHA ANGUSTIFOLIA Lesser bulrush/*Anea*	H M	Brown	*	10 - 20cm	H
10. ZANTEDESCHIA AETHIOPICA Water arum lily/*Zantedeschia aethiopica*	H H	White	* *	10 - 20cm	H
B. SUBMERGED PLANTS					
11. ELODEA CANADENSIS Oxygenating pond weed/*Elodea Canadensis*	L H			20 - 100cm	H
12. MYRIOPHYLLUM AQUATICUM (feathery) Milfoil/*Myriophyllum aquaticum*	H H	White	*	20 - 100cm	H

2. Cyperus Involucratus
3. Iris Pseudacorus
5. Mentha Aquatica
6. Pontederia Cordata
7. Ranunculus Aquatilis

4.14 — POND PLANTS

NAMES *BOTANICAL* English - Spanish	HEIGHT AND SPREAD	TYPICAL FLOWER COLOURS	When Flowering S S A W	DEPTH IN WATER	F R
C. FLOATING PLANTS					
13. NYMPHAEA Water lily/*Nenufar*	H H	Many	* * *	20 - 100cm	H
14. EICHHORNIA CRASSIPES Water Hyacinth/*Eichhornia crassipes*	M H	Pale blue/Mauve	* *	Floating	L
15. PISTIA STRATIOTES Water lettuce/*Pistia stratiotes*	L L			Floating	L

COLUMN CODES:
HT = Height: L = low (less than 10cm); M = medium (10 – 20cm); H = high (over 20cm).
SP = Spread: L = little (less than 10cm); M = moderate (10-20cm); H = spreading wide.
WHEN FLOWERING: S = Spring; S = Summer; A = Autumn; W = Winter.
FR = Frost resistance: L = low; M = moderate; H = high.

8. Schoenoplectus
10. Zantedeschia Aethiopica
11. Elodea
12. Myriophyllum Aquaticum
13. Nymphaea
14. Eichhornia Crassipes
15. Pistia Stratiotes

4.15 HEDGES

NAMES BOTANICAL English - Spanish	HEIGHT AND SPREAD	Growth Fast, med, slow	TYPICAL FLOWER COLOURS	When Flowering S	S	A	W	EVG	FOLIAGE	PERFUMED	BY SEA	INTERNAL	BOUNDSRY	DR	FR
1 BERBERIS — Barberry/Berberis	M M	M	Yellow/Orange	*	*			*	Purple, Green				*	H	H
2. BUXUS — Common box/Boj común	M L	S	White	*				*	Green	*	*	*	*	M	H
3. CALLISTEMON — Bottlebrush/Callistemon	M M	M	Red		*			*	Green		*	*		H	H
4. CHAMAECYPARIS LAWSONIANA — False Cypress/Ciprés falso	H H	M						*	Green, Yellow		*		*	M	H
5. CUPRESCYPARIS LEYLANDII — Leyland cypress/Ciprés leylandii	H M	M						*	Green, Golden		*		*	M	H
6. EUONYMUS JAPONICUS — Spindle tree/Evonimo	L M	S						*	Green, variegated	*	*			M	M
7. HIBISCUS SINENSIS — Chinese Hibiscus/Hibisco Sinensis	M H	M	Many	*	*	*		Sm	Green	*			*	M	L
8. LAURUS NOBILIS — Bay-laurel/Laurus	M M	M	White	*				*	Green	*	*	*	*	H	H
9. LANTANA CAMARA — Lantana/Lantana	M M	F	Many	*	*	*			Green		*	*	*	M	H
10. LAVANDA — Lavender/Lavanda	L L	F	Pink, Purple	*	*			*	Green, Grey	*	*	*		H	H
11. LIGUSTRUM — Privet/Aligustre	H H	M	White	*	*			*	Green	*		*	*	H	H
12. MYPORUM LACTUM — Good-for-nothing/Gandula	H H	F	White followed by black berries	*	*			*	Green	*			*	M	H
13. NERIUM — Oleander/Adelfa	H H	F	Many		*	*	*	*	Green variegated	*			*	M	H
14. PITTOSPORUM TOBIRA — Japanese mock orange/Pittosporum	M M	M	Cream	*	*			*	Green	*	*	*	*	M	H

2. Buxus
4. Chamaecyparis
5. Cuprescyparis
6. Euonymus Japonicus
7. Hibiscus Sinensis
8. Laurus Nobilis

4.15 HEDGES

NAMES *BOTANICAL* English - Spanish	HEIGHT AND SPREAD	Growth Fast, med, slow	TYPICAL FLOWER COLOURS	When Flowering				EVG	FOLIAGE	PERFUMED	BY SEA	INTERNAL	BOUNDSRY	DR	FR
				S	S	A	W								
15. PYRACANTHA Firethorn/Espino de fuego	M M	S	Red/Orange berries			*	*	*	Green		*		*	M	H
16. ROSMARINUS Rosemary/*Romero*	L M	S	Blue	*	*			*	Green	*	*	*		H	H
17. SPIRAEA CANTONIENSIS Spiraea - *Spiraea*	M M	M	White	*	*			*	Green		*	*	*	M	M
18. TEUCRIUM FRUTICANS Bush germander/*Teucrium*	M M	M	Blue	*	*			*	Silver, Grey	*	*	*		M	M
19. THUJA OCCIDENTALIS Cedar/*Cedro*	H H	S						*	Green, Yellow		*		*	M	H
20. VIBURNUM Viburnum/*Viburnum*	M M	M	White	*	*			*	Green	*		*	*	M	H

Many climbers can be used to cover wire mesh fences to create dense boundary hedges. These are referred to in Chapter 4.6. In addition bougainvillea glabra can be grown as a free standing hedge as shown in last photograph.

COLUMN CODES:
HT = Height: L = Low (less than 50cm); M = Medium (50 – 100cm); H = High (over 100cm).
DEP = Depth: L = Little (less than 50cm); M = Moderate (50 – 100cm); H = spreading wide.
WHEN FLOWERING: S = Spring; S = Summer; A = Autumn; W = Winter. PERF = Plant has pleasant perfume.
BY SEA = Plants suitable for gardens near the sea. INTERNAL = Suitable for internal hedging.
BOUNDARY = Suitable for boundary hedging. DR = Drought resistance: L = Low; M = Moderate; H = high.
FR = Frost resistance: L = Low; M = Moderate; H = High.

9. Lantana
10. Lavanda
11. Ligustrum
12. Myporum
13. Nerium
14. Pittosporum Tobira
16. Rosmarinus
18. Teucrium Fruticans
19. Bougainvillea Glabra

4.16 NAYA PLANTS

The following plants are generally plants that you would have called house plants in northern Europe

NAMES BOTANICAL English - Spanish	HEIGHT AND SPREAD	TYPICAL FLOWER COLOURS	When Flowering				FOL	WHERE	GHB	WATERING NEEDS	DR	FR
			S	S	A	W						
1 AECHMEA (bromeliad family) Aechmea/*Aechmea*	M M	Many	*		*		*	SS		Moderate. Water down through centre of plant	M	L
2. AESCHYNANTHUS Aeschynanthus/*Esquinantus - columea*	M M	Orange	*		*		*	SS SH	*	Keep damp	L	L
3. ANTHURIUM Flamingo flower/*Anturio*	H M	Red & others		*	*			SS		Keep damp and spray regularly	L	L
4. ASPIDISTRA Aspidistra/*Aspidistra*	H H	Tiny white	*				*	SS SH		Keep damp	L	L
5. AZALEA Azalea/*Azalea*	H H	Many	*		*			SS SH		Water well from base when flowering. Less when dormant	L	H
6. BIGONIA REX Bigonia Rex/*Bigonia Rex*	M H	Pink	*				*	SS SH	*	When it dries out	M	L
7. CALADIUM Elephant's ears/*Caladium*	M M	Greeny/White	*				*	SS		Keep damp	L	L
8. CALATHEA Calathea/*Calathea*	M M	White	*	*			*	SH		Moderate	L	L
9. CATTLEYA Orchid/*Orquídea*	H M	Many	*	*				SS SH		Daily plus mist spray	L	L
10. CODIAEUM Codiaeum/*Croton*	M M	Yellow	*				*	S SS		Water well in summer. Less in winter	L	L
11. DIEFFENBACHIA Dieffenbachia/*Diefenbaquia*	H H	Greenish white	*	*			*	SH		Let soil dry out between watering to avoid rot	M	L
12. DRACAENA FRAGRANS Dracaena fragrans/*Dracena fragrans*	H L	Cream	*				*	SS SH		Moderate. Keep leaves clean	M	L
13. EUPHORBIA PULCHERRIMA Poinsettia/*Poinsettia*	M M	Many				*	*	SH		Keep moist	L	M
14. FICUS BENJAMINA Ficus Benjamina/*Ficus Benjamina*	H H	Unlikely					*	SS SH		Moderate. Keep leaves clean	M	L

1. Aechmea
2. Aeschynanthus
3. Anthurium
4. Aspidistra
5. Azalea
6. Bigonia Rex
7. Caladium
8. Calathea
9. Cattleya
10. Codiaeum
11. Dieffenbachia
12. Dracaena
13. Poinsettia
14. Ficus Benjamina

4.16 NAYA PLANTS

The following plants are generally plants that you would have called house plants in northern Europe

NAMES *BOTANICAL* English - Spanish	HEIGHT AND SPREAD	TYPICAL FLOWER COLOURS	When Flowering S S A W				FOL	WHERE	GHB	WATERING NEEDS	DR	FR
15. FUCHSIA THALIA Fuchsia thalia/*Fuchsia thalia*	M M	Orange	*	*	*		*	SS		Keep moist	L	M
16. HOSTA Hosta/*Hosta*	H M	Pale pink	*			*	*	SH	*	Moderate	M	L
17. MARANTA LEUCONEURA Prayer plant/*La Maranta*	M M	White		*	*		*	SS SH		Moderate	M	L
18. NEPHROLEPIS Fern/*Helecho*	H H	None					*	SH	*	Keep moist	L	L
19. PHILODENDRON Bread plant/*Filodendro*	H H	Yellow		*			*	SH		Moderate. Less in cooler months	M	L
20. PLECTRANTHUS Money plant/*Planta de dinero*	M M	Lilac, White		*	*		*	SS SH	*	Keep moist	L	L
21 POTHOS AUREUS Pothos/*Potos*	H H	Insignificant					*	SS SH	*	Moderate	M	L
22. SANSEVIERIA Snake plant/*Lenguas de tigre*	H L	Greeny/White		*			*	SS SH		Do not overwater	M	L
23. SPATHIPHYLLUM Spathiphyllus/*Espatifilo*	M M	White		*	*		*	SS SH		Keep moist	L	L
24. STREPTOCARPUS Streptocarpus/*Estreptocarpo*	M M	Many		*	*		*	SS		Keep moist	L	L
25. STROMANTHE Stromanthe/*Stronmanthe*	H H	White, Pink, Mauve		*	*		*	SS		Moderate	L	L

Notes:
1. These plants can also be grown in the shade of porches and under trees.
2. A number of other good naya plants are included in other sections e.g.,
Spider plant (4.4), Clivia (4.10), Ficus elastica (4.8), Howea (4.9), Hydrangea (4.5) and succulents (4.11).
3. A single or collection of Bonsais can be attractive on a naya, but need specialist
daily care. Orchids are included in the list in view of the number now sold but they also need more care than most
others if you are to keep them over winter.

15. Fuchsia Thalia
17. Hosta
18. Nephrolepis
19. Philodendron
20. Plectranthus
21. Pothos Aureus
22. Sansevieria
23. Spathiphyllum
24. Streptocarpus
25. Stromanthe

COLUMN CODES:
HT = Height: L = Low (less than 10cm); M = Medium (10 – 20cm); H = High (over 20cm). SP = Spread: L = Little (less than 10cm); M = Moderate (10 – 20cm); H = spreading wide. WHEN FLOWERING: S = Spring; S = Summer; A = Autumn; W = Winter. WHERE: S = Likes full sun; SS = Likes semi shade; SH = Likes full shade. FOL = Plant has an attractive foliage. GHB = Good in hanging baskets. WATERING = Guidelines for watering. DR = Drought resistance: L = Low; M = Moderate; H = high. FR = Frost resistance: L = Low; M = Moderate; H = High.

4.17 PAINTING WITH PLANTS

The basic design of your garden will have given it shape, space and privacy and included those features that you consider essential to your use and enjoyment of the garden through out the year. But beyond the basics it is the choice, and placing of plants relative to each other, that will achieve the mystique, magic, 3-D effect and interest of a great garden, however small or large.

The 350 plants presented in the preceding fifteen chapters present you with an amazing choice of colours and colour combinations. Their varying heights and widths enabling you to assemble masses of a single colour or intimate mixes of calming or exciting colours.

A. USING COLOURS

The main form, perspective and depth of the garden will be achieved by the bold and subtle use of the many shades of green. The dominant colour of most gardens through out the year. Something Clodagh has no problem remembering coming from Ireland. The colours of flowers providing the hot and cold spots, the sparkle, the vitality, the brilliance of fiestas and the calming *siesta* effects.

We sketched out this chapter over breakfast on a June morning. In the part of the garden we could see we counted 60 shades of green including lime greens, blue greens and grey greens. We counted only 40 other colours – 15 pinks and reds, 10 yellows and oranges, 10 blue and mauves, 5 shades of white plus the creams, greys and yellow ochre of rocks and stone chippings. Beyond the garden the varied hues of roof tiles and mature trees filled the foreground while the browning mountainside beyond was a mix of misty browny and bluey greens. The sort of combined internal/external vista that caused Dick to some years back start to regard gardening as 'Panting with plants'.

The art of choosing, co-planting and combining into a pleasing whole;

- The seven colours of the rainbow – red, orange, yellow, green, blue, indigo and violet.
- The colours of the artists pallet including many shades of whites and creams.
- The hundreds of hues and shades of individual flowers, leaves and trunks. Some occurring naturally and others developed by plant breeders by cross pollination.
- The colours of young new growth and maturity, especially on evergreens.

The effectiveness of the final colour scheme will depend on how you decide to separate or combine plants.

Basic choices include:

a. A mixed bed of annuals, perennials, shrubs and bulbs designed to achieve the most vivid late spring kaleidoscope effect.

b. A mixed bed planted to give year round colour. As one type of plant stops flowering another picking up the baton. E.g. Freesias, followed by irises then by gazanias and purple lantanas.

c. Beds, banks and walls of colour in a variety of combinations and moods.

The following chart offers some thought starters for a number of differently conceived displays.

THE SEVEN 'C's' OF COLOUR COMBINING

1. COMMON COLOURS	Planting a single type or mix of plants with a single common colour of flower and similar foliage colours to create a mass effect.	e.g. A bank of purple lantanas; a wall covered with purple bougainvilleas; a bed of single colour gazanias; a single pink oleander hedge; a bed of bright red geraniums. A pine garden with only pink hydrangeas.
2. COMPATIBLE COLOURS	Planting plants with different but close shades or hues of a colour in the flowers and foliage.	e.g. A bed of varied coloured gazanias; a bed of San Diegos; side by side pastel coloured pink and yellow water lilies alongside the delicate mauve of the water hyacinth; a bed of soft pink and mauve small pin-cushion zinnias.
3. COMPLEMENTARY COLOURS	Co-planting several different plants with vivid contrasts but harmony between the flower or flower and leaf colours.	A view of yellow heliopsis, red geraniums, blue agapanthus, bright green geranium leaves, orange leonotis, red/orange lantana and a pink flowering oleander hedge in the background.
4. CLASHING COLOURS	Purposely close planting a number of plants with violently different colours at either side of the artists pallet and the rainbow.	e.g. An orange leonotis underplanted with bright red geraniums and bright red crocasmias in front of a purple bougainvillea and orange bignonia on a wall. A bed of mixed colour large spiky headed zinnias.
5. CALMING COLOURS	Purposely co-planting plants whose flower and foliage colours create no clashes but rather a sense of restful harmony between flowers and foliages or foliages.	e.g. Purple lantana under planted under an old tree stump covered in a white/blue passion flower; the dark greens in a mixed corner of oleander, bay and pistachio; grey green foliage of curry plants, gazanias, echiums and santolina.
6. COLD COLOURS	An extension of '6' with a mix of cold white and mauve flowers and grey blue leaves that look cool even at midday on a mid summers day.	e.g. White bugle lilies, agapanthus and gladioli in front of a wall of white solanum;white irises alongside a white flowering echium with white alyssum in front.
7. CALIENTE (HOT) COLOURS	Purposely mixing the most vivid reds, oranges and yellows to create a garden hot spot.	Red, yellow and orange lilies, beneath a red and yellow devils tongue. alongside yellow lantana and orange leonotis with a background wall of purple and red bougainvilleas and an orange bignonia.

The choices are yours. Nothing is right or wrong and after all its your garden. Consider some bold daring colour schemes as well as more subdued traditional ones. Consider colour schemes for each season of the year. Map out the colour scheme of each bed, wall and internal vista as if you were completing a jigsaw puzzle while still drawing the picture.

Use your imagination. Use plants already in the garden or in a garden centre to help you start to develop ideas.

Try the following experiments

1. Wander round the garden with a tray or flat basket. Collect a leaf of every colour you can find and a flower of every form, size and colour.

Then attempt to produce two examples of each of the 7 C's. Finally consider whether your ideas can be implemented by transplanting some plants or reducing or increasing the number of others.

2. As a simplification of '1' collect the four or five brightest coloured flowers in the garden and then decide where they could be co planted to create a dramatic effect. Like wise collect twigs of the coolest grey or grey green leaves and see where a calm bed would best fit in if it does not already exist.

3. Before you repaint a wall or the house next time try out a number of colours to check which set up your favourite wall plants or tall self standing plants best. Include yellow ochre in your colours it can be even better than white.

4. Next time you visit a garden centre think about buying plants in groups rather than individually. Pick out some plants that interest you and place them in a group. Add others and remove some until you achieve a pleasing effect. Consider which of the seven C's you have followed or achieved and where the combination of plants would best fit into the garden. The garden centre may take an interest in what you are doing and may even offer to help. After all they may have a happier customer this way and end up selling more plants.

They might even start displaying plants in unusual but practical groupings.

B. ARCHITECTURAL SHAPES

Architectural plants can be as interesting as colourful flowering plants. Like a still life painting or live sculptures in the garden.

A wonderful garden, or mini garden, can be produced with just one or a mix of the following.

a. An oasis of palms.

b. A glade of cordylines.

c. A stone chipping area or rockery planted with a collection of euphorbias.

d. A corner or boundary of tall flowering agaves.

e. An area of mature cacti and aloes.

f. A tall hedge of prickly pear cacti.

g. A row of aeoniums in pots or planted as a dedicated bed.

Lastly have fun with painting with flowers whatever the size of your garden. Your selections don't have to be complex. In a small garden your hottest (caliente) spot may be a pot of orange oriental lilies in front of a scarlet bougainvillea and the coolest a container of white petunias. The plants listed in the previous chapters are the most popular and accessible plants so you should have few major problems.

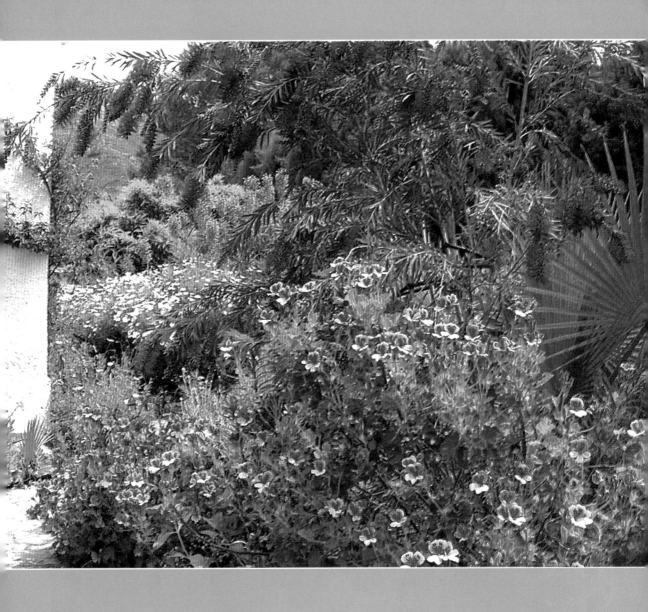

GARDENS
FOR DIFFERENT
SITUATIONS

5.0 GARDENS FOR DIFFERENT SITUATIONS

OVER THE LAST 30 years, several hundred thousands of northern Europeans have purchased properties for permanent or holiday homes in Spain in a wide range of situations – some hot and totally sheltered and suitable for the full range of subtropical and tropical plants grown in Spain, and others in more exposed, higher and more northerly places too cold during the winter for such plants.

More and more properties are being purchased and gardens laid out in inland valleys and even on mountainsides, as stretches of the coastal plain become overbuilt and overcrowded.

Recognising this migration, we consider here the design of gardens in a wide range of very different situations, from coastal apartments to inland mini estates.

At first, some of the situations may seem very hostile, but over the past 30 years amazing gardens have been created from the southern tip of the Gran Canarias to the foothills of the Pyrenees – in situations where before there was nothing other than windswept sand dunes or solid rock..

All that was needed was a regular supply of water and new settlers with creativity, patience and perseverance, the last quality being very important as gardens take some years to mature and be at their best.

When you visit botanical gardens, remember that most of them were laid out 100 years ago by plant collectors who travelled the world looking for interesting species. Luckily, we can now take advantage of their early endeavours, as nurseries and garden centres are fully stocked with the species and varieties they brought back – and many more.

The table next page provides a summary of the general practicality of the plants included in the previous section describing 350 popular plants – as well as the 14 different kinds of situations covered in this section.

PRACTICALITY OF DIFFERENT TYPES OF PLANTS

Situation of garden	General practicality of types of plants included in previous section															
	A	P	H	GC	FS	CS	FT	ET	Pa	B	S	C	G/C	PP	H	N
1. Coastal Plain a. small	*	*	*	*	*	*	R	R	R	*	*	*	*	*	*	*
b. large	*	*	*	*	*	*	*	*	*	*	*	*	*	*	*	*
2. Patios	*	*	*	R	R	R	R	R	R	*	R	R	R	R	R	*
3. Nayas	*	*	R	-	R	R	-	-	R	*	*	R	-	-	-	*
4. Apartments	*	R	*	*	*	R	*	R	*	*	*	R	-	-	-	*
5. Penthouse	*	R	*	R	R	R	-	R	R	*	*	R	R	R	R	R
6. Mobile Home	*	*	*	*	*	*	R	R	R	*	*	R	R	*	*	-
7. Woodlands	R	R	*	R	*	*	*	*	R	*	R	R	*	*	R	*
8. Giant tree	*	R	R	R	*	R	-	-	-	*	R	R	R	-	-	*
9. Inland valley	*	*	*	*	R	R	R	*	R	*	*	*	*	*	*	R
10. Mountain side	*	*	*	*	R	R	R	*	R	*	R	R	*	R	*	R
11. Central plain	*	R	R	R	R	R	*	*	R	*	R	R	*	R	*	R
12. Saline/Barren soils	*	*	*	R	R	R	R	R	*	*	*	*	*	*	R	*
13. Window boxes	*	*	*	R	-	-	-	R	-	R	R	R	-	-	-	R

CODES:
A = annuals: P = Perennials: H = Herbs: GC = Ground cover: FS = Flowering shrubs
CS = Climbing shrubs: FT = Flowering trees: E = Evergreen trees: Pa = Palms:
B = Bulbs: S = Succulents: C = Cacti: G/C = Grasses and canes: PP = Pond plants:
H = Hedges: N = Naya plants. * means most plants in group appropriate. Any restrictions
are related to the amount of shelter that can be given to the more delicate varieties.
– means generally not practical.
R means choice restricted by: a. Size in situations 1 to 6 and 3.
b. Lack of shade in situations 7 and 8.
c. Salinity in situation 9, 11 and 12.
d. Frost in situations 9 to 11.

5.1 HOMES ALONG THE MEDITERRANEAN AND SEMI - TROPICAL COASTS

Many expatriates buy properties along the Mediterranean coastline of mainland Spain and on the Balearic and Canary Islands, mostly in areas with an enviable climate throughout the year, where homeowners can create wonderful gardens.

In the warmer south and more-sheltered northerly areas it is possible to grow a wide assortment of the most delicate subtropical and even tropical plants, provided the soil is enriched and well watered.

From the tip of the Gran Canarias and the tropical gardens of Orotava in Tenerife to sheltered areas in Blanes and Lloret de Mar on the Costa Brava, there are exceptional gardens with amazing collections of plants thriving in their microclimates. We refer to them as being on "semi-tropical" coasts because their climates are not truly sub-tropical.

They do not have the true climatic conditions, especially the pattern of rainfall or constant humidity of the sub-tropics, but provided your garden has south-facing, totally sheltered pockets, you will be able to grow the following plants:

- Tropical plants such as frangipani, bananas, papayas, pineapples and poinsettias.
- The more delicate of sub-tropical plants such as white and yellow bougainvilleas and euphorbias in the sun and jungle bromeliads and orchids in the shade.
- Provided you have shade, the plants used as house plants in northern Europe, or naya plants in more exposed situations. These include ficus, pothos, philodendrons, aspidistras, anthuriums, fatsia and staghorn ferns, which can grow to impressive sizes in gardens.

Not all situations along the coastlines or in the centre of the islands are suitable for such plantings, including:

- Gardens perched on low coastal cliffs that have no tall hedges and are exposed to gales and salt spray.
- Gardens further away from the sea that do not have high hedges to totally shelter the garden and provide a balance between sun and shade (some of the special plants prefer shaded jungle conditions).
- North facing hillsides that lose the sun early, especially in the winter, and have the occasional frosts.
- Windy ridges exposed regularly to strong winds – the type of situation that will be vulnerable to the next generation of wind generators.
- Very dry, arid areas where the hot drying winds make it difficult to maintain a sufficiently humid microclimate within the garden for the tropical and sub-tropical plants.
- Situations with an unreliable water supply, especially during the spring and summer months, for watering and spraying plants to maintain the humidity around their leaves.

THE SUCCESS FACTORS

Against the above background, the following conditions are essential for the successful and relatively easy growing of tropical and sub-tropical plants:

- Rich loamy water-retaining but well-draining soil, achieved by improving the soil you inherit.
- A sheltered south-facing garden with particularly sheltered niches.
- A property surrounded by high hedges, walls or banks of trees, depending on the size of the property, to protect it from all strong winds, especially from the north.
- A garden that is not exposed to sea spray or ∫ frost.
- A constantly good water supply for watering the roots of plants and spraying them to raise the humidity around their leaves.

Major constraints that can hold you

back from success include the following:
- The size of your garden, which can range from 100 square metres belonging to a small townhouse to 20,000 square metres on a rural finca.
- The time you are able and willing to put into the development and maintenance of the garden.
- The extent of your creativity in making the best of the garden area you have.
- Whether you are able and willing to employ a gardener for some hours in a small garden or fulltime in a larger estate.
- The extent of your budget for construction work, equipment, soil, plants and water.
- Your own creativity.

Following are some creative ideas for gardens of various sizes, keeping in mind that even if your garden is not totally sheltered, most of the other plants in Section 4 will be suitable.

SMALLER GARDENS

Although garden areas may be small, they still provide you with the opportunity to create a number of different styles of interesting gardens. In sheltered but sunny spots, some of the most tender plants can be grown in the ground or in large pots. Following are some practical suggestions:

A small front garden:
- A basic design – A low hedge, a monkey-puzzle tree or cordyline (as they are both slow growing), a bougainvillea up

the wall, and a round bed of annuals in the centre of a square of stone chippings.
  • A more creative design – Make the garden appear bigger by covering the whole area from the house to pavement with a wooden pergola. Cover the walls and pergola with climbing plants. Have wrought iron railings that are not totally enclosed to avoid making the area claustrophobic. Pave the short path to the front door with a bright attractive finish. If the path is in the centre with two small square areas on either side, brighten up one side with a small fountain or an interesting group of pots, and the other side with a small wrought iron round table and chairs.

A small back garden:
  • A basic design – Lay crazy paving from wall to wall. Install a blind for shade, an oblong table and chairs, and a collection of potted plants.
  • A more creative design – Cover half the area with a colourful canvas awning and the other half with a metal or wooden pergola. To save space, build two bench seats in a corner along the boundary wall or fence, and a table and chairs for the other side. Grow climbers in narrow, deep-raised beds and restrict the number of potted plants on the limited floor space, but be courageous in your choice. If the area is half shady and half sunny, create a mini subtropical garden. In the far corner from the table, construct a pond or fountain or install a mini Jacuzzi. White walls will make the area look larger and feel cool. Brighten unplanted walls or fences with coloured plates, murals or artefacts. Add style by tiling the terrace with large light-coloured terracotta tiles. (Read chapters 5.2 on patios and 5.3 on nayas for more detailed ideas.

Four-metre-wide side passageways:
  • A basic design – Use as thoroughfares with perhaps a few potted plants. Stack chairs and bikes and cover with plastic.

  • A more creative design – Design one passageway as a narrow, sheltered and cosy eating area, leaving more room in the back garden for perhaps a mini table tennis table. Roof over half with a pergola and arbour for climbing plants, or a canvas-roofed gazebo. Leave the other half open to the sky so that the table can be moved into the sun in the winter. There will be little room for potted plants, so decorate the space with petunias in wall pots. Design the second passageway as a work and storage area with a covered walk-through shed for tools, beach things, folded garden furniture, etc.

A single four-metre-wide passageway:
  • A basic design – Decorate with a few potted plants. If there is no garage, build a place to store tools and folding furniture.
  • A more creative design – Create either an eating or stage area or a combination of the two, if there is no garage.

A roof terrace:
  • A basic design – create an area for sunbathing and drying washing.
  • A more creative design – Add a collection of succulents or cacti and a table and chairs for moonlit dining.

A first floor terrace:
  • A basic design – Fit an awning or blind for shade, and have a collection of ivy-leafed geraniums in pots.
  • A more creative design – Install a metal pergola and cover with climbers grown in large pots. If you are an avid gardener, develop a colourful mini/garden with plants in pots and hanging baskets.

400 TO 1000 METRE PLOTS
One way to approach this size of garden is to surround three sides with three/metre/wide, cantilevered, wrought iron pergolas, with their posts concreted in around the boundary.

  The pergolas, when covered with a variety of climbing shrubs and vines, would create a continuous, covered walkway some 30 metres long around three sides of the garden. When mature and in flower, it will create a very dramatic effect, with shade for terraces and shade loving plants.

Other suggestions include:

• **A basic design** – A boundary hedge, large terrace and pool, areas of stone chippings, a couple of palms and a few pots of geraniums, annuals and succulents. A barbecue beside the pool terrace, and umbrellas for shade.

• **A more creative design** – A boundary of colourful climbers and trees, some of the latter to give fruit and others to give spring flowers and shade. Create different styles of garden on each side of the house – for instance, a courtyard/patio at the front, a pool garden on one side, a garden shed and work area on another side, and the main flower garden with perhaps a central pond and fountain in front of the main terrace or naya.

It could be a tight squeeze perhaps with only 500 square metres, but with double that size you could even fit in a small vegetable garden, a greenhouse, garden frame and an area for poultry and rabbits – creating the complete small garden, interlaced with a meandering network of paths and terraces, and with a number of choices as to where to eat, entertain or take a siesta.

1000 TO 3000 METRE PLOTS

• **A basic design** – This is often a blown up version of the 400 to 1000 metre plot, with an added lawn, larger pool, second terrace, carport and a more dedicated orchard.

• **A more creative design** – An expansion of the basic design, perhaps with herb, cacti and water gardens as well as a succulent-based rockery garden, separated from the perennial and shrub garden by internal hedges or patches of taller shrubs. Mature trees, including palms,

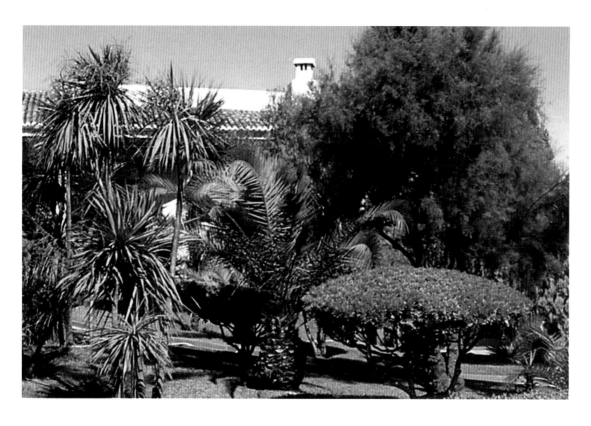

could provide cool and cosy corners in the summer and, as there is now more space, you could allow some shrubs to grow to their full mature height. There is also enough room for a larger vegetable plot and soft fruit garden.

LARGER PROPERTIES

• A basic design could be a wire and post enclosure with the house in the centre surrounded by an inner circle of lawn, terrace, pool and garden totally 4000 square metres. The rest is left wild, with a few trees and perhaps a copse, unless it is agricultural land still being worked or rented out.

• A more creative design could include the following:

1. An inner series of flower gardens. The wide choice includes a cool garden, hot garden, herb garden, perfumed garden, textured garden, cactus garden, rockery,

palm garden and water garden. Create a special area in the garden for the most tender and spectacular of the tropical and subtropical plants. Restrict the whole area to 1,500 square metres and surround it with a 25-30 metre-deep wood of a wide variety of deciduous and evergreen trees. The more evergreen and non-fruiting trees there are, the easier the annual cleanup will be.

2. Banks of plants such as spreading purple lantana, pelargonium graveolens, artotis, osteospermums, marigolds and lantanas camara. With luck, some of them will self seed, and you will have the space to allow them to grow wild.

3. Full size shrubs and trees. The big advantage of your large garden is that you will be able to allow shrubs and trees to grow to their mature height without the major winter cutback essential in

smaller gardens to keep them under control.

4. Maturing natural woodlands. Consider the ideas included in chapter 5.7 (In the Shade of Trees) or chapter 5.8 (Under the Umbrella of a Giant Tree).

5. A sizeable, organic vegetable garden.

6. An adjacent and comprehensive orchard and soft fruit garden.

7. A pool area including a Jacuzzi and sauna hut.

8. A lawn for games (putting green, croquet, petanc court) and guard-bird peacocks.

9. A hard-surface games area for basketball, table tennis, etc.

10. An area for animals and poultry.

11. Paddocks for grazing, surrounded by trees for protection against winds.

12. A large natural and wilderness area.

The possibilities are endless but, as with all sizes of garden, maintenance is in direct proportion to the size and complexity of the garden. A basic 1000 metre plot probably needs a gardener for two hours a week, while a fairly complex layout on a 10,000 metre plot could require a fulltime gardener once the garden is established.

5.2 PATIOS AND COURTYARDS

Patios have been popular in Spain for over a thousand years, since the Moors incorporated an open-air inner courtyard into the design of their townhouses, fortified farms and palaces. Originally the townhouses would have had no other garden space, so the patio was of major importance to their lifestyle. The best patios were beautiful gardens, attractively furnished for outdoor living and maximising the benefit of deep shade in the summer and any touch of sun in the winter, though some in deep wells received no sun.

The concept continues and the best features of the original and the new can be incorporated into a wide range of homes, including:

a. The small inner courtyard of traditional townhouses.

b. The larger courtyard of country *cortijos* (farms).

c. The rear-walled corral of a terraced village house originally used for the mule and chickens.

d. The small rear-walled back garden of new terraced townhouses.

The concept is now also applied to any terrace surrounded by three walls, fences or trellis.

In this chapter we concentrate on the original inner courtyard concept. The key features can be readily adapted to other situations as appropriate to your lifestyle.

DESIGNING A PATIO GARDEN

When designing your patio garden, keep the following points in mind:

1. Decide on what sort of patio you want.

2. Design and maintain it as an important place in which to relax, eat and entertain.

3. Combine all the skills of gardening and interior design.

4. Use the limited space available to the maximum. Think three-dimensional. If the patio is ten metres square it has a floor area of only 100 square metres, but if you add in the surface of four walls seven metres high you have another 280 square metres to work with.

It is amazing what you can do if you make the most of the space available. Some people achieve more in a small patio than others achieve in a large garden.

If you are tempted to go the patio route, consider the following before going into action:

1. To what extent will the patio be important to your daily lifestyle?

2. What will be the maximum and minimum annual temperatures? The warm walls of the patio may raise the temperatures just those few degrees required to

prevent winter frost damage but in the summer the south facing wall could become hot and turn the courtyard into a furnace.

3. Where is the natural shade? Recognize that the larger the courtyard the lower percentage of shade and the greater the exposure to the sun in the summer and swirling cold winds in the winter.

4. Where can the rainwater from the roof and floor run to? Decide whether it can be harnessed by fitting gutters and a cistern. The water can then be used for plants and topping up the water features.

The best patios all have certain key features that are indispensable to the full enjoyment of patio living. They include:

1. SHADE – provided by trees in the centre or one or more corners of the patio. Popular choices are olive, orange, palm, ficus, fig, jacaranda, judas tree, galan de noche and cordylines. Remember that leaves, flowers or fruit need to be swept up.

2. PLEASANT SOUNDS – the soothing and cooling sound of water cascading from a wall fountain or from one crowning a miniature pond in the centre of the patio.

3. COLOURFUL AND PERFUMED WALLS – achieved with window boxes and wall pots trailing pelargoniums/geraniums, petunias, fuchsias, carnation, vincas and nasturtiums; and with climbers such as bougainvilleas and the less rampant bignonias, wisterias, jasmine, roses, honeysuckle, passion flower, clematis, stephanotis and plumbago.

4. COOL EVERGREEN PLANTS – placed in the shady parts of the patio, the choices including ferns, aspidistras, spider plants, pothos, philodendrons, succulents, mother-in-law's tongue, cacti, bamboos and bonsais of various types.

5. FLOWERING PLANTS IN POTS – such as kalanchoa, fuchsias, begonias, pansies, busy lizzies, azaleas, hydrangeas, some bulbs such as clivias, cyclamens, freesias, irises, lilies and agapanthus – and groups of herbs for their texture, perfume and culinary/medicinal uses.

6. COMFORTABLE AND COMPATIBLE FURNITURE – sufficient for relaxing or dining alone or with company. For comfort, why not a canopied swing chair and perhaps trellised screens to create quiet corners and covered pergolas for shade when the sun reaches down into the well of the patio? Remember it may rain, so choose furniture that won't spoil easily.

7. FLOOR COVERING – large stone slabs or terracotta tiles are amongst the best.

5.3 COLOURFUL NAYAS

The nayas – or arched covered terraces – of old country homesteads and barns were originally built for drying and storing crops and agricultural equipment. Many are now popular features of converted properties and newly built houses – and for good reason.

As gardeners we see the naya as the first part of the garden rather than the last part of the house. If its design includes a display of colourful flowering plants along the shaded inner wall and the east and west ends, and there are uninterrupted views of the garden through the open arches, the naya can literally catapult one into the garden.

Unfortunately, if all the plants are along the outer edge across the arches or there are heavy balastrades, the effect can be the opposite. One can then feel hemmed in towards the house.

Nayas provide an ideal microclimate for a wide range of semi shade and shade loving plants. They retain moisture longer, therefo-

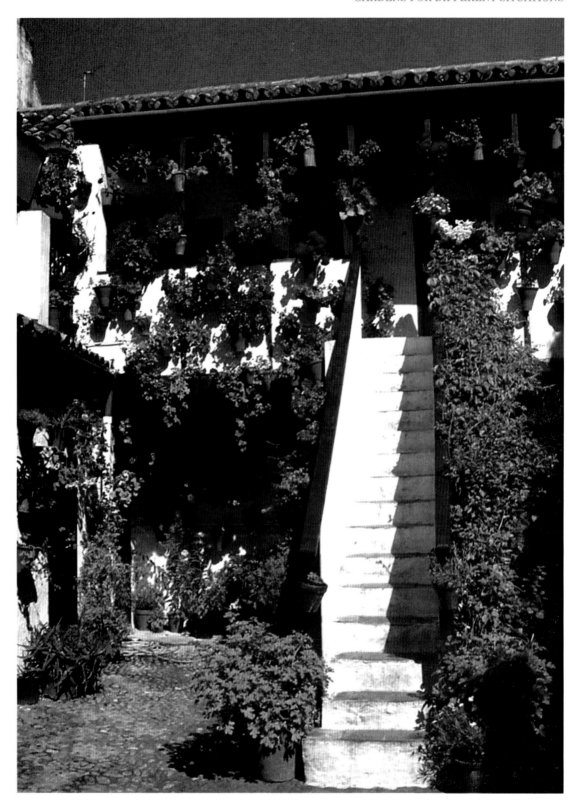

re needing less frequent watering than those in the full sun. Some of our favourites are as follows:

a. If south facing – fuchsia thalia, begonia rex, streptocarpus, aechemea, succulents, amaryllis, lilies, dicliptera, ivy leafed geraniums, petunias and stephanotis.

b. If north facing – hydrangea, cyclamen, azalea, authurium, aeschynanthus, clivia, streptocarpus, philodendron, calathea, pothos, ferns, kalanchoa and minature palms.

Whether a naya has one, two, three or even six arches, it provides an interesting outlook not only to the garden but also to the landscape beyond. Most nayas face south because they were designed for drying crops. Nowadays, they are ideal as an outdoor room and can be regarded as patios for design and living purposes. The low arch keeps out the high sun in summer and lets in the low, warming sun in winter. Open-ended nayas are even more attractive as the low morning sun can shine in at the eastern end and you can enjoy the evening sunsets through the western arch.

If the ends are glazed in, nayas become more sheltered from the wind during the winter without losing the morning and evening sun, but the impact and essence of a naya can be lost if it is totally glazed in.

For the gardener, the naya continues to be an ideal place for drying herbs, garlic, onions, red chilli peppers, tomatoes and raisins – as well as a convenient place for starting off winter seed trays.

They are the natural home for many geckos that do a good job of nightly reducing the population of mosquitoes and other flying insects. Geckos love hiding behind one or two large bunches of herbs hung in the top shady corners.

If you are an absentee gardener, the naya can be first place to brighten up with temporary plants during your visits. Using the garden before you have created some shade and a terrace or two could be difficult during June, July and August. Potted plants in nayas dry out more slowly than they do in the full sun, however, they do need to be kept just damp.

5.4 APARTMENT TERRACES

One can soon gain an impression of what can be done to create an interesting and colourful apartment terrace by looking up at a number of apartment blocks or, better still, looking down from a top apartment or terrace onto the terraces below. The best stand out very clearly, but are few and far between.

There are ten main ingredients for creating an interesting and colourful terrace:

1. The owners see the terrace, however small, as extra living space and as an elevated covered patio. They provide for its maximum pleasurable use.

2. Keen gardeners have no problem in continuing their hobby on a small scale. They overcome the limited floor space by training plants up walls and trellis, and along the ceiling.

3. Colourful flowering plants and evergreens are used to provide a year-round impression of being in a garden environment and are planted in attractive pots and containers – square and oblong rather than round being used for economy of space.

4. The plants used are appropriate to the direction the terrace faces.

5. Plants are planted in a combination of window boxes attached to the terrace walls or railings, in pots on top of end sideboard cupboards, hanging baskets and wall pots as well as in floor pots, especially for climbers trained up the wall on hooks or attractive trellis.

6. The owners are resident and enjoy plants. The watering of plants is their first priority in the early morning and late evening. In the summer, south-facing pots may need watering twice a day as well as deadheading most days. Dead flower heads will be more evident in a small space than in a large garden.

7. Blinds are fitted to protect the display of plants from the hottest sun as well as creating shade for an afternoon siesta or other activities on the terrace.

8. On north-side terraces, outer trellises are used to support plants to give some protection from the chillier breezes.

9. Plants are supplemented by tasteful ornaments and artefacts displayed on the walls. A mini self-contained water feature may add the magic of trickling water – or a painted or tiled wall mural may brighten up a wall between windows.

10. The terrace area is small and furniture is selected for its aesthetic appearance, colour, comfort and, most importantly, compactness. A matching table and chairs, rocking chairs and end cupboard units for storage and to provide waist high surfaces for a major display of potted plants is sufficient to enjoy a garden terrace to the full.

If you are a resident apartment owner, consider such a transformation. If you are an absentee owner living in the apartment for only a few weeks or months a year, consider buying colourful plants for the terrace as the equivalent of buying cut flowers for the house at home. Buy them on the first day of each visit and remove them when you leave, unless a friendly neighbour or porter will water them for you during your absences. We recommend removing them when you leave as dying plants soon give a forlorn appearance and advertise the fact that you are not in residence.

If you are a frustrated ex-allotment owner, why not grow a few vegetables and herbs in pots and containers on the terrace? Try tomatoes, peppers and the herbs you use for cooking or infusions as starters.

The table below gives you a number of planting options, but whatever you do, plant well, water regularly and watch out for and combat bugs and diseases.

lived for some years in a penthouse with a large terrace on three sides of the house with vistas of mountains, valley and sea. We walked through panoramic sliding doors onto the terrace. The wind blew hard. Dried

SOME SUGGESTIONS FOR APARTMENT TERRACE PLANTS

FACING DIRECTION	PRACTICAL PLANTS
EAST (*)	Petunias, portulacas, bizzy lizzies, pansies, herbs, geraniums, orchids, fuchsias, aloes, bulbs, bougainvilleas, plumbago, potos, kalanchoas, succulents and carnations.
SOUTH (*)	Geraniums, pansies, petunias, portulacas, succulents, cacti, aloes, freesias, herbs, bulbs, plumbago, bougainvilleas, and carnations.
WEST	Petunias, pansies, herbs, aloes, begonias, geraniums, bizzy lizzies, tronco de brasil, bulbs, fuchsias, spider plants, potos agapanthus, and miniature conifers.
NORTH	Azaleas, cyclamen, herbs, clivias, bizzy lizzies, pansies, geraniums, bulbs, aloes, herbs, miniature heathers, dwarf conifers, small palms, a collection of bonsais and traditional house plants such as kalanchoe, asparagus ferns, aspidistras, hostas, capisicum, veronica, skimmia, cinerias, bromeliads, ivies, money plant and potos.

(*) Blinds on the east and south sides will help to protect plants from the hottest low suns.

5.5 WINDY PENTHOUSES

Penthouse gardens are at the top of the gardening world. Large terraces with 360-degree views await the creativity and care of a keen gardener. Some interesting and restful rooftop gardens undoubtedly exist – but so do some disasters.

Recently we visited friends who have

out plastic pots of herbs bounced across the terrace, although only watered a few hours earlier. The original boundary beds had been converted to seats some years earlier as water had seeped through into a downstairs flat. Seaward geraniums showed signs of salt burn and in only one sheltered shady corner did some succulents and annuals survive well.

Across on another block we could see a verdant rooftop garden with container palms, bougainvilleas, oleanders and conifers, etc., – but the owner had problems with windbreaks attached to the outer railings that broke community regulations.

The two gardens highlighted the special challenge faced by rooftop gardeners, which can include the following problems:

1. The intensity of the direct and reflected rays of the sun that cause normal plant pots and even larger containers to dry out very quickly.

2. The danger of wind-blown salt burn if the property is on the sea front.

3. Winds from all directions, often constant and stronger than at street level, blow anything light around or over.

4. Thermal uplifts similar to those that rise up the faces of mountainsides and cliffs (but a cliff top house has a cliff on only one side).

5. The danger of moisture, even running water, seeping through the terrace into the ceilings of the flats below.

6. The regulations of community associations and town hall planning departments, particularly in respect of high screens around the perimeters.

7. The transporting of plants, ornaments, pots and materials to the top floor by lift or crane.

8. The limited weight bearing properties of wide terraces that overhang the building line of flats below which may restrict the installation of a Jacuzzi, swimming-pool, pond or large earth-filled containers.

9. Many owners are non-resident, only visiting for holidays.

As with all gardens, you should first review your life style needs and ask some very pertinent questions. If you could provide more shelter from the sun and wind, would you sit, eat, exercise and siesta on a more regular basis on the roof terrace? Or do you prefer to look at your panoramic views through the windows of your panoramic, air-conditioned lounge – cool in summer and warm in winter. And ask yourselves these questions:

● Would we enjoy the sound of a fountain to compete with the whistling wind?

● Would an electric raclette or hot stone cooker make more sense than a barbecue or paella ring in the windy conditions?

● Would a modern lightweight Jacuzzi be used regularly?

● Do we want to spend time preparing and tending for plants in pots and containers, or would we be best with a minimalist garden?

Be creative in your design. Consider:

● **For protection** – strengthened glass windbreaks around the windiest sides and surrounding the cosiest corners, and a gazebo with terraced sides and a canvas roof. Awnings or a large umbrella on a heavy base with safety guy lines. A euonymus, pittosporum, thuja, bougainvillea or bottle brush hedge planted in a line of large pots.

● **For comfort** – comfortable dining chairs, rocking chairs and sun loungers. Why not a colourful Brazilian hammock hung on a wooden or metal stand or a traditional swing seat with a sun canopy?

● **For interest** – Metal trellises around the outside walls and as internal dividers, partially covered with climbing plants. Groups of interestingly shaped, textured and coloured ceramic or terracotta pots and ornaments. A mini rockery in a large container; ceramic murals, modern or traditional sculptures, statues, a collection of coloured tiles or plates on the walls.

● **For relaxation** – the sound of water from a mini water feature, fountain or cascade between two small ponds.

● **For colour** – plants. Walls painted in interesting colours, Astroturf over the terrace tiles (or painted in an attractive colour with industrial grade polyurethane concrete floor paint), attractive cushions on seats and benches, and coloured pots.

● **For romance** – interesting lighting effects. A cosy corner with a good night view sheltered by a perfumed climbing shrub.

If you decide to have plants:

- Plant them in plastic pots with a diameter of twice what you would normally use at ground level. This will increase the moisture holding capacity of the soil around plants four fold.
- Place the plastic pots inside larger earthenware pots. This will stop pots from rolling in the wind and shade the inner pots from direct and reflected solar heat. Select a range of pots that will look good individually or in groups with compatible sizes and designs. Ensure pots have wide and deep watering trays.
- As an alternative, plant plants in earthenware pots that have been pre-sealed on the inside to prevent speedy drying out by evaporation. Unsealed pots dry out very quickly.
- Use a good water-retaining potting mix but not one that becomes water logged, causing root rot. It is a good idea to include vermiculite, lava lumps, pieces of water absorbent foam plastic and a little of a proprietary absorbing gel in the soil.
- Mulch the surface of the soil in all pots with a centimetre or two of small stone chippings, grit or lava balls.
- Instead of a group of pots, consider plastic or sealed earthenware troughs, 1-2m long and 30 to 50cm wide and deep. The best come with excellent deep watering trays.
- If your new or existing pent house terrace has built-in raised flower-beds, perhaps as part of the outside barrier of the terrace, ensure that they are waterproof before you plant and water. Empty the beds, which may be sizeable and deep, of all soil and builders rubble. Then clean the inside thoroughly. Fit a line of drainage tubes along the base to run off excess water from rain or watering. Paint 3 or 4 times with a high quality bitumen paint or swimming-pool paint, designed to give a secure waterproof layer. Then fill the beds with 10cms of rock chippings for drainage, topped with a good potting mix.

Plant the pots and troughs with plants that will withstand high temperatures, winds and wind-blown rain and they will provide greenery and flowers for most if not all of the year. For example:

- Flowering succulents and cacti.
- Zonal and ivy-leaved pelargoniums/ge-raniums in the sun.
- In the shady corners clivias, lilies, ficus, aspidistras and other naya plants.
- Herbs for perfume, flowers, leaf effects and cuisine.
- Controllable climbers such as bougainvilleas of various colours, plumbago and jasmines. Plumbago grows well in a large pot when pruned as a shrub.
- Lantanas kept pruned to shape when flowers die off or grown as standards. Yellow varieties stay more compact.
- Soft leafed yuccas, cordylines and small palms for their architectural form, height or shade.
- Slow growing evergreen shrubs such as bottlebrush, pittosporum and variegated euonymus.
- Include annuals only if you are happy to water twice daily in the summer.

There are plenty of plants to choose from to create controlled or kaleidoscopic colour schemes. It is important to water and feed plants regularly, and keep the following points in mind.

- To ensure that water gets down to the roots of shrubs and small trees, plant lengths of 2 or 3cm plastic tubing adjacent to plants and water through the tube.
- If you are likely to be away, install a timer-controlled watering system. Set the system at the lowest setting just to keep plants damp. Thoroughly test the system to ensure that excess water does not run out of drainage holes during or after watering, as it could drip down onto lower properties. It is better to water for 3 minutes twice a day than 5 minutes once a day.
- Remember that plants will need more dead heading and pruning than in the garden. The more you plant the more

work you will create, and untidy plants look worse on terraces than in the open garden.

If you have a suspect terrace surface you have two possibilities:

- Take up all the tiles, reseal the roof and then retile.
- Thoroughly seal the suspect tiles and cover with Astroturf to provide a non-slip, protective layer
- Cover part of the terrace with wood slat paving.

By using some of the above ideas you could lay out the rooftop as two or three mini gardens, separated by metal trelliswork with planters in front and perhaps connected via tunnel pergolas.

5.6 MOBILE HOME SITES

More and more mobile home parks are being opened as less expensive alternatives to town houses or small villas. Some parks are a mass of greenery and colour. On others, only the sites of enthusiastic small-scale gardeners stand out.

The challenge is obviously to create a small complete garden that provides year-round colour, perfume and a degree of privacy. The main obstacles to achieving this are as follows:

1. The restricted size of the plot.
2. Site restrictions on what can and cannot be done, especially where the park owners plant hedges between plots and trees for shade.
3. Often the sites are on bedrock with shallow soil or a substantial thickness of hardcore to create a stable level site resistant to the effects of heavy rainfalls.
4. The need for a separate watering system to the general system put in by the park management.
5. The need on some basic sites to do everything from scratch as no framework of hedges around plots and trees are provided.

6. The problems created by neglected adjacent gardens owned by absentee owners. For instance, geraniums attacked by the geranium moth being left untreated, resulting in other plots becoming infested.

Possible solutions include:

1. Provide privacy by (a) planting a hedge around the site, keeping it trimmed to keep it tidy and narrow so that it takes up the minimum of space, (b) construct a white or green-painted, open panelled or trellis wooden fence if you don't want to be totally enclosed and the park regulations do not allow a hedge, or (c) construct a green wire mesh fence and grow a climber on it.
2. Plant a lawn if you have good soil, or terrace the area leaving space for a flowerbed in front of the hedge or fence.
3. If there are no pre-planted trees, plant a tree in each front corner of the site to provide summer shade in addition to the front awning of the mobile home. As trees and climbers grow, check that they are securely supported.
4. Decide whether you want to plant plants in a flowerbed around the site or in a number of large pots or containers. The latter is the better solution on a rocky site. Even trees can be planted in large deep containers as long as they are regularly watered.
5. As your space is limited, plant plants that are not too vigorous.
6. Decide whether you want a permanent display of flowers or a seasonal display to give variety.
7. Invest in good potting compost for flowerbeds and pots/containers.
8. Install a battery controlled watering system to avoid having to water daily during the hot dry periods of the year.
9. Deadhead and prune regularly to keep everything in order.
10. Spray weekly against the geranium moth and also spray plants on adjacent plots if the owners are absent.

5.7 WOODLAND SITES

Many traditional Spanish houses were built amongst trees, especially summer homes where the cool shade was once considered essential from June to September for both people and many plants. Most Spaniards continue the tradition, but it seems many expatriates are happy to fell the trees to build a larger swimming-pool and terrace, and to avoid having to sweep up falling leaves and fruit. They seem to prefer air-conditioning to the natural coolness of shade trees.

Depending on where you live in Spain, the woodlands may be oak (perhaps even cork with the wonderful orange of their stripped trunks brightening up the garden), chestnuts and walnuts in the south, beech in the north, and pine – the last being the most prolific, especially along the coast.

The following are four possible woodland sites:

1. A well-kept woodland garden. Maintain it well for a year to see what plants appear and flower season by season before considering changes or making additional plantings.

2. An unkempt garden previously used only in the summer. Give it an early winter clean up to see what is underneath the layers of pine needles or leaves. If reasonably attractive proceed as above. If it turns out to be a disaster, start a new garden from scratch.

3. No garden at all because either you have a new house or the previous owners preferred the natural woodlands to a manmade garden. If you prefer the latter, gradually enhance the site.

4. Woods exist, but some of the trees are diseased and dangerous. Hire a qualified tree surgeon to fell and prune as necessary and then plant in the glades.

Above all, if the trees are attractive and safe, preserve the shade and design your garden accordingly. There is often sufficient light coming through the trees to have a good lawn. You may have to rake up fallen leaves but the grass will be sheltered from the burning sun.

If you do no more than plant a good hedge around the property, add a lawn and some pink hydrangeas, you would have a pleasing garden. A few cycas and containers of colourful begonias, busy lizzies, vincas and aganpathus in the centre of the lawn and on the terrace around the house would add interest and colour and still be easily maintained.

If you want to do more, first check on the depth and quality of soil. Woodlands often grow in an amazingly thin layer of topsoil, over a stony or rocky subsoil. When a tree falls in a storm, the root ball may be six metres across but less than half a metre deep.

If the woodlands are old you may be lucky that there is a good depth of peaty soil rich in humus but perhaps on the acid side. You can take advantage of the acidity by planting plants that have an affinity for such soils, such as camellias, hydrangeas, aspidistras, rosemary, lavender, thyme, sage and rockroses. Roses also seem to do well. If the woodlands are new, the soil may be very shallow and you will need to import soil to fill large planting holes and raised beds, or provide the base for a rockery.

In woodland glades, both original glades and those created by cutting down one or two trees, plant a mixture of woodland plants and bulbs that thrive in the semi shade with occasional sun. The mixture could include:

a. Herbs such as rosemary, lavender, thyme and sage.

b. Smaller trees that add interest such as bay, ginko biloba, strawberry tree, jacaranda, magnolia, small palms, fig, and small decorative conifers, thuja and horizontal junipers.

c. Shrubs such as oleander, hydrangea, pittosporum, lantana, broom, echium, viburnum, soft leaved yuccas and rock roses.

d. Climbing shrubs such as ivies, bignonias, clematis, honeysuckles, jasmine, wisteria, passion flower and roses where the sun shines on trunks.

e. Perennials such as leonotis, argyranthemum, senecio and euryops.

f. Patches of irises, lilies, agapanthus and grape hyacinths.

If there is a rocky outcrop or gully, consider creating a rockery with succulents, aloes or cacti. And don't forget forest fruits. In a dappled shaded area, try planting alpine strawberries, raspberries and blackberries. Dig in plenty of well-rotted manure and compost before planting.

When walking in the autumn, we often meet Spaniards out collecting setas (wild mushrooms). If you like this delicacy, try and obtain some spawn to seed an area of the woods.

No woodland is complete without a natural pool. One can be easily constructed with a plastic liner. Add natural reeds, bulrushes, bog irises and other marsh loving plants and you will soon have an interesting feature, hopefully full of frogs and toads.

If you long for home grown organic vegetables, prepare a raised bed in a clearing or on the edge of the woods. New potatoes can easily be grown in a damp pile of pine needles or leaves.

Woodland sites do have their problems. Mature trees are thirsty and might leave little moisture for other plants, so you will need to install an irrigation system until new plants are established. Pine needles and leaves can suffocate low-growing plants, so you will need to clean up regularly.

Large trees can become unstable in gale force winds. Check for any movement of root balls when you wander through the woods – and, at the same time, look for any signs of disease from wood-boring beetles or fungi.

Woods, especially pinewoods, can be fire hazards. Put up "no smoking" signs, have a hose that reaches the edge of the property and locate fire brooms at various visible points in the woods. Cut off branches to three metres above the ground and keep dry, wild undergrowth under control. And never have a bonfire!

5.8 UNDER THE UMBRELLA OF A GIANT TREE

Some gardens are dominated by a giant tree – a monster that has grown amazingly fast in a damp spot or is centuries old with a gnarled trunk and branches. Some olives were even planted by the Romans two millenniums ago and are now sold at extravagant prices as the centrepieces of large courtyards or terraces.

Olives, carobs and evergreen oaks provide heavy shade throughout the year. Others, such as fig, mulberry, plain and weeping willow, being deciduous, drop their leaves in the winter but create welcome deep solid shade in the summer. Pine trees are continuously dropping needles and cones. Often, old trees have been trained when young to create an abnormally wide umbrella of leaf, by pruning and hanging weights on the branches to make them grow horizontally rather than upwards. All of them provide maximum shade – that vital ingredient for a truly enjoyable Spanish summer – yet are often forgotten in today's rush

towards a pool, terrace and air conditioning.

If you are lucky enough to inherit an old tree, how ever big, think twice before lopping or felling it. It is worth more than the value of its logs.

Start by deciding how best to use the shade while at the same time recognising the risks.

A big tree gives you the chance to create a cool place for siestas and fiestas. You can hang a hammock or sky chair from a heavy bough and install a weighty wooden table and chairs for outdoor dining and partying. You could even build a circular seat around the trunk.

The only risks involved are falling figs and mulberries and wasps, but these inconveniences only last for four to six weeks a year. The problem of falling carob pods or bees pollinating the flowers is again only short lived, and olives and acorns don't fall until the late autumn.

The area under any tree can be brightened up with pots of flowering plants or a flower-bed around the drip line – as well as deep-shade-loving evergreen house plants in a bed around the trunk or in hanging baskets from the boughs.

Unfortunately, few plants will flower successfully in full shade, but there is a solution to this problem -- the colourful jacaranda, especially in warm coastal situations where it does not lose all its leaves in the winter and so provides dappled shade all year round.

The jacaranda can grow to 20 metres with a spread of 25 or more metres.

So how can we best use its special shade once its wonderful early summer display of enormous blue bunches of flowers has faded?

First see the shade as having three distinct zones, each one worthy of special treatment to create an overall integrated, magical mini garden:

• **The deepest shade around the trunk** – the place for plants in pots, as the root system will prevent satisfactory plantings. Many plants, including aspidistras, ferns, and ficus benjamina would be suitable, but you can also train a jungle climber, such as a pink dipladenia, up the trunk to create a central colourful heart, and tie bromeliads to some of the branches. Run a narrow stepping stone path a few metres from the trunk and brighten up the spaces between the evergreen plants with raised pots of colourful orchids and trailing fuchsias.

• The inner circle of dappled shade – plant shade loving plants in the soil and infill with a wide assortment of colourful plants in pots with a meandering path running through. There are many plants to chose from for this semi-shade, humid microclimate: shrubs such as camellias, hydrangeas, azaleas and datura; perennials such as orchids, fuchsias and succulents; bulbous plants such as clivias, lilies and agapanthus; annuals such as trailing petunias, busy lizzies,

salvias and nasturtium. Create humidity by the natural heat and the moisture of an extensive drip irrigation system and, in summer, a mist spray several times a week. This type of garden is not for the faint hearted or the absentee gardener, as it will require a watering system with several hundred individual drip heads.

• The outer circle – plant shrubs such as the devils tongue, lantanas, hibiscus, dwarf salmon flowered oleander, datura, cassia/senna and bottlebrush; perennials such as argyranthemums, leonotis, lavandar and heliopsis for summer colour and echiums, euryops and rock roses for spring colour; and patches of freesias, irises, lilies and agapanthus.

Overall, this is an amazing mix of semi-jungle-loving plants as a stand alone garden or a set piece in a broader landscape.

Such a garden could obviously not be

created in a windswept situation.

It would need to be surrounded by high boundary walls, fences or hedges for shelter from both summer and winter winds, the former preferably covered with brightly flowering climbers such as bougainvilleas, bignonias and wisterias, and the latter perhaps with a mixed-coloured oleander hedge. In a larger property it could be a mini garden – the jacaranda garden – enclosed within high hedges or walls.

If, like most of us, you are not lucky enough to inherit a large jacaranda tree, you could move towards the same effect under a group of maturing palm trees or a group of young jacaranda or albizia trees.

5.9 IN AN INLAND VALLEY

Developing a garden in an inland valley presents some special opportunities as well as some particular problems.

SOME SPECIAL OPPORTUNITIES

Besides the obvious one of having good views along or across the valley, other special opportunities a garden in an inland valley can offer you include:

1. Old terraces that can be used to create a garden on several levels.

Each terrace wall can be developed into a

feature. For instance, plant the face as a rockery with plants growing between the rocks or plant ground cover plants on the top to cascade down the wall.

2. The depth of soil behind walls. Terraces were generally built and then in-filled behind to grow crops such as grapes, olives, almonds, cherries and vegetables as well as apples and pears in cooler areas of the country.

3. Good deep soil on the valley floor, especially if a river runs through it.

4. Sheltered south and east-facing valleys can provide opportunities to create microclimates where semi tropical and tropical plants, including fruits, can be grown – provided the valleys are below the general frost line or your garden is facing south and is 50 to 100 metres above the valley floor.

5. Valleys at 200 metres or more above sea level are generally a few degrees cooler than the coastal plain – and experience more morning dew – provided breezes blow through them.

6. Many north slopes have springs. You may be lucky enough to inherit one in an old garden.

7. Established pines, oaks, carobs, olives, almonds and chestnuts will provide shade.

8. Fruit trees, bushes and vegetables often grow well if the soil is improved.

9. Terraces or a slope of wild herbs, rock roses and bulbs may exist if the land has not been bulldozed clean.

10. Perennials thrive in the cooler, damper climate.

11. Rocky hillsides can be perfect for natural terraced gardens.

12. Annual rainfall will probably be higher than on the coast.

SOME POSSIBLE PROBLEMS

Early loss of sun on north facing slopes, especially in the winter, is one obvious problem. Others include:

1. Frost, most often on the valley floor and north facing slopes.

2. The chance of snow above 600 metres.

3. North facing slopes can be damp in the winter.

4. Low sheltered valleys can be hotter than the coast in summer.

5. Soil on mountainsides and over large rocks can be shallow.

6. Flash floods can occur after storms, especially where terraces have been bull-dozed away, woodland felled or old waterways filled in.

7. Natural plant cover on a rocky plot on a south-facing slope can wither in the summer.

8. Soil is often heavy, orange clay that needs stabilising if bulldozed by builders and if the terraces have gone.

9. Topsoil could have been removed or buried when site was levelled.

SOME SUGGESTIONS

Retain all natural features such as stone terraces, well heads, large rocks and mature trees, and design your garden to make best use of them. Other suggestions include:

1. Maximise the planting of frost hardy plants. If you are above 400 metres on the mainland or in the Balearic Islands, try growing banks of daffodils, peonies and Christmas roses.

2. Give special attention to creating warm sheltered spots for sitting in the winter sun and planting some of the less hardy shrubs.

3. Retain as many established healthy trees as possible for shelter and shade and plant a thick hedge.

4. Don't plant delicate plants until you have established sheltered areas that are protected from the wind.

5. Build a spectacular rockery.

6. Build a series of ponds with waterfalls between to attract the valley wildlife.

7. Site a number of terraces with tables and chairs at different levels for interest.

8. Frame the best vistas so that they can be enjoyed from the places where you are most likely to sit.

9. Plant fruit trees and grow a terrace of vegetables.

10. Build a garden frame and greenhouse for growing early plants and over wintering delicate plants.

11. Check when you lose the winter sun and whether you get frosts before considering whether to plant sub tropical plants.

12. Protect tender shrubs in the winter from possible night frosts.

13. Take advantage of the slope to channel rainwater to where it is most needed.

14. Don't build paths and terraces right up to the boundary. Leave space for planting a hedge to provide privacy and to act as a windbreak.

5.10 HIGH UP ON AN INLAND MOUNTAINSIDE

As the coastline becomes overbuilt, more and more people are moving inland, seeking existing houses or building sites on the slopes of mountains – a challenge to even the most dedicated and determined gardener. Good gardens can, however, be developed if you recognize and respond to the following positive and negative aspects of such locations from day one.

ALL HILLSIDES

The positive factors for home sites on all hillsides are good vistas, cooling breezes, naturally growing plants, peace and quiet, and perhaps a spring, fed by higher-up melting snows. The negative factors can be full-sun parched areas in summer, possible frost or snow in winter, hot and cold drying winds, possible steep slopes, and erosion by wind and rain.

NORTH FACING HILLSIDES

The additional positive factors of hillsides facing north are more early morning mist and dew, more chances of natural springs, cooler temperatures in summer, higher rainfalls and less need to water, losing the sun earlier.

The negative factors can be many days of frost, colder temperatures in winter, a shorter growing season, and non-survival of tender plants.

TEN BASIC GUIDELINES

Here are some tips to improve the chances of your hillside garden being a success:

1. Retain as many existing natural herbs and shrubs as possible. They obviously enjoy the microclimate and have probably taken years to establish themselves. Clear unwanted vegetation from around them, mulching with stones and trimming lightly to shape.

2. Decide how to best incorporate existing plants into your future garden.

If you are lucky enough to inherit an intact hillside with a good mix of native herbs, bulbs and shrubs, do nothing except for a few carefully considered enhancements, such as pathways and terraces in natural stone.

If your hillside is not totally covered with native plants, use what there is as the main framework for an interesting and colourful garden. Even a few pockets of existing plants may be worth keeping as special features.

3. Decide on a budget for developing the garden. The main costs will be buying plants and building materials for constructing walls and terraces as well as importing good soil, compost and manure if on a dry, rocky hillside.

4. Decide whether trees are advisable to provide a windbreak and shade or as specimens to provide focal points in shaping the garden. Look around the area and check what trees grow naturally or are being imported successfully by neighbours at your height on the mountainside. Check out from what size the latter were grown (50cm high saplings or mature specimen trees). Also check what depth of soil your neighbours have compared with your own.

5. Decide on what plants will give shape, colour and perfume. The choices include

brooms, rockroses, santolina, rosemary, sage, thyme, rue, lavender etc. Many perennials can be grown successfully, especially if planted below a wall or bank. Aloes can survive high up and grow into spectacular plants.

6. Select planting places carefully. First try and map where you have:

- Solid rock, less than a metre below soil level.
- Deep soil between outcrops of rocks.
- Holes or hollows that could be filled with good soil.
- Areas of fine sedimentary soil washed down by of years of rain.
- Areas of rock that could be cleared down to soil level, keeping the rocks for a rockery or mulching.
- Places where you could sink a plastic barrel to fill with soil for planting a conifer or large shrub. The purple flowering bougainvillea can grow even in exposed situations if protected in the winter.
- Natural rain waterways.
- Consider terracing part of the garden with dry stone or concreted rock-faced walls in-filled with local or imported soil.

8. Decide whether to have a small vegetable and soft fruit garden. Raspberries grow well in the Alpujarras in Andalucía at up to 1,800 metres.

9. Provide extra colour by planting pots and window boxes. There are plants appropriate for both the summer and the winter.

10. Plant subtropical plants in pots for their summer splendour, but ensure that you take them inside to a well-lit window during the winter months. There they can provide an interesting winter display.

5.11 EXPOSED ON THE CENTRAL PLAIN

The wide-open plains of La Mancha and Aragon can be hostile places to live but,

increasingly, more and more newcomers are settling there. The plains can be hot and dusty in summer, erosion dust storms sometimes blocking out the landscapes, and in the winter, winds can be cold and wet with many areas experiencing frost and snow. These are the high plains of Spain – around 1200 metres above sea level – surrounded by higher mountains where ski resorts are open most winters.

Properties on the plains are either isolated farmhouses and cottages – many of them abandoned since their inhabitants moved away to villages and cities – or houses in lonely villages, such as those in La Mancha that Don Quijote passed through in his travels.

Summer gardening in these parts is not that different from elsewhere, but in winter plants will need to be more frost resistant, and temperate trees such as planes, mulberries, oaks, conifers, weeping willows, laburnum, philadelphus and walnuts are more usual than chorisias and jacarandas. Vines are more normal than lemons; spring peonies and hellebores more in evidence than echiums and acacias. Garden soils are often good, having served as the yards for sheep and goats for centuries, and vegetables should grow well in the sheltered village gardens.

Out in the open it will be a different story. With no mutual protection from other houses, windbreaks will be the number one priority. If you have struck lucky, your house will have a walled yard waiting to be turned into a combined flower and vegetable garden, and an outhouse or two that can be used as a workshop, storeroom or a place to keep a few hens and rabbits.

If your property is just a cottage, we suggest you first build a high-walled area around both the front and back of the house, if the plot and local regulations allow. If there is space, you could build a high wall around the whole property in which to develop a walled garden. Winds can hop over walls, so plant some trees as a windbreak either within the embryo walled garden or just outside the wall if you can. Check around the surrounding 50 kilometres or so to see what trees survive and where you can buy some sizeable saplings. Choose trees that will grow fast with the help of some animal manure and regular watering.

Make a feature of any wellhead, trough or washbasin you inherit – and an old farm cart if you can find one. Consider adding a sheltered terrace, if planning regulations allow, and build a frame and greenhouse in order to grow plantlets for planting out as soon as the frosts are past.

It's now the time to consider what sort of garden you want, bearing mind that your lifestyle will probably be rather different than on the Costas, at least in the winter. Aim to have a mixed garden because, being isolated, it makes sense to be as self sufficient as possible.

Grow vegetables in the spring, summer and autumn (the winters will probably be too cold) and plant fruit trees and bushes. Nuts, apples, pears, plum, raspberries and peaches should be possible crops – but a lemon tree will need to be well protected in winter if it is to have any chance of survival. Within the garden a herb area would make sense, as well as frost resistant perennials and shrubs. Train a grapevine over a traditional iron arbour in front of the most south-facing doorway.

Brighten up the summer garden with pots and window boxes of bright coloured annuals. Develop a rose garden and grow climbing roses up walls and over pergolas rather than the bougainvilleas and bignonias of the coast. Grow delicate shrubs in large pots and take them inside for the winter as one would in Madrid, which has a similar climate.

MADRID

The climate in Madrid will be very hot in summer and cold in winter, as on the open plains, although high and dense building gives protection from winds. Sheltered gardens will be like an oven in the summer, so a wide variety of plants can be grown (including sub tropical plants) if watered well and maximum use is made of any shade.

Anything that is not frost resistant needs to be planted in pots and taken into the house or apartment during the winter and placed in front of a south-facing window. Remember what you used in northern Europe to give winter colour – even if it was only varied shades of green. Maximise the planting of temperate evergreen shrubs, trees, roses, herbs and bulbs, and brighten up spring, summer and early autumn gardens with colourful window boxes, pots and hanging baskets.

5.12 SALINE AND BARREN SOILS

Fewer and fewer new houses are built on good soil. Increasingly, saline or barren land is being used for building, as it is of no use for agriculture, fruit growing or vines. Sometimes land is classified as *tierra de secano* – to be left as dry, non-irrigated land to go wild. Many such areas are rural and have enviable views, but initially there are two problems that need to be overcome.

First it is important to understand why your land is said to be saline or barren. There are four main causes of salinity:

a. Seawater entering the water table along the coastal strip during a period of several years of drought.

b. A rising water table over salty sub strata as a result of the felling of trees and therefore less extraction of water by plant roots, especially where native trees grew previously on the slopes of a valley.

c. The over use or deepening of a well.

d. The irrigation of soil with salty water over a number of years which. eventually kills fruit trees and vines.

There are four main causes why very little or nothing will grow in certain situations. They are:

a. Builders have stripped all the topsoil

off your plot and all you have left is very infertile sub-soil.

b. Serious salinity.

c. Years of very little rain resulting in desert land, although in reality the desert-like soil may be rich in nutrients.

d. Pollution of the land by factory effluent and the inclusion of industrial waste tips.

What can be done to improve the soil? Obviously you need to reduce the salinity in the soil, and you can do this by:

a. Stopping the use of saline water immediately.

b. Having the extent and type of salinity checked and then searching out a suitable and economic desalination unit.

c. Washing through over a number of years by watering with collected rainwater or imported tankers of spring water.

d. Enriching the soil where you will be planting flower-beds and trees by
mixing in large quantities of well rotted manure and compost.

e. Replanting/planting salt resisting trees such as pines.

f. Installing a magnetising water improvement unit to treat well or piped water.

g. Installing a mini reverse osmosis or evaporation desalination unit.

To improve barren soil, you need to do the same as in 'b' above and irrigate well, import loads of good soil and grow plants in raised beds in enriched new soil rather than directly in the ground.

Other steps you can take are to design the garden with large terraced and paved areas to minimise the areas to be planted, situate shrub beds under the eaves so that they catch all the rainwater; slope the surrounding terrace towards the bed to increase the amount of fresh water; and plant things that are reasonably tolerant to low levels of salinity.

What can be planted in saline situations? If you walk along many beach areas, you will often find:

a. palms and tamarix being grown on the beach,

b. yuccas, cordylines, pittosporum, aloe, arboresens (red hot poker), agaves, prickly pear cacti and succulents such as aeoniums and messembryanthemums growing at the edge of the beach,

c. ground covers such as carpobrotus, aptenia, morning glory, asteriscus maritime covering sand dunes,

d. bamboo thickets in damper areas,

e. pines that adapt to the salty situation.

The best thing is to start with the planting list above before mass planting other shrubs. Plant a few and see how well they grow for a year.

5.13 WINDOW BOXES AND LINES OF POTS

Window boxes or lines of pots planted with colourful or evergreen plants make attractive mini gardens on the window sills and front edge of the balconies of houses, apartments and penthouses. Sadly, window sills and balconies are under utilised in this way, even though garden centres stock a much better selection of suitable containers these days – and an example has been set by many inland villages.

When they are planted well and cared for, plants in window boxes or lines of pots can do the following:

1. Brighten up the outlook from windows and the doors onto balconies and terraces.

2. Provide a screen from prying eyes.

3. Brighten up the overall appearance of a building from the outside, from both the garden and the street.

4. Be colourful all the year round with either permanent or seasonal plantings. Tiers of window boxes on four storey village houses or even taller apartment blocks can create an amazing Hanging Gardens of Babylon effect, even during the winter months when house fronts can otherwise look drab and communal gardens are not at their best.

5. Brighten up dull courtyards when placed on windowsills, hung on walls or positioned on low walls.

6. Brighten up the semi shade under large trees – perhaps where you eat or take a siesta – by hanging window boxes from boughs or supported on hanging shelves.

7. Give the appearance that the house or apartment is lived in. Walk past a few blocks of apartments in traditional village streets or through a few urbanisations and you will notice that the properties with window boxes stand out, especially if cared for.

In principle, anyone can have window boxes. Traditionally built houses often have wide external windowsills that give space for window boxes between the window frames and wrought iron security grills. Some also have balconies with metal or wooden railings.

Many new houses have plastic or aluminium windows with integral double-glazing and security blinds that often have only very narrow sills or none at all. Fortunately, many garden centres now stock window boxes with metal supports that can be hung below the windowsill in much the same way window boxes can be attached to railings of an apartment terrace.

Provided you are able to water them regularly you can have window boxes anywhere, from the seashore to the mountaintop. The need for hand watering can be minimised by rigging up a mini drip system. In sheltered situations, the heat loss from windows is often sufficient to create a mild microclimate that stays just above freezing, even in high up villages above the frost or snow line. In more exposed situations, window boxes can be planted with frost resistant plants or left empty during the winter months. Absentee owners can plant up the day they arrive.

TYPES OF CONTAINERS

Traditionally, Spaniards have used a wide assortment of long planters, painted terra-cotta pots, empty tin cans, jars, glazed earthenware containers, lengths of deep water guttering and even large dried gourds, the choice depending on ingenuity and budget.

For most of us it is more practical and aesthetic to buy specially manufactured terracotta, ceramic or plastic window boxes. They are now available in a wide range of lengths and widths to fit various sizes of window sills and to produce a continuous bed along the edge of balconies. You can buy them with matching or integral drip trays and built in self-watering reservoirs that hold sufficient water for several weeks. The containers can be plain or decorated, though the extra cost of the latter might not be worth it, as trailing plants will soon cover the box.

There are pros and cons for each type of material. Traditional terracotta pots can cool down the roots of plants by surface evaporation if not covered by trailing plants, while non-porous materials lose water less quickly, but can get hot if not covered by trailing plants.

WHAT TO PLANT?

The following plants are amongst the most reliable:

1. FOR FLOWERS – all the year round: trailing ivy leafed and regal pelargoniums/geraniums, except in the heavy frost/snow belt where they need to be put in a cold frame or greenhouse for the winter.

Spring, summer and autumn: trailing petunias, portulacas, carnations, felicia, tradescantia, verbena and in the shade fuchsias and busy lizzies.

Spring: pansies, trailing sweet peas, verbena, primulas and freesias.

Autumn and winter: heathers, kalanchoa and pansies.

Winter: cyclamens, poinsettias, stocks and bulbs such as hyacinths and daffodils.

2. FOR COLOUR – all the flowers listed above, as well as the colour that can be provided by the fruit and foliage of plants.

Fruits: the fruits on mock pepper and mini pomegranate plants can look very attractive during the autumn, once annuals are past their best.

Foliage: begonias, spider plants, variegated ivies, succulents, cacti, herbs and dwarf conifers all have interesting foliages.

3. FOR THE ABSENTEE GARDE-NER – if you are an absentee gardener, restrict your window boxes to trailing ivy leafed geraniums, succulents and cacti. If your visits are very infrequent and short, replant your window boxes with seasonal annuals each time you visit and let them die off when you leave. In this case, remo-

ve the boxes to an invisible place so as not to advertise your absence.

WATERING, WATERING
AND WATERING!
The soil in window boxes needs to be constantly damp to get the best out of your plants. You can achieve this by:
* Filling the window boxes with a rich water-retaining but free-draining compost. Being waterlogged can be as bad as being too dry. Use a 5:5:1 mix of good soil, home made compost and sharp sand with a little water retaining gel mixed into the bottom half of the compost.

• Watering while taking into account the type of plant and whether the window boxes are in full sun or in the shade. For instance, annuals in full sun will need watering every day, while ivy leafed geraniums on the shady north side of the house will only need watering once or twice a week in the summer and once a fortnight in the winter.

• Planting less thirsty plants.

• Mulching the top of the compost with ground lava, grit or stone chippings.

• Using self-watering window boxes. But do watch the level indicator and top up the reservoir before it is empty!

• Making handy self-watering drip bottles from 1.5 or five-litre water bottles (as illustrated). Make a small hole two centimetres above the base. This will be above the curve and will allow any sediment to settle without blocking the jet. Push the end of a joiner used to join five- millimetre irrigation tubing carefully through the hole. Seal the connector to the bottle with a blob of waterproof glue and leave to set overnight. Then cut a length of irrigation tubing just a little shorter than the length of the window box. Fit drip feeds to the tube, using T-junction pieces and to the end so that there will be an even distribution of water. Check for leaks and then place on top of the soil at the side of your window box. Adjust the drip to release just sufficient water to keep the soil damp a finger depth into the soil.

FEEDING

The roots of plants in window boxes have a relatively limited amount of soil in which to search for nutrients. This will be used up relatively quickly, so feed plants regularly – monthly in the autumn and winter and weekly in the spring and summer. A weak feed at this frequency is better than a strong occasional feed in order to achieve steady rather than a stop-go development of the plants.

Ensure that you use a balanced feed and one not too high in nitrogen. The latter can stimulate too much green growth in preference to flower buds and long lasting flowers. Also, fast growing green growth can be fleshy and weak and therefore susceptible to pests and diseases. In general, change the compost every second or third winter.

DEADHEADING AND PRUNING

Deadhead regularly to stimulate continuous flowering. Remove dead leaves and stems as soon as they appear to prevent the chance of fungal diseases. Trim plants to shape to improve the overall appearances of your boxes, but don't over prune cascading plants such as petunias and trailing geraniums. If you live in a front line apartment and your window boxes are burned by salt spray, wash the plants regularly with water and cut out any branches that have been seriously damaged.

HEALTH CARE

Plant only strong plants and keep them healthy by not over watering and over feeding them – or of course forgetting to water them at all. Watch for any sign of insect damage or disease. Cut out damaged leaves and stems and spray appropriately.

CARING
FOR PLANTS

6.1 PREPARING THE SOIL

LIKE THE FAMILY CAT, plants have nine lives, each one of them easily lost and largely irrecoverable. The more lives lost, the less chance of having strong, healthy and colourful plants in your garden. The nine lives are:

1. The quality of the seed or cutting used to propagate the plant.

2. The ambient conditions in which the seedlings are grown into plants in nurseries for sale to the public or, if home grown, for planting out.

3. The ambient conditions during the transfer of plants from the grower to the garden centre – increasingly by trans-European pantechnicons and international airlines.

4. The pre-sale care of plants in the garden centres, especially during the winter and summer months, and the quality of advice given regarding the planting and ongoing care of those you buy.

5. The selection and purchasing of plants.

6. The acclimatisation of plants before planting in their final positions.

7. The selection of their planting positions.

8. The planting and aftercare.

9. The quality of the soil in which your plants are planted.

The quality of the soil is the most fundamental issue and often ignored until too late. Many plants in Spain are in a permanent state of survival due to a combination of poor soil and watering.

Numerous surveys we have carried out on the problems of expatriate gardeners in Spain have destroyed the myth that all Spanish gardens have good soil. Response to surveys by people living between Valencia and Cadiz classified their soils as follows: excellent 5%, good 30%, poor 50% and very poor 15%.

Many of those claiming excellent and good soils did so because they or their predecessors had improved the soil. Soils were poor for the following reasons:

1. Clay soil, heavy to work when wet and impossible to work when dry and baked. It is often rich in minerals but they are not easily extracted by roots of plants. It dries out quickly in the sun and roots can be compressed by the drying clay.

2. Sandy soil that drains quickly and can be acidic. It is light in nutrients as millions of years of rain have dissolved and washed away many of the minerals to the subsoil or water table.

3. Shallow soil, sometimes just two or three centimetres over bedrock. Some gardeners use a Kango hammer to create planting holes, while others resort to raised beds.

4. Soil full of stones or rocks, sometimes even large flat rock slabs within 30cm of the surface.

5. Soil full of builder's rubble.

6. Topsoil removed by builder and not replaced.

7. Topsoil bulldozed under subsoil.

8. Barren soil due to over use or no rainfall.

9. Soils that have become saline by over use of wells or felling of forests.

10. Acid soil low in nutrients.

Plants may survive in poor soil but they will not be at their best. They will only remain alive with regular watering and feeding, so check your soil and improve it, whatever its current condition. But first what is a good soil? For most plants the ideal soil is one that is:

a. Crumbly and friable, high in humus (decomposing vegetable matter) and allows roots to spread and go down deeply in search of moisture and minerals

b. Water retaining, due to the humus

content but sufficiently gritty and open to allow excess water to drain away.

c. Attractive to and retains earthworms that process humus and improve the draining and oxygen penetration of the soil.

d. Rich in micro organisms and minerals required for the healthy growth of plants.

NUTRIENTS REQUIRED BY PLANTS

1. Carbon dioxide taken in through the leaves at night to create chlorophyll.

2. Moisture taken in by roots and leaves. Together with micro- organisms, water extracts nutrients from the soil and causes plant cells to swell to provide rigidity and strength in stems, branches and leaves.

3. Nitrogen (N), required for the development of green plant structures (stems, branches and leaves) and for root growth.

4. Phosphorus (P), often known as phosphate, essential for the development of strong root structures.

5. Potassium (K), often known as potash, essential for the development of flower buds, flowers, seed heads and fruit – and to enhance the drought and disease resistance of plants.

6. Minerals and trace elements that maintain health and vitality. The most important are as follows.

a. Magnesium, which prevents yellowing of leaves between veins.

b. Calcium, essential for cell growth and resistance to diseases.

c. Sulphur, which promotes general plant health when in the soil and increases soil acidity to enhance the extraction of minerals. Fed on the surface of the leaves, sulphur also prevents mildew and fungal diseases.

d. Iron, which helps create chlorophyll and prevents bleaching of leaves between veins.

e. Zinc, which prevents leaves from developing yellow spots.

f. Manganese, which prevents yellowing of leaves between veins.

g. Boron, copper and molibium, which contribute to the development of cell structures and natural disease control.

All are found in Spanish soils although not always in the right balance, so they need to be supplemented by the addition of manures, compost, seaweed, comfrey and nettle feeds, and proprietary organic and inorganic fertilisers.

Get to know your soil. To improve it, try the following:

1. Dig holes in several places in the garden and check the depth of the darker topsoil before you get down to a lighter-coloured subsoil or rocks.

2. Water a few square metres of soil for two minutes, wait until the surface water has drained away and the surface is firming up, then dig down to find out how far the water has penetrated. Repeat this until you get water down to 30cm.

3. Leave the area to dry out for two days and then dig down to find how far it has dried out. Repeat every two days for a week.

4. If the top soil is less than 20cm and the water drains away or dries out quickly, deepen the soil with earth from other parts of the garden or brought in and work in plenty of compost and manures to improve its fertility, water absorbing properties and openness.

5. If the water does not soak away and the soil becomes waterlogged in the top 10 or 20cm, loosen the soil down to a depth of 50 to 60cm and mix sharp sand or grit into the soil at the same time you add the compost and manures.

6. Another way to test the composition of the soil before and after making manure/compost additions is to put a handful of earth in a tall thin glass, fill it with water, place your hand over the top and shake. Then leave to settle. The solid matter will settle in layers – the heavier larger stone particles at the bottom, the smaller stones and grit in the middle

and a dark layer of fine particles and light organic humus on top. You should notice a big difference in your soil after you have enriched it.

7. If you are taking over an existing garden and the earth is poor, you have four options.

• Mulch the surface of the soil around plants with well-rotted compost/manure and work it into the surface of the soil with a hoe and harrow after rain.

• Clear each bed in turn and enrich the soil before replanting with the plants you took out or with new plants.

• Make new, perhaps raised, flowerbeds in another area and, if feasible, transfer existing plants to the new bed. Use the original area for a terrace or special feature such as a pond or rockery.

• Reduce the areas of the garden used for flowerbeds by clearing the least attractive ones or those in the wrong position.

• In new gardens, aim to add two 20-litre plastic buckets of compost/manure to each square metre of poor soil to be used for flowerbeds. Add one extra to sandy soils and add a bucket of sharp sand/grit to each square metre of waterlogged soil. In all cases, work the additions into the top 20 to 30cm of the soil. To save time and money don't bother to enrich the soil where you have no intention of planting anything.

9. The preparation of the soil alongside walls needs special attention. Often you will find a large quantity of builder's rubble buried there. This causes two problems. Firstly the soil drains instantly and secondly the buried mortar makes the soil too alkaline for favourite wall plants such as bougainvilleas and bignonias. So dig deep alongside walls and remove most of the rubble before changing or enriching the soil.

10. If you have good soil, most permanent flowering plants in the garden will rarely need extra feeding. Annuals will, however, as well as potted plants, vegetables and fruit trees.

11. Some plants, such as camellias, blue hydrangeas, irises and rock roses, like acid soil, as found on wooded or cleared sites, especially pine woods.

12. If you are planting acid-loving plants in normal soil, either plant in large buried pots full of acid potting compost, the compost from under pine trees, or develop a special acid mix for a bed that is preferably in the semi shade.

13. If you have a small garden you may want to restrict the growth of some plants while encouraging others to grow rapidly. For instance, you may want a cactus/aloes bed, but not with huge mature plants. In this case plant them in poor soil but add sand/grit to ensure that it is free draining. Just enrich the beds for your prize shrubs and other plants.

CHECK YOUR SOIL ACIDITY

Most Spanish garden plants will grow well at acidities on the pH scale of 6 to 7.5, with an optimum of around 6.5. Acid-loving plants will be happier at a pH of 4 to 5. The pH scale runs from a high acidity of 1 to a high alkalinity of 14, with 7 regarded as neutral. The difference between two numbers on the scale indicates a tenfold difference in acidity.

If interested, buy an inexpensive soil testing kit or ph meter from a garden centre or a roll of litmus paper (pH papel) from a chemist. Using litmus paper is easy. Put an inch of soil in a jar, half fill with water and shake. Let it settle for a few minutes and then stick one end of a strip of litmus paper into the water. Leave for a minute and then check the colour against the colour chart provided. Just one precaution: check the pH of the water you use before doing the tests as this could distort the results.

The issue of soil fertility and acidity is more important in the growing of vegetables and fruit. Chapters 7.7 and 8.4 therefore provide further guidance.

6.2 GUIDELINES FOR BUYING PLANTS

Whether you purchase plants or propagate your own, only plant out strong healthy plants. The following are guidelines for buying plants:

1. Select plants that match your local microclimate and the style of garden you have decided to develop. Most plants sold are suitable for planting along the Costas, but there can be big differences in the winter microclimate between coastal gardens at sea level, five kilometres inland, inland valleys, north facing slopes and mountainsides. Temperatures often vary by one degree centigrade per 100 metres of height on normal days, but this can rise to two or three degrees per 100 metres during wintry weather. Two hours of frost every three years can make the planting of tropical and the more tender subtropical plants very disheartening. Also recognise that some plants love acid soil such as found on plots near to pine trees.

2. Select and purchase strong healthy plants that have:
- No sign of disease or infestations,
- A good shape with strong joins between the branches and trunk,
- A good root ball in relation to the size of the growth above the soil. If a plant is top heavy, the small root structure may struggle to extract sufficient moisture and nutrients from the soil to support the super structure when planted in the harsher conditions of the average garden compared to those in a propagating house. We often prefer to buy a smaller, balanced plant and bring it on at a realistic rate in the garden.
- Plenty of new, unopened flower buds. Purchase a plant with just one or two open flowers in order to check the colour,

with many buds that will open later in the garden, unless you need instant colour as in-fills for a special occasion. If you buy a plant in full flower with few oncoming buds, it will soon finish flowering, as the plant's priority when first placed in the garden will be to put down roots. Yes, many garden centres do market plants in full flower and some now charge more for budded but un-flowered plants.

• Good supporting canes and ties which have not started to rub or cut into the bark. This is especially important when selecting tall shrubs and trees.

3. Do not buy plants that show signs of being:

• Wind or frost burnt, especially when purchasing during the winter or early spring.

• Seriously root bound. However, if buying a tree, there is an advantage if strong roots have grown through the bottom of the container into the soil beneath.

• Very recent propagations, as yet without good root structures. This is especially important with climbers sold in very small pots.

• Stressed by heat or having been allowed to dry out.

• Waterlogged, and therefore perhaps susceptible to fungal diseases.

4. Don't buy very early annuals unless you have a very sheltered garden or a cold frame in which plants can be hardened off.

5. When buying something unusual, check that the garden centre can tell you how to care for the plant. If not, ask them to find out before you buy.

6. If the garden centre does not have the variety or colour of flower you want, ask if they can order it for you.

7. When purchasing very large plants such as palms or old olive trees, check that the garden centre is able to deliver and plant for you at a reasonable cost.

8. Search widely for good and unusual plants. Recognise that there is a wide range of sources as illustrated in the "Some Useful Sources of Plants" table below.

9. If plants seem expensive, check at a number of other places. Prices can vary widely.

10. Recognise that unlike most other purchases, no warranty normally comes with plants. Few outlets will readily replace plants that die. It is up to you to manage the transfer of plants from

---

SOME USEFUL SOURCES OF PLANTS

1. Nurseries that propagate most of the plants they sell.
2. Garden centres and supermarkets that buy in all their plants.
3. Weekly markets, rastros and garden club stalls where enthusiastic amateurs sell some of their own propagated plants.
4. Agricultural cooperatives – especially for fruit trees and vegetable plants.
5. Swaps with friends or gifts.
6. Self-seeded plants on the roadside or in the garden.
7. Neighbours about to either replant a garden or add a swimming pool.
8. Jobbing gardeners who propagate to produce in fills in the gardens they maintain.
9. Mail order catalogues – especially for roses, bulbs, speciality shrubs and vegetables.
10. You own propagation from seeds or cuttings.

where you buy them to your garden – avoid transferring them in a hot car in mid July/August – and plant them well and nurture them into the best specimens in the neighbourhood.

11. When your garden is fully planted, ensure that the unplanned, impromptu purchase of a special/unusual plant that catches your eye can be fitted in by replacing an existing plant, re-planning part of the garden or adding yet another pot to a mounting collection.

Remember that they all need to be cared for.

6.3 PLANTING EFFECTIVELY

New plants should be planted in as near an ideal position as possible using the best available soil. Under those circumstances each plant has the best chance of speedily developing the deepening and spreading root system necessary to extract the nutrients and moisture essential to achieve the strong, healthy, and continuous growth.

POSITION
Select planting sites appropriate to each plant. For instance:
- In the sun, semi shade or shade.
- In sandy, chalky, stony or rich-in-humus soil.
- In swampy or free draining soil.
- In acid, neutral or alkaline soil.

When deciding where to plant, recognise that situations such as alongside a drive, terrace, path or stone chipping area will provide roots with a natural damp shelter, once they grow sideways and downwards, searching for moisture and dissolved nutrients.

TIME
Plant at the optimum time of the year, preferably after a period of rain and, if sunny,

late in the afternoon. If you garden according to the lunar calendar, take note of the special planting days for flowering and evergreen leaf plants.

Although most plants are now sold in pots with a well developed root system and not dry rooted (although the latter still occurs), the best time of year to plant perennials, shrubs and trees is during the cooler months of October through March. However, if your garden is in a frost belt, delay the planting of any delicate plants until after the last frosts.

PREPARATION OF THE SOIL
Prepare flowerbeds and areas for trees as outlined in first chapter of this section entitled "Preparing the Soil".

PREPARATION OF PLANTS
Water all plants the evening before planting so that the compost around the root ball stays as firm as a ball when you remove the pot.

PREPARATION OF PLANTING HOLES
Prepare planting holes carefully. If you are lucky enough to have a garden with a light, good draining loamy soil it will normally be sufficient to dig a hole slightly larger than the size of the root ball. Fill the hole with water and let it drain away. Carefully transfer the root ball from the pot to the hole, working some compost into any air holes left.

If you are unable to fully prepare beds in this way, dig a hole twice as wide and deep as the pot containing the plant. Fill with water and let it drain away. Then line the hole with a 50:50 mix of soil and well-rotted compost or a water-retaining planting compost from a garden centre. If the planting hole drains away quickly or your soil normally dries out very quickly, add a teaspoon of a water-absorbing gel into the compost at the bottom of the hole. Firm the compost at the bottom of the hole and add more until the depth of the hole is equal to the depth of soil in the pot containing the plant.

PLANTING

Remove the plant from the pot, taking care not to disturb the root ball, and place in the planting hole. If the plant was root bound in the pot, loosen some roots before putting in the hole.

Infill the hole around the root ball with the 50:50 planting mix mentioned above. Firm each five centimetre layer until you reach the level of the surrounding soil. Then mulch with two centimetres of loose, well-rotted garden compost or purchased compost. If you are planting acid loving plants such as camellias, hydrangeas, rock roses and conifers, use acid planting composts.

If strong roots were coming through the bottom of the pot, or the soil in the pot was very loose or fibrous, cut off the pot rather than try to pull the plant out of the pot. After planting give the soil around the plant a good watering.

STAKING AND PROTECTION

If the plant needs a supporting cane or post, knock this firmly into the ground before planting and tie up the plant as soon as planted. Likewise, fix screw eyes into a wall if the plant is to be tied against it. Ensure that plant ties leave plenty of room for the stem and branches of the plant to expand and that they do not chaff or rub.

If you are planting in a sunny position, cover the surrounding area with woven plastic sheeting and mulch with stones, chippings or wood bark to keep the soil cool and moist and to make it difficult for weeds to establish themselves.

If planting in a windy position, protect plants with a woven plastic screen until they are established.

WATERING NEW PLANTS

If you have an irrigation system, fix a drip feed for each new plant. Check the soil regularly to see that it is moist and that you can push a finger down into the soil. Recognise that a plant can die from the bottom upwards just as easily as from the top downwards, so a deep watering down to the base of the roots will be better than a shallow watering three times a week. It helps to push in a 20cm length of 5cm diameter plastic tubing beside the plant, and then water down it to get water to the roots.

Be especially careful to water sufficiently during the first summer. By the second and third year most shrubs and trees will have their roots well down towards the water table, so you should be able to reduce the watering progressively.

FEEDING

If you enriched the flowerbeds and planting holes, plants should find sufficient nutrients in the soil to sustain their continuous growth. However, if plants are yellowing or become stunted even though you are watering properly, give the plants a boost with a liquid comfrey/nettle natural feed or an organic general fertilizer for flowering plants or evergreens as appropriate. If using the latter, we recommend using half the indicated strength and applying it twice as frequently. From then onwards, give your plants a light slow release granular feed each spring. Water in well if it doesn't rain within a day.

EARLY CARE

As the plants grow, keep a wary eye out for pests and diseases and treat promptly. Prune plants lightly during the first year to achieve an attractive balanced shape.

PLANTING BULBS

Plant bulbs according to their recommended depths. Typical planting depths in Spain are as follows:

- Small bulbs and corms such as crocuses, anemones and grape hyacinths 3 or 4 centimetres.
- Shallow rhizomes such as miniature irises, 2 or 3 centimetres.
- Medium sized bulbs and rhizomes such as daffodils, tulips, San Pedro and gladioli, 8 to 10 centimetres.
- Large bulbs such as lilies and dahlias, 10 to 12 centimetres.

• Large rhizomes such as flag irises and canna lilies, 3 or 4 centimetres.

6.4 USING EFFECTIVE TIES AND SUPPORTS

Many plants need to be tied to walls, fences and trellises or to supporting canes or stakes. Trunks and branches can be strangled or severely chaffed if tied or supported poorly and branches may be lost or plants, including maturing trees, die. To prevent this, we recommend you take the following actions:

1. Recognise that the diameters of the main stems and side branches of climbers planted against the wall of the house, boundary walls or fences or mid garden terrace soon expand, especially after the first year. For instance, a bougainvillea planted with a thin one-centimetre stem may have a thick five-centimetre diameter trunk within five years.

Unless ties are loosened or replaced as the plant grows, strangulation soon starts, with tie wires being absorbed into the new flesh and eventually killing off the branch or entire plant. It is all too easy to fix a few metal eyes into a wall, tie plants tightly to them with small-gauge round or flat garden wire and, at the same time, wind wire around branches to train them straight – and then assume that all is well.

Go into your garden now and examine all your climbers. You may be surprised at how many wires are already cutting in, even being totally enclosed by new woody growth. Remove all immediately, pulling out any sealed wires if possible.

Replace all such ties with a length of garden wire passed through an appropriate length of the 5, 10 or 15mm diameter black plastic tubing as used for drip irrigation systems. Use the narrower tubing for small plants and the wider for thicker trunked and branched shrubs and trees.

Note that the flat garden ties, even if plastic covered, can be worse than round ties as they act as saws on windy days. This problem is very critical for absentee gardeners who may only see plants in full flower and leaf and not when bare in the winter after leaf fall or the winter cut back.

2. The supporting canes and tight ties on plants in the garden centres are designed to ensure that plants are not damaged in transport to or from the garden centre. Rarely are they intended as a long-term support for the plants when planted out in your garden.

If you purchase a plant with one or two plastic strips held firmly to a cane by metal staples, remove both the cane and strips as soon as planted. If necessary, especially with climbers, get someone to hold the plant firmly while you insert a more appropriate support stake and tie.

Very often the cane supplied by the garden centre is too thin to stay firmly in the ground in high winds. Replace it with a thicker and taller cane so that you can push the cane into the ground for 30 centimetres and not just the few centimetres in the original plant pot.

3. If you have plants, including young citrus trees, planted in the garden still with the original canes and ties, examine them carefully. In many cases you will find that the tie has started to chaff the bark, especially if the metal staple is touching the trunk

4. When planting larger trees, obtain thick canes or poles to support them, long enough to be able to knock into the ground for 30 to 50 centimetres. If the trunk is thin, support it at several places.

Fix each tie first to the support post, and then loosely around the trunk to avoid cutting into the bark and to allow the trunk to recognise that it needs to build up its girth to support the tree in the wind.

Yes, you can purchase proprietary

plastic tree ties, but wire and rubber tubing is less expensive and you can size each tie to match the diameter of each tree. When making the ties, allow enough spare wire to be able to let out the ties as the girth of the trunk increases.

5. Lastly, but most importantly, check all ties once or twice a year. Adjust or replace as appropriate and add more ties to climbers as they grow.

6.5 ECONOMICAL WATERING

Watering is required to replace moisture lost by evaporation, to cool the earth and support the cellular growth of strong healthy plants. Water needs not only to reach shallow roots seeking nutrients in the surface soil but, more importantly, to the larger and deeper tap roots. Many plants will survive drought for a time but they will rarely become the best specimens in the garden.

Watering can be both time consuming and expensive, and water prices are forecast to rise in many areas of Spain in the future. It therefore makes sense to follow the waterless gardening practices below to save time and money:

REDUCE REQUIREMENTS

1. Plant plants that require the least water.
2. Plant deep-rooted rather than shallow rooted-plants.
3. Make major new plantings in the autumn and not later than March.
4. Minimise the planting of annuals.
5. Keep plants in pots and containers in semi shade rather than full sun.
6. Increase the percentage of the garden that is covered by paths and terraces.
7. Water at the drip line of trees rather than around the trunk, to stimulate spreading root balls.
8. Plant on the north side of the house, especially if you are an absentee gardener.

9. Stop watering for awhile after rain.
10. Water non flowering plants to just keep them alive in August. Three times the amount of water won't bring them back into flower until temperatures drop in September and October.
11. Don't water mature plants unnecessarily (to help, insert 20cm lengths of 5cm plastic tubing alongside deep rooted shrubs and trees when planting and water through the tube).
12. Sweep rather than washing down terraces.
13. Install an automatic time-controlled watering system with an adjustable drip feed to each plant needing water
14. Turn off or remove redundant drips.
15. Check watering system every week to make sure there are no leaks and losses of water.
16. Reduce the size of the lawn, or better, don't have one.
17. Plant alongside paths and around terraces so that roots can travel underneath to seek water and retain shade.
18. Use perforated tube irrigation systems along lines of vegetables.
19. Design a minimalist garden with a few or no plants.
20. Don't leave hoses running unnecessarily.

IMPROVE THE QUALITY OF WATER

1. In recent years trials at the Royal Botanic Garden Kew, in Spanish horticultural units and elsewhere in Europe have demonstrated that the quality of water can have a significant impact on the growth of seedlings and strength of mature plants. Water from both reverse osmosis and energized watyer units can be of particular benefit to amateur gardeners. Econimic and hand held garden hose energized water units can be obtained by mail order from Vi-Aqua, Ireland (*www.viaqua.ie.com*), Tel 00 353 872500181.
2. Check and adjust the acidity of the

HOW TO CONSTRUCT A DRIP IRRIGATION SYSTEM

CODE:

1 = Automatic timer
2 = 15mm tube
3 = T-piece
4 = Tap
5 = Bend
6 = Connector
7 = Spray Head
8 = Hole Punch
9 = End Stop
10 = 10mm Tube
11 = 5mm Tube

The main features of this basic design illustrated above are:

a. Adjustable drip heads (red) to each plant.

b. 5mm diameter tubing to feed heads from main pipe.

c. 15mm diameter tubing for a main distribution pipe.

d. Joiners to go round corners.

e. A whole range of different sized tubing, connectors, stoppers, drips, etc., to suit your needs.

f. In a larger garden, the 15mm tubing will need to be joined to a 3cm mains to get the necessary pressure of water.

g. A battery operated timer or a more complex mains electricity computerized timer for a multi zone system in a large garden.

h. A filter on the watermain in addition to the filter built into the timer will help prevent the blocking of drip heads.

Alternatives to mains water are a pump feed from a cistern or a gravity feed from a header tank at the highest point of the garden.

water you use for watering to a ph value of around 6.5 for most plants.

IMPROVE THE RETENTION OF WATER

1. Enrich the soil with compost and manure before planting.
2. Add water-retaining gel to the bottom of planting holes and compost in pots.
3. Build at least a low wall around the entire garden to prevent water loss over the boundary.
4. Build a secure retaining bank around vegetable plots that are watered by flooding.

REDUCE EVAPORATION

1. Water in the late evening rather than in the morning or midday.
2. Plant trees for shade or semi shade.
3. Plant closer together and use ground-cover plants to reduce the areas of bare soil exposed to the sun.

4. Plant through holes in plastic sheeting and cover with a mulch.
5. Keep potted plants in the semi shade to reduce evaporation.
6. Paint or varnish the inside of pots and containers to stop evaporation through the sides.
7. Mulch window boxes with a thick layer of moss, grit or stone chippings.
8. Underlay stone chipping areas of the garden with plastic sheeting.
9. Leave fallen leaves under shrubs and hedges as a natural mulch.
10. Mulch vegetables and soft fruit.
11. Soak newspapers in a thin water/flour paste and lay as a blanket around established shrubs, then cover with earth.
12. Water deeply down to the lowest roots. Shallow watering stimulates shallow roots turning back to the surface.
13. Lay woven plastic around shrubs and mulch with stones, pebbles or shredded tree bark.

14. Lay a mulch of crushed volcanic rock around succulents and cacti in rockeries and containers.

15. Lay light coloured terraces rather than dark to reduce the amount of reflected light evaporating water from the leaves.

COLLECT AND REUSE

1. Locate major shrub beds under the eaves of the house.

2. Fit guttering and collect rainwater in a cistern or butt and use for watering the garden.

3. Set up used eight-litre water bottles with the tops cut off to collect rainwater with a drip tube to a recently planted shrub or tree.

4. Channel rainwater from paths and terraces to where it is most needed.

5. Slope the drive so that valuable water is not lost into the road.

6. Use eco detergents and washing up liquid then reuse the cool water for hardy plants and vegetables.

7. Use cooled water from cooking or steaming vegetables for pot plants.

8. If you have a natural spring, collect the water in a large holding pond and distribute to the garden.

9. Create a concrete volcanic landscape with 30cm planting holes for a desert like mature cacti and aloe bed. Tint the concrete with a sand colouring and texture the surface with ripples like a wind blown sand dune (useful in absentee minimalist gardens).

10. Place trays under potted plants.

The use of a few of these ideas should reduce your water bill as well as allow you more time to enjoy the garden.

6.6 SEASONAL FEEDING

Your initial improvement of the soil will have built up the reservoir of nutrients and also made it easier for the roots of plants to access and extract those nutrients at a natural rate, the rate necessary to support healthy and sustained growth and flowering.

For those plants that stay in the ground year after year – perennials, shrubs and trees – the initial soil enrichment and an annual or biannual topping up with a mulch of well-rotted manure or compost, or a light feed of natural slow release bone meal or other organic fertilizer, should be all that most plants will require to continue growing steadily, flower profusely and cause no major health problems.

There is no point in overfeeding as it makes plants grow too quickly, resulting in excessive foliage needing frequent trimming, weak growth susceptible to pests and diseases and an earlier maturity than occurs naturally.

Gardeners with smaller gardens will find plants big enough without attempting to grow giant specimens. Gardeners with large gardens can plant larger specimens and let them grow at natural rates for decades.

Anyone who had a total instant garden laid out with mature shrubs and trees with regular heavy watering and an inline system for adding fertilizer will know the amount of over vigorous growth that soon needs to be pruned back to keep the originally pristine mature garden under control.

There are, however, some exceptions. Shrubs that are slow to come into flower or produce very few flowers even after one or two years could benefit from a high in potassium liquid feed to stimulate the reproduction cycle. There are many organic and inorganic products available.

Plants that have been caught by a frost can benefit from a high in nitrogen foliar feed to stimulate new green growth, after first cutting out the damaged foliage. We use a dilute nettle feed.

Annuals need regular feeding to stimulate a long flowering season, for the following reasons:

1. They have relatively shallow and short roots and therefore search for moisture and nutrients in the top 10cm of the soil.

2. They have been able to obtain sufficient nutrients without trying hard in the nursery greenhouse where they have been fed continuously hydroponically.

3. They can probably extract sufficient nutrients from the soil to support one flowering and seeding natural reproductive cycle, but we expect more from annuals. We want large bushy spreading plants that flower continuously for six to nine months, which is quite possible, providing we dead head regularly to avoid any seeds forming, water to keep the plants rigid in hot weather and give the plants a regular fast acting general flower plant fertilizer to stimulate the growth of roots, foliage and new flower buds. We use a comfrey, nettle, compost natural cocktail. Don't use an unbalanced feed, very high in nitrogen, as this will stimulate greenery at the expense of flowers.

The other plants that need ongoing watering are perennials, shrubs and trees in containers as they can only search for nutrients in the relatively small volume of compost in which they are planted. As the plants grow, the initial reservoir of nutrients is soon consumed and the roots get larger and larger to frantically find the last crumbs. In the end, the plant becomes root-bound and starved.

Feed either with an annual spring slow-release general fertilizer or establish a

regular feeding cycle – monthly in the winter, fortnightly in the summer and autumn. Use a general fertilizer, except in the spring and summer when a high in potassium feed will stimulate flowering. Naturally give a high-in-nitrogen feed to non-flowe-

ring evergreens, but only at diluted strengths to avoid too fast-growing, lush and potentially unhealthy plants.

Do not under any circumstances give a double-strength feed just because you are going on holiday. The fertilizer could well burn the roots.

Finally, don't only feed pot plants when they become unhealthy. If they are attacked by insects or diseases give them a fast-acting nitrogen foliar feed before treating the plant with insecticides or fungicides.

6.7 DISEASE AND PEST PREVENTION AND CONTROL

Most gardens suffer from only a few pest and disease problems but it would be wise to take the following precautions:

1. Plant only healthy plants, whether from garden centres or your own propagation.
2. Don't force plants by over watering and over feeding them. Fast sappy growth can be susceptible to attacks.
3. Don't let plants dry out and become weak.
4. Be constantly vigilant. Examine plants when you water them.
5. Act as soon as you see any sign of an attack by pests or diseases.
6. Move unhealthy potted plants to a semi-shaded nursery area.
7. Remove any badly affected, dying or dead plants from beds and pots and seal in a plastic bag. Burn on a bonfire if possible.
8. Recognise that roots as well as leaves, flowers, buds, branches or trunks can be attacked.

The ten most common problems and suggested ecological treatments are summarised below. The treatments listed are our DIY approaches except for Neem, which is a commercially available oil based product extracted from the seeds, leaves and roots of neem trees. If you don't like the idea

MOST COMMON PESTS AND DISEASES

Common Spanish garden pests	Main plants affected	What to look for	Causes	Suggested treatments
Ants *(Hormigas)*	Potted plants, Newly planted grass seed.	Soil being sifted out from base of plant pots. Trails of ants carrying seeds to nests. Ants feeding off aphids on plants, which is beneficial.	Ants looking for moisture and food.	**a.** In pots, drown with heavy watering. **b.** Find their trail and sprinkle with cayenne pepper or spray with 25ml water and a few drops of essential oil of lemon or rosemary. **c.** Keep newly sown grass seed continuously wet. Find nests and pour down boiling water. **d.** As a last resort use ant powder.
Aphids *(Pulgones)* a. Greenfly	Oleanders, roses, lady of the night, chrysanthe-mums, hibiscus.	Countless tiny sticky green flies on stems, leaves and flower buds. Usually ants are feeding off their sticky excretion.	Too little water. Too much nitrogen feed.	**a.** Spray twice weekly with a solution of either Potassium soap, nettle or garlic. **b.** You can add a few drops of Neem. When insects feed on it, it effects their reproduction cycle.
b. Whitefly *(mosca blanca)*	Geraniums, begonias, roses, garde-nias, indoor plants.	Tiny white flies on underside of leaves. Leaves wither and die.	High humid tempera-tures and poor soil.	"
c. Blackfly *(mosca negra)*	Nasturtiums	Masses of small black on tips of stems and flower buds. Too little water. Too much nitrogen feed.	High humid tempera-tures and poor soil.	"

MOST COMMON PESTS AND DISEASES

Common Spanish garden pests	Main plants affected	What to look for	Causes	Suggested treatments
Geranium moth. (*mosca africana*)	Zonal and ivy leafed geraniums.	Small black holes in stems where they lay their eggs. Small insipid brown moths hovering around plants in spring and summer.	Over watering and feeding too much nitrogen produces a weak fleshy plant.	**a.** Don't water plants until they almost dry out. **b.** Don't wet leaves and stems. **c.** Spray twice weekly from March to October with solution of either geranium oil, garlic or proprietary sprays. **d.** Cut out damaged stems and burn.
Mealy bug (*cochinilla*)	Euonymus, stephanotis, citrus, cacti, succulents, indoor plants.	Sticky white bugs on stems and underside of leaves.	Dense foliage and weak plants.	**a.** Clean off with a toothbrush or cotton wool soaked in soapy water. **b.** Spray weekly with solution of horsetail with a few drops of Neem.
Processionary caterpillars (*oruga procesionaria*)	Pine trees.	**a.** Winter fluffy white nests hanging out of branches. **b.** Feb/Mar caterpillars file down from nests. **c.** Appear in lines along ground and up walls. (They are blind and follow the leader).	Attracted to pine trees. High humid temperatures and poor soil.	**a.** NEVER allow caterpillars or the green dust left below their nests to touch you or your dog's skin. Can produce serious allergic reactions. **b.** Cut down with care and burn nests within easy reach **c.** Remove from ground and burn. **d.** Wash tools thoroughly. **e.** If trees are badly affected, seek professional advice.
Slugs (*babosas*)	Young annuals and fleshy plants.	Remains of eaten plants or a missing plant.	Young and juicy plants are very tempting.	**a.** Put down beer traps. **b.** Spray garlic solution around plants. **c.** Encourage birds, toads and frogs into the garden.

MOST COMMON PESTS AND DISEASES

Common Spanish garden pests	Main plants affected	What to look for	Causes	Suggested treatments
Snails (caracoles)	Bulbs, narcissus, iris, young plants, some succulents.	Bitten leaves and stems and slimy snail trails.	Rain followed by sun.	a. Collect at night. b. Place bran and cabbage leaves around garden to attract snails and collect. c. Use snail traps. d. Use slug bait as last resort.
Spider mite (acaro)	Roses, privet, oleander, annuals, ficus, indoor plants. Pine trees.	Yellowing leaves and underside of leaves covered in silk-like web and tiny spiders.	High temperatures and too much nitrogen.	a. Where possible wipe off. b. Spray regularly with solutions of Potassium soap, nettle or Neem.
FUNGAL DISEASES (HONGOS)				
Botrytis (botrytis)	Petunias, zinnias, dahlias, heliopsis, lilies, annuals, euonymus, roses.	Fluffy grey mould with black blotches.	Damp conditions.	a. Don't over water plants and avoid wetting leaves. b. Clean up affected plants. c. Spray with solutions of horsetail or Neem. d. Plant a garlic clove at the base of rose bushes.
Mildew (mildiu)	Chrysanthemums, heliopsis, annuals, geraniums, dahlias.	Pale yellow blotches on leaves and white powder on leaves.	Damp conditions and high temperatures.	a. Don't wet leaves when watering. b. Don't feed plants too much nitrogen. c. Spray twice weekly with solution of horsetail or Neem. d. Dust lightly with sulphur.
Oidio (oidio)	Roses, euonymus, dalias, margaritas, cacti, indoor plants.	Leaves curl up and get covered with white mould.	Humid warm temperatures.	a. Don't wet leaves when watering. b. Spray twice weekly with solution of horsetail or Neem. c. Improve ventilation.

MOST COMMON PESTS AND DISEASES

Common Spanish garden pests	Main plants affected	What to look for	Causes	Suggested treatments
Rust *(roya)*	Regal geraniums, roses.	Orange/brown pustules on leaves.	Damp conditions.	**a.** Spray in spring with solution of horsetail, tomato leaves or Neem. **b.** Don't wet leaves when watering.
Rotting off *(De pudrición)*	Roses, privet, oleander, annuals, ficus, indoor plants. Pine trees.	Discoloured wilting leaves.	Too much moisture with bad drainage.	**a.** Not much you can do except throw out the plant and start again. **b.** Always spray young seedlings and plants with horsetail solution.
Scale and fungal diseases *(escama y hongos)*	Bay, oleander, citrus.	Scales on leves and black mould on branches and leaves.	Humid conditions. Lack of light.	**a.** Wipe off with horsetail solution where possible. **b.** Prune back hard in autumn. **c.** Twice weekly spray with solution of potassium soap, horsetail or neem. **d.** Citrus – only prune hard as a last resort.
Fungal disease in conifers *(hongos)*	Conifers and hedges.	Browing and dieting plants	Poor drainage and watering too close the base of plants	**a.** Aerate soil around base. **b.** Don't wet trunks when watering. **c.** Spray soil and trees with horsetail and neem solution.

Note: Potassium soap is often now referred to as insecticidal soap and in Spain is often referred to as jabón negro.

of preparing your own sprays, there are now many effective proprietary biological/ecological products on the market.

PREPARATION OF NATURAL SPRAYS

When you are preparing natural sprays, be sure always to use unchlorinated rain or well water in recipes. The following are some recommended natural sprays:

6.8 DEADHEADING AND PRUNING

The deadheading and pruning of plants are two essential ongoing jobs in the garden.

DEADHEADING

The removal of dead flower heads as they form has several benefits:

NATURAL SPRAYS

Name	Uses	When to spray	Preparation
Garlic (ajo)	Insect repellent.	Fungicide and builds resistance to disease.	Cover 50gr of chopped garlic with boiling water. Leave covered to cool. Filter and add 1 litre of water.
Horestail (cola de caballo)	Fungicide and builds resistance to disease.	Early morning or late evening when dry.	**a.** Simmer 25gr of dried horsetail in 1 litre of water for 30mins. Stand for 24 hours. Strain and use. **b.** Gently boil 100gr of fresh horsetail, without roots, in 3 litres of water for 15mins. Cool, strain and use.
Nettle (ortigas)	Insect repellent and builds resistance to attacks.	As above	**a.** Simmer 25gr of dried nettle in 1 litre of water for 30mins. Stand for 24 hours. Strain and use. **b.** Fill bucket with young leaves and cover with water. Cover. Leave one week to ferment. Filter and dilute 15.1 to use.
Potassium soap (jabón de potasio)	Insecticide	As above	Melt 100gr of potassium soap in 5 litres of hot water. Cool and use. If it thickens add more water.
Tomato (tomate)	Against rust	As above	Pour one litre of boiling water over a handful of leaves. Cool, strain and use.
Geranium	Insecticide	As above	To 1 litre of water add 2 drops of essential oil of geranium.
Neem oil	Insecticide Fungicide		A couple of drops can be added to any of the above for extra effect or it can be used alone. (Read instructions on bottle).

Note: dried herbs can be purchased at most good herbalist shops or at local markets.

- A continuity of flower buds and flowers as the plant attempts to produce seed a second and third time, only to be thwarted each time by your efforts. This is particularly important with plants that are able to produce a continuous display of flowers for some months, such as roses, annuals, perennials, all the daisy flowered varieties, gazanias, carnations, heliopsis, and pelargoniums/geraniums.
- A second flowering a month or two later from some shrubs such as oleander, plumbago and lantanas.
- Tidier plants and a tidier garden once the dead heads and stems have been removed from plants that only flower once a year, such as lavender, rue, and sage.
- Stronger bulbs for the next year by the removal of dead flower heads as they form from bulbous plants. Leave the stem to die back before cutting off, even if a little untidy for a few weeks. This will stimulate the plant to put all its energy into developing a good bulb for next year rather than a ripe seed head that would weaken the bulk (e.g. daffodils, tulips, gladioli, lilies, irises and canna lilies.

If you want to collect seeds for next year, leave some strong and healthy flower heads and allow them to produce seed for you to harvest once dry. Mark the selected stems in case you trim them off a week later. Easy ones for starters are hollyhocks, marigolds, yellow lantanas, nasturtiums and sweet peas.

PRUNING

As well as removing dead flower heads, trim untidy ends of branches and water shoots on an ongoing basis. The benefits are:

- A tidier garden. Just look around weekly and see what is starting to look out of place or getting in the way.
- More naturally shaped plants.
- Control of height and width of plants.
- Special architectural shapes through the trimming and wire shaping of topiary.
- Stopping vigorous plants from swamping smaller, slow-growing plants.

- Stronger plants by cutting out any water shoots that grow from the base of bougainvilleas, jasmine and roses.
- The stimulus of the flowering and fruiting side shoots for the following year.
- A safer garden by removing hazards such as the pointed ends of low-growing branches and yucca leaves, cacti branches and low palm fronds near pathways, terraces and in shrub beds where you need to work.
- To remove branches and twigs damaged by gales, frost or sun-burn.
- The retention of external and internal views.
- Allowing passage on outside pavements. This may mean removing flowering branches of vigorous hedges such as oleander, honeysuckle, bougainvilleas and bignonias.
- To stimulate larger fruits. If fruit bushes or trees have a very heavy crop, remove some fruits on each branch to stimulate larger fruits.
- To continue to see the fish in the pond. Regularly remove excess aerating weeds and some water lily leaves.
- To maintain neat hedges, such as Conifers, pittosporum and privet.
- To obtain cuttings that can be used to propagate new plants, such as carnations, mock orange, geraniums, messems, oleanders, plumbago, leonotis, hydrangeas and lady of the night.

Use good sharp but safe pruners and saws for the above tasks to reduce the effort required. They are safer than pruning knives. In the summer, prune early morning rather than roasting in the midday sun. Cut ends will seal during the day, preventing the entry of diseases.

6.9 THE ANNUAL CUTBACK AND CLEAN UP

Spanish gardens benefit from a major cutback and clean up each winter rather than in the autumn. For most gardens this is best done during January. There are six reasons for doing it at that time:

1. Shrubs and perennials will have been allowed to continue flowering to give the most colourful Christmas garden possible.

2. Most plants are dormant or at their lowest level of growth. In trees, the sap is down and stable except in early flowering acacias and almonds.

3. Plants allowed to continue flowering beyond December tend to have few flowers and go leggy. If not cutback until March, they will be late to flower in the spring.

4. Plants have a good clean up before starting to bud and grow in earnest when the weather warms up.

5. The soil is cleared of rubbish/weeds and hoed while there is maximum space between plants.

6. The weather tends to be dry and sunny, so you can enjoy the exercise while achieving a tidy garden and an even better one in the coming year.

It is always very tempting not to cut back plants that are still growing strongly and perhaps even flowering, but if you don't do this now, plants will be out of shape and overgrown by the spring and not create the flower and leaf buds necessary for good displays in the spring and summer. So be harsh.

Obviously winter flowering plants such as poinsettias, camellias, acacias, winter jasmine and chrysanthemums are not pruned back at this time as they will be in full flower. They can be pruned as soon as they finish flowering.

MAIN TASKS

The five main tasks involved in cleaning up your garden are:

1. Cut back and prune all perennials, shrubs and trees appropriate to their age, size and format.

2. Divide up and replant large clumps of perennials

3. Clear all weeds and rubbish from the beds.

4. Loosen the surface soil and mulch young plants and plants with shallow roots to prevent weeds from growing, retain moisture and shade roots from the hot sun.

5. Shred all prunings, except thick branches, ready for adding to the compost heap.

The following are guidelines for dealing with a wide range of popular plants.

SHRUBS

The main aim is to cut back to achieve a size and shape appropriate to your garden and to develop strong profusely flowering shrubs.

Bougainvillea – All well established plants benefit from a hard pruning, otherwise they get out of control. When they are in full flower, high winds can tear them away from walls, causing considerable damage. Cut back the side shoots along each of the main branches to stimulate flowering shoots. Cut back the main branches to give shape. Cut out all suckers – these are the paler green straight stems with larger leaves. After pruning, check that the main branches are securely tied. Thread the tying-up wire through an old piece of hose so that it doesn't cut into the stems as they grow. Treat younger plants a little more gently, concentrating on pruning to shape.

Lantanas – One of the most useful plants in a Mediterranean garden. Well pruned, they give colour during most months of the year. Each of the several varieties needs a slightly different treatment:

Low growing – with the purple and white trailing variety, you need to cut back leggy branches by at least half their length and trim to shape. The yellow variety should be pruned lightly to shape.

Medium height – with the yellow, orange/red, pink/yellow, yellow/white varieties you need to cut back all flowering stems to 5 to 10cm from the trunk just above a new budding point. The pruned plants will look very bare but you will stimulate the sprouting of a multitude of new flowering shoots.

Standards – Cut to shape to encourage side shoots and create a round head.

Climbing – The pink/yellow, white, and orange/yellow varieties can be trained to grow up or over walls. Prune side shoots to shape and leave the tallest branches intact.

Hibiscus – Some Spanish gardeners cut these back very hard, but we don't find this necessary. We suggest your shorten the branches by 50cm, depending on the size of the plant, to produce a good shape.

Plumbago and white flowering jasmine – Shorten branches by half their length and tidy up all side shoots to produce a well-shaped bush. The yellow flowering winter jasmine should be cut back later after it has finished flowering.

Oleanders – To prevent them getting very tall and leggy, prune back very hard every second or third year to stimulate new shoots and side branches. In other years keep them tidy and cut out any suckers. Wear gloves when pruning as the sap and flowers are poisonous.

Bignonia – The large flowered pink variety is the most prolific and needs to be pruned right back leaving woody lateral branches for next year's growth. Just trim other varieties back to shape.

Passion flowers, solandras and solanum – Cut to shape, hard if necessary.

Galan de noche – Cut back hard to a basic fan or standard shape.

Roses – Cut back bushes to two or three buds on each stem and cut out any suckers growing from the base. Cut out the old and weak stems that have few flowering shoots from climbers and ramblers and then shape.

Tall herbs – Lavender, rosemary and sage should be trimmed to shape and cleaned up underneath.

PERENNIALS

Daisy flowering types and rock roses – Cut back leggy growth to produce a more compact and cluster flowering plant.

Gazanias and arctotis – Remove dead leaves and prune untidy side shoots and runners to shape. These can be used to propagate new plants. Pull out any totally dead plants. If they have any life left in them, leave well enough alone as they will normally re-leaf and bud in the spring.

Pelargoniums/geraniums – Clean out all dead leaves and stems. Also look out for signs of geranium moth damage and cut out these stems at a healthy node.

Zonal – Cut back to shape if leggy

Ivy leafed trailing – Trim to shape.

Regal – Cut back hard to shape if very woody and leggy. They will sprout from the old wood.

Graveolens Scented – Cut back hard to shape. Grows rampant.

Leonotis, Rudbekias, Ajania, Valerian and other perennials that flower best on new growth from the base – Cut back to 5cm from ground. Prune chrysanthemums similarly when they have finished flowering in February or March.

Low growing herbs – Remove any dead wood and trim to a shape and size that blends with adjacent plants. Do likewise with herbs in pots.

PALMS

Cut out some lower fronds, taking care to avoid the spikes, and generally tidy up. The heads of taller Canary Island palms should be trimmed to look like giant pineapples.

CORDYLINES

Pull off all dead leaves and cut off dead flower heads.

YUCCAS

Cut off unsightly and dangerous/top heavy branches and dead flower heads. For self preservation and the safety of others, cut off the spiky tips of all leaves within reach a n d then cut off or pull off the lower leaves on the stems to create a palm like effect.

ALOES

Remove suckers. Cut out dead flower stems

and dead plants. Cut off unsightly and dangerous lower leaves.

CACTI

Cut off unsightly and dangerous/top heavy side shoots. Cut out any rotting parts of small cacti. Make sure you clear away any rubbish from within and around the cacti that could cause fungal diseases to set in.

SUCCULENTS

Trim to shape if necessary, using the cuttings for propagation. Leave sappier varieties until after the last frost if in the frost belt. Remove dead flower heads if not done in the autumn.

BULBS

Remove dead leaves and rubbish from around irises and the dead leaves of any autumn flowering bulbs. Carefully clean up the surface of flower beds where you know spring bulbs will be shortly coming up.

HEDGES

All types benefit from a close cut. Cut the top to a height that gives you privacy without being impossible to prune safely. Trim both sides to tidy and reduce the overhang over adjacent shrubs and flowerbeds. A good cut also stimulates flowering shoots on those that flower. If the hedge is getting leggy, cut out some of the hard thick internal branches (privet or oleander), or cut back to the hard internal framework (myporum, bay and hibiscus) to stimulate new and denser growth.

FLOWERING TREES

Many need to be hard pruned to keep them down to manageable size for small and medium sized gardens and to develop pleasing architectural shapes. This will also stimulate new flowering side branches. Always cut out any dead or dying branches as well as any heavy branches that could cause shallow rooted trees to become top heavy or lopsided and therefore liable to being blown over in gales. Leave the winter

flowering acacias until they are finished flowering. Be aware that the jacaranda and albizia trees thrive best when left to grow to maturity without pruning. Any pruning of branches tends to stimulate new lower growth and reduce flowering.

EVERGREEN TREES

Trim to shape and size. This is time to start and maintain any topiary shapes. Clean up dead foliage under trees to reduce chance of fungal diseases.

POND PLANTS

Cut back and thin reeds and irises. Also every couple of years lift out the clumps to keep their size under control by splitting and cutting back the root ball. Lift out potted plants such as water lilies and trim off the dead top growth and reduce the size of the protruding root ball. Cut back and remove excess growth of oxygenating weed beds.

PLANTS IN POTS AND CONTAINERS

Remove any dead and untidy growth. Clean the surface of the soil and wash off algae from the outside of pots and the water tray with vinegar and water to maintain a hygienic environment.

PILES OF PRUNING AND WEEDS

You can propagate them. Although not an ideal time, try potting up some healthy cuttings and putting them in the greenhouse or garden frame. After all, the cuttings are free so nothing is lost.

You can shred parts of them. Don't bother with fibrous material such as palm fronds or aloes, as they will block the shredder. Shredded material is very useful in the garden as raw material for the compost heap, mixed with leaf mould and manure in preparing raised beds for vegetables and raw as a useful mulch around shrubs – especially where it won't be easily seen – and for creating soft pathways in woodlands and the vegetable garden. So are palm fronds if you first cut off the spiky ends.

You can take them to the local Eco

Composting Unit. Some gardeners are lucky enough to be able to sell their prunings and other garden waste to a local composting unit and afterwards leave with bags of inexpensive final compost.

Now take a week's rest from gardening before you start to sow seeds and prepare the vegetable plot for the spring. If you want to enjoy a good garden in the spring, summer and autumn, the winter is a busy time.

6.10 SPRING CLEAN POTTED PLANTS

All pots, window boxes and other planted containers benefit from an annual internal and external spring clean. The spring clean should be thorough and aim to remove anything that might attract diseases or pests, to improve the fertility and moisture retaining properties of the compost within the pots, and improve the appearance of the pots themselves.

We recommend the following ten actions.

1. Thoroughly wash any used pots with washing up liquid in water and then rinse in a dilute disinfectant or vinegar solution to prepare them for reuse.

2. Clean up all potted plants as follows:

a. Prune all dead leaves and dead or diseased branches.

b. Prune to shape if out of balance.

c. Remove all dead leaves, flowers and other rubbish from the surface of the soil.

d. Scrape out the top 3cm of the compost and replace with new.

e. Replace any grit or chippings that you had used as a mulch.

f. Give the drip trays a good wash.

g. Wash the outside of the pots to remove grime. Algae can be removed from terracotta pots by wiping with a dilute bleach solution or vinegar and water. Protect the plant in a plastic bag while washing. Leave the pots to dry and then wipe lightly with a cloth dampened with olive oil.

3. If potted plants have been in the same compost for several years and you have become unhappy with the plant, re-pot, using new compost. First clean the pot as above or use a slightly larger pot.

4. If you find that the plant or plants are root bound, re-plant in a pot several sizes larger.

5. When re-potting use new compost. Also take the opportunity to incorporate a little water retaining gel into the lower part of the soil. Don't use too much or the gel will push the plant up and out of the compost.

6. Give all plants a spring feed with a weak solution of a general flower plant fertilizer or a comfrey/nettle feed if gardening organically.

7. Clean grimy leaves on evergreen plants by first brushing lightly with a soft paint brush, and then wiping with a solution of milk, beer and liquid nettle fertilizer. If you have no nettles substitute, a few drops of a nitrogen foliar feed

8. Put any plants still covered with spring pine pollen out in the first rain to freshen them up. At the same time, collect spring rainwater in a water butt for summer watering.

9. If there are any signs of an ant nest in a pot, re-pot removing all compost from the root ball and washing the roots before re-potting to remove the last ant. Put some ant powder in the drip tray under the pot to prevent a reinvestation

6.11 PRODUCING GOOD COMPOST

Compost is an invaluable addition to the soil in Spanish gardens. It adds nutrients and useful micro organisms and improves the structure and water- retaining properties of naturally poor or over-worked soil, the sort that many of us have initially.

There is evidence that plants grown in healthy compost-enriched soil are less prone to disease and grow stronger. During the long hot summers, a rich friable loamy soil will lose less moisture through capillary evaporation than a hard-baked poor soil.

Compost can be added to the soil by mixing it into flower and vegetable beds before planting seeds or plants – or as a mulch around plants to help retain moisture and keep the roots cool.

WHAT IS COMPOST?

Compost is the natural decomposition of kitchen and garden waste to achieve a fine, sweet-smelling, crumbly, loamy soil rich in water-retaining humus and plant nutrients, and ready to mix into potting/seed composts, flower beds and vegetable plots.

An ecological recycling of waste, it is less expensive and is of better quality than many commercial brands of compost. It also involves less municipal cost for disposing of household and garden rubbish, and the use of fewer plastic rubbish bags.

Compost is produced by mixing organic waste materials from the kitchen, garden and vegetable plot in a suitable container and then leaving to decompose naturally. All the waste will eventually rot down with the help of heat, moisture, oxygen, micro organisms, insects and worms. Just let nature take its course.

Even so, there are a few tricks to the trade. We list below the factors that contribute to the making of good compost in our generally hot and dry climate:

1. Design of composting bins. Boxes or bins are essential here in Spain, as the open compost heap of a rainy northern Europe would soon dry out in the hot Mediterranean climate. Construct two or three composting boxes at least 1 1/2 m in width, depth and height. It is difficult to build up essential heat at the heart of smaller boxes. Two boxes are better than one because during the process of composting the decomposing material needs to be turned. A third box would allow you to start a second heap while the first is maturing. A homemade box can be easily constructed by using four posts and wire netting or three old pallets. The front is most easily closed with a wire netting gate or removable wooden slats for ease of access. To increase aeration you could use a fourth pallet as the base, although broken twigs are just as effective. Never place on a concrete base as you need to encourage many small insects, worms and micro organisms from the soil into the heap.

2. Positioning of compost bins. The compost heap needs to retain moisture and build up heat. Ideally it should be situated in a semi-shaded corner of the garden.

3. Line the bin and cover. To retain moisture and internal heat, line your box with cardboard from old boxes or thick layers of newspaper as you build up the waste materials. Don't make air holes as you would have done in northern Europe as this will only result in the rapid drying out of the outer layers. Keep the top covered with a layer of damp newspapers topped with a square of old carpet.

4. Layering the different raw materials. Don't just throw the waste materials into the bin willy-nilly. If you do,   the decomposition will be patchy and essential heat will not built up. Build up the heap layer by layer as follows:

- Start with a 15cm layer of coarse twiggy material to create air circulation and help start the aerobic decomposition process.
- 10 – 15cm of manure or half decomposed compost. This will attract worms and essential microorganisms.
- 10 – 15cm of green waste.
- 10 – 15cm of brown waste.
- 4 sheets of wet newspaper laid over the top. Worms love it, but avoid colour printed pages.
- 10 – 15cm of manure.
- A sprinkling of wood ash.
- Repeat (c) to (g) adding natural accelerators to the layers until the compost bin is full.

5. A good mix of raw materials including:

• **Green waste** – vegetables, fruit (avoid too many orange peelings as they are too acidic), crushed egg shells, weeds, soft green cuttings and prunings, grass cuttings, disease free leaves and stems of vegetables that have finished cropping, dampened and torn-up paper packets, newspapers, cardboard in centre of toilet rolls and kitchen towel rolls. Don't use cooked kitchen waste, cheese, oil or raw meat, fish, etc., as it may attract vermin and flies in the height of summer.

• **Brown waste** – dry fibrous materials such as shredded, hard prunings, branches and cuttings, flower heads, stalks, dry leaves, waste from the vacuum cleaner, animal and human hair. It is preferable not to add cuttings from bay, conifers, acacias and oleanders as their residues can be toxic to other plants.

• **Wood ash** – a little will add valuable potassium and lime.

• **Manures** – horse, sheep, goat, rabbit, chicken and pigeon. Stack the latter two to rot down separately, as they are very strong, and then only use in small proportions.

• **Accelerators** – Seaweed, comfrey, borage, dandelion and nettle in leaf or liquid form are all good accelerators, as well as adding essential nutrients to the heap. The liquid forms can be prepared by steeping leaves in water for two or more weeks. If you don't have access to any of the above, use sulphate of ammonia or a proprietary powder. Diluted human urine is also very effective!

• **Water** – essential to the whole process.

6. Moisture control. Dampen each layer where necessary as you build up the heap. This is the best time to add your prepared liquid accelerators. Dilute them 10/1 before use. There is no point in leaving material dry because it won't rot down. But don't over-soak as it will then become slimy and smelly. It is just a matter of trial and error.

7. Temperature control and Decomposition. It is important to line and cover the heap to build up the temperature necessary for bacterial action. Ideally, it should be at 50 to 60 degrees centigrade to kill off weed seeds, etc. It will still decompose at lower temperatures, but at a slower rate. The fast rate, referred to as "aerobic", requires oxygen. If the heap is well mixed with dampened materials, it will decompose in six to twelve months. The slower rate, referred to as "anaerobic", causes the material in the heap to become smelly, slimy and compacted as a result of being over wet. The solution is to turn the heap, at the same time layering in new dry materials.

The aim is to achieve a totally aerobic process, but even in the best heaps there will be odd corners of anaerobic decomposition taking place.

8. Turning. It is advisable to turn your heap after six months to re-aerate it. Prepare your empty bin as for starting a heap. Then fork over the decomposing heap to the empty bin, mixing in any dry materials left on the outer edge or over wet compost in the centre. Remove the lower part if it is ready to use. It should be fine and sweet smelling. At this stage you top up the partially composted material with fresh materials, and then repeat the process in six months time.

9. Worms. Worms play an important role in the compost heap. Firstly they eat damp waste material and excrete processed waste, and secondly their burrows aerate the heap. They will be attracted by the heat and dampness, but do add in any you find around the garden and always put back any left in the finished compost. They will leave the compost if it is too dry.

10. Problems and solutions. Rats – don't include any raw or cooked meat, fish, cheese, oil or salads dressed in oil. Flies – always top kitchen waste with a layer of dry materials and cover. Ants – in a drying heap, ants will look for moisture in the form of retreating worms. Find where their trail is coming from and put down ant powder.

11. Be patient. One is always short of compost in the garden – but don't try and take a shortcut by using the heap before it is fully decomposed, unless you are using it only for mulching or preparing bean and pumpkin trenches. Our approach to composting in a hot dry climate is based on many years of trial and error. Yes, it does take time, but just think of the end result – all that lovely, inexpensive, fine loam and the fact that you have made the best use of your garden and household rubbish, as well as helping the environment.

6.12 PROPAGATING NEW PLANTS FROM OLD

Propagating new plants from old has several advantages. It is easier than growing them from seed, it is an inexpensive and interesting way to multiply plants in the garden, it is a way of collecting unusual varieties by obtaining cuttings from friends and it can produce stronger, less forced, plants than the ones you buy. You can start cuttings at any time of the year and once potted they take less time to grow than plants grown from seed.

In Spain there is generally no need to use a propagator as the average temperature is higher than northern Europe, but in the hotter months cuttings dry out fast.

Below is a list of different types of plants and information on how to propagate them:

1. Stem cuttings from soft wooded plants, e.g., lavender, sage, plumbago, fuchsias, pelargoniums/geraniums, gazanias, margaritas, etc. Pull off a side shoot (preferably non-flowering) with a heel. Pinch out the growing tip to leave a cutting about 10–15cm long with a leaf node at the top and base. Remove any flowers or buds and all the leaves except four towards the top.

Pelargoniums/geraniums benefit if left to dry out for a day before potting. An alternative way of taking cuttings from trailing geraniums when you are pruning them is to cut off 10cm, keeping at least three nodes from the tip. Pinch out the tip, remove any flowers or buds and leave two leaves.

2. Stem cuttings of more delicate plants. Busy lizzies, fuchsias, pothos, etc., do better if they are placed in water or wet vermiculite and allowed to produce roots before being planted. Break off a piece from the plant and place in a narrow container in a warm place. Fill with non-chlorinated water. Add a small piece of charcoal to keep the water fresh. Top up water regularly. Cuttings will take anything from a day to a month to produce roots.

Alternatively, wet some vermiculite and fill a clay pot. Insert your cutting and keep the contents moist. We don't recommend using plastic pots as they don't breathe and the vermiculite often goes mouldy. This method produces stronger root systems.

3. Cuttings from cacti and succulents. The prickly pear and Christmas cacti variety of cacti and all succulents can be easily propagated by breaking off a piece, leaving it to dry for a couple of days and then planting.

4. Stem cuttings from hard-wooded plants, e.g., lantana, bougainvillea, hibiscus, rose, oleander etc. Cut off a woody branch and cut into 10cm lengths. Leave a bud node at the base and top. Cut off any flowers and leave about four leaves. They can be rooted before potting by putting in dark wine or beer bottles to which a drop of fungicide has been added. Leave in semi shade and top up with water when necessary. They can also be started off in slit trenches in the vegetable garden if kept damp.

Rooting can be accelerated by dipping

the bottom ends of cuttings into a proprietary rooting powder. It is helpful to follow the Spanish custom of slitting the base of rose cuttings and sliding in a dried sweet corn kernel. The growth hormone in the sweet corn helps stimulate the formation of roots. Try doing the same with other large-diameter, hard- wooded cuttings.

5. Rooted runners. Spider plants, some succulents and aloes produce rooted runners. Detach carefully and plant up in small pots.

6. Babies. Plants such as aloe vera, succulents, cacti etc., produce babies. Remove carefully and pot.

7. Leaf cuttings. Plants such as sedums, echeveria and streptocarpus can be propagated by cutting a healthy leaf and sticking the stem end in damp vermiculite. A new plant will grow from the base.

8. Division of roots. Clump forming perennials such as chrysanthemums, gazanias, agapanthus, coreopsis etc., can be divided in early spring and either planted directly into the ground or potted. Others, such as ground cover purple lantanas, ivies and grey leafed creeping gazanias, put out roots on their spreading branches. Rooted ends can be potted or transplanted.

9. Air Layering. Rubber plants and solandra can be reproduced by sliding a plastic bag with the end cut out over a branch that is getting too long and would otherwise be pruned. Make a cut at a leaf node and with the help of a second person press a damp moss/compost mix around the branch until it is like a 10 to 15cm diameter sausage roll with the branch in the middle and the cut leaf node in the centre. Seal with cello tape at both ends to prevent moisture escaping

and leave for a year, allowing a root ball to develop. Then cut off and root.

POTS AND CONTAINERS

Any 8-10cm diameter pot with a drainage hole is suitable for planting single cuttings, and a 12-15cm diameter pot is suitable for planting groups of cuttings. Cut the base of a 1.5 or 5-litre water bottle three quarters of the way up. Keep the lid to create a mini greenhouse. Put some wet gravel in the base and sit your pot on it. Fit the lid over the top to seal.

There are many other containers that can be adapted, for instance milk and fruit cartons with the tops cut off, plastic containers used for packing fruit in the supermarkets, yoghurt cartons, plastic cups and soft drink cans. Just use your imagination.

PLANT IN GOOD COMPOST

When planting a cutting it is important to use good compost, following the guidelines below:

1. For most plants, make a mix of 7 parts light compost, 3 parts peat substitute and 2 parts sharp sand. Dampen evenly in a large container. For succulents, aloes and cacti add a further 3 parts of fine grit.

2. Take a plant pot and put a few pieces of broken pot or polystyrene at the base and fill with compost. Press down lightly.

3. Plant cuttings in prepared pots or bottle containers. If large enough, you can put three or four in each, but if you only put one, they won't need to be divided later.

4. Dip the end of cuttings into hormone rooting powder before potting.

5. Always spray the soil with an ecological fungicide or an infusion of horsetail.

6. Remember to label your cuttings. The vanes of old plastic blinds cut into strips and marked with a waterproof pen create inexpensive labels.

7. Put each pot in a clear plastic bag and prop up the bag with a length of old black watering hose, so that the leaves, especially grey ones, don't touch the plastic. Close with a tie, and cover those in cut-off water containers with the cut-off top half. These methods will create a mini greenhouse that maintains a constant humidity on the leaves and saves you watering the cuttings every day. Also, the enclosed module protects plants started during the autumn and winter.

8. Alternatively, use polystyrene fish boxes – most supermarkets throw them out. Wash well and make holes in the base for drainage and cover with a damp layer of compost/soil mix about 3cm deep. Place potted plants on top or fill the box with potting compost and plant lots of small cuttings. Special plastic module trays can also be used. Fit these into a polystyrene box on top of a 3cm compost base. When using fish boxes, enclose the cuttings and box in a white plastic envelope, secured with clothes pegs to maintain a constantly humid microclimate and the plants won't need watering until they are ready to pot.

9. If you don't use the microclimate method, prepare as in methods 1 and 2. Then line plastic trays or a similar container with 3cm of dampened compost/soil mix. This helps the plants form good roots. Stand prepared pots on soil. Then place in semi shady place or garden frame that is protected from the hot sun. Keep pots and soil underneath damp.

10. Succulents and cacti need a more gritty and free-draining compost than most other plants.

11. If you have a suitable area of bare soil and an automatic drip tube irrigation system, it is possible to propagate a large number of cuttings in full sun as commercial nurseries do. Plant one cutting to a pot. Line the pots up on capillary matting in full sun and place a drip on each pot. Ensure that the com-

post used is very free-draining to allow the plants to be watered twice a day and at times to be rained on without becoming waterlogged. This method is especially suitable for perennial herbs and shrubs, such as oleanders and plumbago, but not for succulent or cacti varieties.

ONGOING CARE

1. Place in shaded greenhouse or frame. They need light but direct sunlight will broil.
2. Check regularly that cuttings are neither too dry nor too wet.
3. When watering always add a fungicide.
4. Remove any rotting leaves regularly.
5. Do not be too hasty to remove a doubtful cutting. They can appear dormant one day and start sprouting the next.

POTTING ON AND HARDENING OFF

1. If 8-10cm pots are used, you should be able to plant the plants directly into the ground.
2. Once cuttings grown in groups in a pot or a planting tray have rooted well, divide them carefully and pot individually into 8-10cm pots. Seal in plastic until they show signs of growing strongly again.

HARDENING OFF

1. If plants are grown in a greenhouse or frame, harden off in the semi shade and the sun before planting out.
2. If grown in the semi shade of a tree or the north side of the house, expose to sun before planting out.

FEEDING

Water with a very dilute plant feed containing potash to stimulate root formation, potassium to stimulate a strong plant structure and flowers and nitrogen to stimulate leaf formation. We generally use a very dilute natural nettle and comfrey feed.

Good cuttings grown annually will expand and thicken your plantings. A 70% success rate will be good, so at all times plant more cuttings than you need. If you achieve more, you can always swap spares with friends.

6.13 GROWING PLANTS FROM SEED

Growing plants from seed can be an interesting and rewarding pastime, but it can also be very frustrating when failures occur. Even so, the pleasure and sense of achievement when your own hand-raised plant flowers for the first time makes all the effort worthwhile.

Your own plants can be healthier and stronger specimens than those forced in huge commercial greenhouses. Growing them from seed gives you the possibility of growing popular varieties in larger quantities at lower cost as well as growing unusual plants and building up a rare collection relatively inexpensively.

We recommend that most seeds are first grown in trays and pots for planting out later, especially where spring seedbeds can suffer from wide variations between night and daytime temperatures, drying winds, torrential rain, hail and attacks from snails and slugs.

GROWING PLANTS FOR PLANTING OUT

● **Obtain good seed** - Buy seed from reliable suppliers that have a regular turnover of seeds. Always check the condition of the packet and the "plant by..." date to ensure they are fresh. Also read the plant description carefully to ensure that you are buying what you really want. Plant breeders are continually developing new strains that offer new colours, dwarf or giant plants, bushy and cascading specimens.

It is fun to try some of the new varieties. We buy a combination of Spanish seeds and others through various mail order seed catalogues. You can also save seed from your own and friends' plants. Either collect them as they ripen or cover the seed heads with a paper bag and let them fall. If some are not quite dry, cut off whole seed heads and spread them on a tray in a warm, semi shaded place.

● **Store seed carefully** - Always store seed packets in a dry cool place, never in a greenhouse, tool shed or warm room. Ideally, once opened the packets should be firmly resealed with cello tape, put in an airtight container and stored in the refrigerator. Put your self-dried seeds in brown or kitchen paper and store in the same way. Don't forget to label them clearly.

● **Use a good planting medium** - As with propagating from cuttings, it is important to have a suitable medium for sowing seeds. Seeds need a light, aerated, moisture-retaining, low nutrient compost, preferably soil less. Buy a special seed compost from a garden centre or make your own. We prepare ours with 2 parts sterilized garden compost, 1 part peat substitute to improve moisture retention, 1 part sharp sand to ensure good drainage and 1 part vermiculite to lighten, aerate and prevent the mix from drying out.

Before mixing the above, sieve the garden compost through a 1cm sieve to remove any lumps, twigs etc., and then sterilize it by putting a layer on your oven tray and bake at 200ºC for 30 minutes. Cool and add to your potting mix. Alternatively you can sterilize it in the microwave, using a roasting bag – puncturing the bag before heating up so it doesn't explode.

Wet the peat substitute separately and then add the remaining dry ingredients. Mix in well and add more water if necessary. The mix should be neither too wet nor too dry – a difficult operation

and a matter of trial and error. Some people prefer standing the filled pots in water until the compost is damp, but we find the first method better, especially when we use various types of containers.

● **Use suitable containers** - When choosing the containers in which to sow your seeds, try to economise and be inventive. The choice is vast:
1. Plastic flowerpots.
2. Plastic cups.
3. Juice and milk cartons with the top cut off.
4. Five litre and 1.5 litre water bottles with the tops cut off to leave a 10cm base, keeping the tops to use as lids (in the 5 litre container, we even off the base with some compost and then sit either one flower pot on top or four 6 x 6cm. plastic modules cut from a seed tray).
5. Polystyrene or plastic planting modules with various-sized planting holes.
6. Polystyrene fish boxes filled with compost and planted up with larger seeds such as decorative gourds. You can also put a layer of compost on the base and then sit separate pots on top, which helps retain moisture and encourages stronger roots.
7. Inexpensive newspaper tubes. These are useful for growing a wide range of larger seeds, especially vegetables ready for planting out. Cut out 7cm strips (or the depth of the box you are using) from stacks of four sheets of newspaper. Roll into 3 or 4cm diameter tubes and secure with cello tape. Sit in a fish tray on top of a 3cm layer of compost and put compost in between each one to the top. At the same time, fill the tubes with seed compost. Plant seeds and then cover completely so that the newspaper does not dry out.

You can turn all of the above into a mini greenhouse by putting 1, 2 & 3 into clear plastic bags and closing. With 4, seal as above or slide the cut off closed bottle tops down over the base and seal with cello tape. With 5 & 6, cover with clear plastic and secure with clothes pegs for easy opening. Make a mini, hooped, wire frame under the plastic to allow the air to circulate and to keep the plastic away from the emerging seedlings. Make sure there are no tiny holes where moisture can escape. In the case of larger seeds that don't need light to germinate, cover with cardboard until they emerge, leaving a 2cm air gap.

Before using them, wash all containers in a dilute mix of vinegar and water so that they are thoroughly clean and disease free.

● **Allow sufficient space** - Recognise that if you start off with a packet of zinnia seeds sown in a 15cm diameter seed container and 50% of the seedlings germinate you might need a large fish box for pricking out the seedlings. You could soon fill a small greenhouse, garden frame or cover the terrace table or floor!

● **Temperature control** - Ensure that the seeds are kept within the recommended germination temperature range, which is generally between 20ºC and 28ºC. Seeds might not germinate, especially in a sub-tropical environment, if day or night temperatures vary widely. A propagator can be helpful if you are trying to grow more exotic plants that need a constant higher heat before late spring.

● **Locating containers** - Containers can be placed almost anywhere:
● In the semi shade of a south facing enclosed terrace or a semi shaded window sill. Beware once the weather heats up, as it could be too hot, especially on a south-facing window sill.
● In a garden frame, for less delicate seeds.
● In a greenhouse with a thermostatically controlled heater for the more delicate seeds when started early in the year.

Yes, temperatures do fluctuate in Spain. Nights can drop to 5ºC, having been 25ºC at lunchtime. The greenhouse and frame need to be shaded once temperatures rise. Without shading, the daytime temperature in the greenhouse could reach 50ºC, even in March.
● In an airing cupboard, for seeds that don't need light.
● In a warm, semi shaded corner of the garden.

● **Sow at the right time** - When to plant seeds depends on:
● The germination temperature required.
● The time from germination to first flowering.
● Whether you want to provide for continuity of flowering by planting out several successive batches of plants.
● The frost resistance of the seedlings.

Sweet peas, for instance, are best sown in pots or directly in the garden in November for flowering in the spring, while zinnias are best sown in a cool greenhouse in March or directly in the garden in April/May for flowering in the summer.

Naturally, if you have a climate-controlled heated greenhouse you can start seeds much earlier and produce annuals for planting out for Easter. Beware of early spring temperatures that can plummet and of heavy rain storms. In many situations it is best to delay planting out tender young plants until May.

● **Sowing seeds** - Some seeds benefit from special treatment to encourage them to germinate. Very hard coated seeds, such as sweet peas, can be soaked in water for at least 24 hours, or alternatively you can make a small scratch on the seed, being careful not to damage the embryo. This is called scarifying.

Seeds such as peas and beans will benefit from being soaked for a couple of hours. Other seeds, such as special trees, shrubs and alpines, need cold stratification. That means planting, covering and putting them in the fridge for a couple of weeks, then transferring to the greenhouse. The idea is that when you take them out of the fridge they will be shocked out of dormancy and germinate in the warmth.

• Labelling - Make labels before starting to sow your seeds. There is nothing worse than not knowing what is in your pot, either because you haven't labelled it or the markers have faded! You can buy plastic markers and special marker pens, but they can be expensive and fade fast in the hot Spanish sun. After experimenting with various methods, we recommend you type a list of seeds on your computer – with the date of planting in bold type. Print it off, cut out each label, seal it in cello tape, push a small length of wire through the label, and attach to a short stick.

• Sowing - First of all, fill your chosen containers with dampened compost to about 2.5cm from the top. Press down lightly to avoid air pockets. Then sow your seeds. The number of seeds to each container will vary according to their size and whether you want to plant the seedlings on. We treat larger seeds, such as decorative gourds, the same as we would treat vegetables such as pumpkins, courgettes, melons and beans. These we sow two or three to a pot and, when strong enough, plant directly into their final position.

A simple rule for sowing is to cover the seeds with compost equal to their size. Very fine seeds need light, so either leave uncovered or sprinkle a little vermiculite over the top. Do not sow seeds too thickly.

Most importantly, spray the soil surface with a fungicide after sowing to protect against damping off. Use a fine hand sprayer or a watering can with a very fine rose.

Once seeds are sown, you need to be very vigilant. Check every day that the compost in uncovered containers is still damp. Those sealed in plastic should stay damp, but still check from time to time.

• Recognise and solve problems quickly - If seeds don't germinate, check to see if the compost has dried out and compacted, or is too wet. If it is dry, spray with a fine sprayer, always using a dilute mix of fungicide in your sprayer. If the compost is too wet inside the plastic, leave it open for a while to dry out a little and then reseal.

Check to see if the containers are exposed to too much direct sun. If they are, move them to a cooler spot.

Ask yourself if temperatures are fluctuating too much. Perhaps you need more heat in your greenhouse at night and less heat during the day. Make sure you have shading on the greenhouse, and be sure to open the ventilation during the heat of the day. Place a small temperature controlled heater in the greenhouse. Do the tiny seeds have sufficient light? If not, plant another batch on the surface.

If your seedlings become too leggy, they might not have enough light.

Once seeds have appeared, remove the plastic cover or cardboard and place them in good light, but not in the direct sun.

If they are rotting or damping off, the compost could be too wet and you might have forgotten to spray them with a fungicide when sowing the seeds. When seedlings rot off at the base and keel over, it means you have a fungal disease. Quickly remove the rotting seedlings and dry out the compost so that it is just damp to touch. Spray the remaining seedlings and soil lightly with a dilute fungicide mix.

• Planting on - Many seedlings will need planting on into larger containers or modules. Make up a planting medium of 7 parts compost, 3 parts substitute peat and 2 parts sharp sand. Dampen as for seed compost but now dampen with a dilute liquid fertiliser. Use a proprietary general fertilizer, liquid seaweed or a nettle/comfrey feed.

Prick out the seedlings when they are big enough to handle. This is normally when they have four leaves. Always hold them by the leaves, never by the fragile stems. Don't disregard smaller seedlings, as sometimes they grow to be the strongest. Transplant and water very carefully and spray with a dilute mix of fungicide. Don't water again until they are just starting to dry out. At this stage they can rot very easily if over watered. Thereafter, feed once a week feed with a weak solution of liquid fertilizer to encourage strong growth.

To ensure plantlets are not eaten by slugs and snails, always keep several bran or beer traps in the greenhouse and cold frame or, as a last resort, sprinkle some slug pellets around.

● **Hardening off** - Plants grown in the greenhouse or undercover will need to be acclimatised in a sheltered corner of the garden for a couple of days before being planted in their final position. Check that the temperatures are not forecast to drop dramatically before moving them out.

● **Timely planting out** - Finally the time has come to plant out your nurtured plants. Make sure you choose the right situation and soil. For example, annuals could die in one day in a very hot sunny spot, whereas succulents will thrive.

Make sure you work good water-retaining compost into flowerbeds and flower containers. Do not plant out plantlets until they have a good root structure. Remove plants carefully from trays or pots and plant to no more than their previous depth. Firm down the soil around each plant and water gently. Slugs and snails love young plants,

so protect them well from the first hour.

● **Sowing seeds directly into the garden** - When sowing seeds directly into the garden, follow the guidelines below:
● Read instructions on seed packets for required temperatures and spacing.
● Prepare beds by digging in plenty of well-rotted moisture retaining compost.
● Make a 4cm trench or hole and fill with seed compost for fine seeds and planting mix for larger seeds. Use the mediums already described above. Firm down lightly.
● Sow seeds thinly to avoid thinning out later. This will be their final position.
● Cover fine seeds with a little vermiculite. Larger seeds are best covered a layer of planting compost equal to their size. Firm down lightly.
● Label and mark your seeds.
● Water well with a fine rose watering can or sprayer.
● Put down some slug protection.
● Don't let your seeds dry out. Water regularly with a fine spray. Heavy watering will quickly damage young stems.

If you are not totally successful in year one, don't give up. The Spanish conditions do take time to get used to.

6.14 BENEFICIAL GREENHOUSES AND GARDEN FRAMES

In spite of the Spanish climate, a greenhouse and garden frame can be invaluable if you grow more than a few plants from cuttings and seeds for the flower or vegetable garden and you have tender plants that need to be moved out of the garden during the winter.

Few Spanish houses have deep inside windowsills that can be used for propagating or over-wintering plants. A south-facing windowsill would be generally too hot.

TYPICAL USES, PROBLEMS AND SOLUTIONS

TYPICAL USES	GARDEN FRAME	GREENHOUSE
Shelter for seed trays	*	*
Late winter sowings		*
Shelter for propagated cuttings	*	*
Housing collection of tender plants, e.g.,cacti, orchids and succulents	* (If temperature never drops below 0ºC).	* (If temperature never drops below 0ºC).
Early tomatoes and cucumbers	*	*
Winter salad crops	*	
Forcing a grapevine		*
Over wintering potted tropical plants		* (Provided it's heated in colder areas.)

TYPICAL PROBLEMS AND SOLUTIONS		
Temperature drops below zero	Seal tops and sides. Cover with blanket or blister wrap at night. (ineffective for long cold periods).	Close ventilators. Line with blister wrap. Install thermostat controlled heater.
Temperature can rise above a 100 ºC.	• Site in semi shade. • Open top during day.	• Cover with woven plastic or slatted shading. • White wash glazing. • Site on west of house. • Open door and ventilators during daytime.
Slow germination or propagation	• Pre-germinate or root in mini propagator before placing in frame. • Ensure that compost is always just damp. • Place pots and trays with seeds or cuttings in sealed plastic bags to achieve constant temperature and humidity.	• Have propagator in greenhouse (with a mist humidifier in a larger greenhouse • Ensure compost is always just damp. • Place pots/trays with seeds/ cuttings in sealed plastic bags to achieve constant temperature and humidity.
Fungal attacks	• Wash all seed trays and pots in dilute bleach and rinse before use. • Empty, clean out and wash with fungicide once a year. • Don't over-water and include fungicide in water. • Remove any affected plants immediately.	
Slugs and snails	• Put beer traps on floor and shelves amongst the plants. • Ensure there are no entry gaps around the base.	

TYPICAL USES, PROBLEMS AND SOLUTIONS

TYPICAL USES	GARDEN FRAME	GREENHOUSE
Aphids	• Hang proprietary sticky strips. • Place/hang bunches of rosemary. • Take out any affected plants, clean off and spray potassium soap solution.	
Drying out of pots/trays.	• Maintain a daily watering routine. Use drip trays or capilliary trays. • Place seedlings and cuttings in plastic bags until well rooted.	

The difference between day and night time temperatures in the spring, when most seeds are sown, can be 20 degrees. Achieving a constant temperature for good germination can be very difficult.

Tender sub tropical and even tropical plants love the spring and summer temperatures but in many inland areas, especially a high meseta, Madrid and the higher coastal mountains, they would die in the winter if left outside.

For all these reasons it's worth having a greenhouse or garden frame. We all love to try and beat nature by planting newly imported varieties raised in hothouses worldwide, but we can be caught out by just an hour of night frost, even in the south of Spain.

In the boxes below we list some typical uses for greenhouses and garden frames as well as some problems you could encounter and their solutions.

HARDENING OFF

Plants grown in the greenhouse can be hardened off in a cold frame or semi- shaded situation. Plants from the cold frame can be moved to the semi-shade. Place them in the sun for a few days when they are almost ready to plant out.

SITING

Unless you have a very big greenhouse it can get very hot in the full sun. If placed on the east side of the house it will be warmed up by the morning sun, but in the afternoon it will cool down before dusk, especially during the winter months. The west side has the advantage of receiving later sun and will therefore be warmed up for the night. We find it beneficial to have one cold frame in the sun and one in semi-shade.

MINIMUM USEFUL SIZE

A 1sq.m horizontal or vertical frame with four 60x20cm shelves is practical and can produce an amazing number of plants if used throughout the year.

A 11/2sq.m base with a height of two metres is probably the smallest practical size for a greenhouse. Naturally, there is no limit to the size, excepting space and budget.

Problems can arise when you install larger units. For instance, where do you fit in all the trays when you prick out seedlings from small cell trays to individual pots? Where do you harden them all off, and where do you plant them all? Remember, considerable time and patience is required to nurse and water hundreds of plants.

TYPES

Both greenhouses and frames can stand alone or be placed against the wall of the house, garden wall or fence. Garden frames can be horizontal with glazed, plastic sides or solid sides (the latter providing better winter and summer insulation).

A large tent cloche made from old wood and plastic sheeting is an ideal frame for raising large seeded vegetables such as pumpkins and melons.

Wooden, metal and plastic covered aluminium frames are all feasible, the latter having the benefit of not rotting or rusting.

Multi-cell, plastic glazing provides better insulation and is safer than glass for both the tops of garden frames and the glazing on greenhouses.

If you have a large vegetable plot, a tunnel greenhouse constructed from heavy grade plastic over a hooped metal tubing frame can be very useful for not only growing plantlets but also for growing early crops of tomatoes, courgettes, beans, melons, etc.

6.15 PHYSICAL PLANT PROTECTION

In all gardens, tender plants need to be protected from the hottest suns and high winds – and from frost in some areas.

There are several practical ways you can protect your plants from the sun. You can protect seedlings and young propagations from cuttings by hardening off in the semi-shade of a tree or purpose-built, woven plastic or cane shade.

Plants that have shallow roots and will dry out fast in the sun should be planted in semi-shaded situations. Don't plant shade-loving plants in full sun. Use the dappled shady areas in the garden to the full when planning areas for flowerbeds and potted plants.

Many new gardens are not protected from hot or cold drying winds or wind-blown rain or hail until boundary hedges, trees and fences are in place.

Protect young hedge plants grown against an open-mesh, wire fence by lining the fence with rolls of woven plastic or cane windbreak material which you can leave or remove when the hedge is mature, depending on what is then on the other side of the fence.

Delay planting delicate shrubs and trees that could be snapped off by strong winds or become burnt by the sun or frost until external and internal hedges and windbreaks are in place. Preferably, plant tender plants against a south-facing wall or in a sunny nook.

If you plan to plant tropical plants, such as the wonderfully perfumed frangipani, ensure that they have the most sheltered position possible. The ideal is against a south-facing wall with large evergreen trees on either side to protect from east and west winds, and with three-metre or more hedges around the garden. If there is any chance of a winter or spring frost, plant in pots and take inside during the risky months.

FROSTS

From time to time we are all tempted to plant one or two of the more delicate of sub-tropical or tropical plants, knowing that this is a risk – if not during the next winter, then sometime during one of the next five, on average. Early in March 2004, for the first time in more than a decade, a single two-hour night frost decimated delicate plants growing just inland from the coast, from Cataluña to southern Andalusia. The frosts of February and March, 2005 affected even seafront gardens.

This can happen annually in some inland valleys and on mountainsides. If you intend to plant tropical plants, such as bananas and frangipani, or more delicate subtropical plants, such as the white and yellow bougainvillea, be sure to plant them against a protected south-facing wall, wrap them in fleece, woven plastic windbreak material or cover them with a plastic-sheet wigwam.

Keep in them pots and take them inside the house or into a heated greenhouse. In cooler situations, it is best to grow them permanently in a greenhouse.

If you plant out annuals or perennial cuttings early, protect them for a few weeks with cloches made by cutting the bottom 5cm off five or eight litre-water bottles. Stick a cane through the top hole into the ground for stability.

6.16 BE A PLANT DETECTIVE

In general, many of the plants that die in expatriate Spanish gardens do so because they were poorly planted, watered insufficiently or drowned, planted in the hottest corners of the garden in midsummer in shallow or hard drying clay soil or were exposed to frosts during the first winter while still tender.

Where a problem exists, it is all too easy to rush to the garden centre for the latest insecticide or fertilizer and give plants overdoses for something they never had. It would be wiser to follow the guidelines below:

Few garden centres offer a warranty on the plants – so be meticulous in choosing the best type of plant for your situation, planting them well in an appropriate soil, and then giving them thorough aftercare.

When a plant looks unhealthy, try and find out why as soon as possible rather than treating the symptoms in an ad hoc fashion. If a plant dies or does not look right there has to be a reason, whether it is just one plant that gives you concern or half the garden. The reason has to be:

- Something you or someone else did or didn't do, perhaps unknowingly.
- Something unusual about how you bought, planted or cared for the plants.
- Something unusual about the source or type of plant.
- Something that is fundamentally wrong with the depth or type of soil – or planting is being done in sun or shade.

For most of us, there are many things that are different when we first come to Spain and we all need to modify or adjust some of our previous gardening practices.

Be aware of the vulnerability of your gardening practices. The next time something goes wrong, analyse the problem carefully. Ask yourself why only this particular plant is affected and not the one nearby or in another corner of the garden.

Think through the history of the plant and its location and ask yourself if you have done something unusual and whether a similar thing has happened before? Look around the garden and decide which plants are doing the best and try to think of any reasons why they should be doing so well.

The moment you think you know why a plant is unhealthy or dead, act to stop the problem – stop it from reoccurring and stop it happening elsewhere in the garden.

Fifty possible causes of plant problems are listed below. Read through the list and tick any statements that are at least partly true. Then go back over the list and count how many statements you have ticked. The higher the number the more vulnerable the plants in the garden!

Poor choice of plants

1. Making a poor choice when buying plants, or being given a present of a plant unsuitable for your soil and microclimate.
2. Buying plants direct from hot houses without them being hardened off.

Over optimism

3. Assuming that native Spanish plants require little or no watering when first planted.
4. Delaying watering because a storm is forecast.
5. Assuming that you will never get an air frost.
6. Assuming that all soils are good, including yours.

Inadequate watering

7. Unclear agreement in the household as to who waters what and when.
8. Failure to remember a special plant in a far away corner of the garden.
9. Watering in full sun, as a busy life prevents watering in the cool of the evening or before the sun is up.
10. Forgetting to water the terrace pots, greenhouse or garden frame.

11. Watering with the hot water lying inside a long hose left in the sun.

12. Watering quickly and shallowly rather than slowly and deeply.

13. No catchment tray under pots.

14. Saline water or highly chlorinated water on tender plants.

15. Watering irregularly rather than using a timer-controlled irrigation system.

16. Letting recently purchased plants dry out before planting in the garden.

17. Not checking the drip irrigation system for leaks or blocked jets.

18. Failure to water annuals daily during the summer months.

19. Allowing the soil to totally dry out when on holiday or when you are an absentee gardener.

20. Failure to improve the humus, water holding property of the soil, so that much water just runs through to the water table.

Poor spacing of plants

21. Planting too close so that faster growing plants smother smaller plants.

22. Planting too far apart so that the hot sun bakes the soil between and the shallow roots of plants.

Poor mulching

23. Not mulching young plants to keep their roots cool and the soil moist.

24. Mulching deeply with fresh manure and encouraging fungal diseases.

Poor planting in pots

25. Using a compost that dries out very quickly.

26. Using thin walled terracotta pots that dry out quickly by surface evaporation.

27. Not mulching the tops of the soil in pots put in the sun with grit or stones.

28. Not re-potting when root bound.

29. Over watering, especially in the winter months.

30. Placing delicate potted plants in full sun rather than semi- shade.

31. Not wrapping up delicate plants in fleece, plastic sheeting or woven cloth.

32. Not taking delicate plants indoors for the coldest months if in a frost or snow belt.

33. Poor windbreaks.

34. Insecure support posts for trees.

Poor plant tie

35. Tight ties strangling or cutting through plants as they grow.

36. Hard or sharp ties acting like saws in the wind and cutting into trunks, stems and branches.

Inadequate weeding

37. Allowing vigorous weeds to starve plants of moisture and nutrients or smothering weaker plants.

38. Using weed killer near delicate plants.

Poor pruning

38. Pruning just before or after frost.

39. Not sealing cuts after major surgery on trees.

40. Not cutting out diseased wood.

Poor insect/disease control

41. Failure to act fast when problems are first seen.

42. Failure to take preventive action against snails and slugs at the time you sow seeds or plant out young plants.

Root disturbance

43. Loosening of plants when pulling out weeds.

44. Being washed out of soil by erosion during heavy rainfalls.

45. Being knocked over by strong winds.

46. Digging up or fouling by animals and birds.

Burning of foliage or roots

47. Watering alkaline-loving plants with the backwash from the swimming pool.

48. Over application of granular general fertilizers in the garden, especially under young fruit trees and on flowerpots.

49. Over-strength foliar feeding, especially when done in full sun and when leaves are very dry.

50. Burning of soft leaved plants by spraying over-strength insecticides and fungicides, especially in the middle of a hot day.

CHECK YOUR VULNERABILITY

Go back through the list and count the number of statements that you have ticked.

0 – 10: Doing well. You are obviously getting it right.

11 – 25: Generally a need to be more thorough and attentive.

26 – 50: The garden centres must love you! Perhaps you need a gardener or you should consider creating a courtyard or paved garden with few plants.

6.17 A FLOWER GARDEN CALENDAR

JANUARY

- Do the major annual cut back and clean up.
- Take cuttings of a range of plants and pot up to propagate.
- Process all manageable prunings, cuttings and weeds through the shredder.
- Start a new compost heap, carefully layering soft and harder materials.
- Cut up sawn off branches and trunks for logs for the stove or fire.
- Obtain a licence for a bonfire, if necessary, or take material that cannot be shredded to local eco park. Some now pay for it!

- Divide and replant large clumps of perennials.
- Take cuttings of chrysanthemums for propagation.
- Clean out garden frame and greenhouse.
- Sort through and wash/disinfect all empty plant pots and trays.

FEBRUARY

- Check and adjust all plant ties and posts.
- Prune early flowering acacias after flowering.
- Stake over-wintering sweet peas.
- Plant non-tender perennials, shrubs and trees.
- Sow first annuals in the greenhouse.
- Clean pond and prune back the roots of vigorous pond plants.
- Plant summer flowering bulbs and rhizomes.
- Mix well-rotted compost and manure into flowerbeds.Cut back poinsettias when they lose their leaves.
- Turn last autumn's compost heap and sieve out fine compost for preparing seed and potting compost mixes.

MARCH

- Start to spray geraniums against the geranium moth.
- Start to mow lawn and give it a top dressing of sand, peat and fertilizer.
- Take cuttings of perennial plants such as echium, leonotis, margaritas and succulents.
- Remove frost protection from delicate plants after last frost.
- Plant hedges and complete the planting of spring and summer flowering shrubs and trees.
- Carry out an annual safety check on the garden.
- Plant summer corms such as begonias and gladioli.
- Divide chrysanthemums after they have finished flowering.
- Take geranium cuttings and pot up.
- Spring clean the tool shed.

APRIL

- As weather warms up, commence or increase watering of young plants.
- Plant out the first summer annuals for Easter colour.
- Start to give plants in pots and containers a monthly feed.
- Sow zinnias for cutting in the summer.
- Trim frost damage on succulents.
- Don´t be impatient with plants such as hibiscus, lantana and bougainvilleas that look as if the frost killed them. They often sprout as late as May or even June.
- Give hedges a good spring cut.
- Watch out for processionary caterpillars.
- Make final sowings of annuals such as petunias.
- Ensure that compost heaps are kept damp.

MAY

- When cyclamens start to die back, place in a cool shady corner of the garden until September.
- Start to mow the lawn weekly.
- Cut off any new sharp ends of yuccas, palms and other thorny shrubs and trees.
- Deadhead any spring flowering plants.
- Water and feed sweet peas during flowering season.
- Plant out new perennials and herbs.
- Fill in gaps in the rockery with new herbs, succulents and cacti.
- Start to feed fish in ponds on a regular basis.
- If the weather is dry, set up the irrigation timer to water daily in the evening.

JUNE

- Deadhead and tidy plants weekly.
- Dig out or hoe wind-blown weeds as they come up.
- Increase watering as temperatures start to rise.
- Check watering system regularly for leaks and to ensure that all drip heads work.

- Watch out for pests and diseases that can appear as the heat and humidity rise.
- Go out with a torch to catch active slugs and snails, especially around newly planted plants.
- Ensure you keep up the weekly spraying and health check of geraniums.
- Top up pond and continue to watch levels throughout the summer.
- Hand weed or hoe areas of stone chippings and only if really necessary use weed killer.
- Feed plants in pots and containers.

JULY

- Increase watering if there are no summer storms.
- Cut and dry herbs for culinary, health and decorative purposes.
- Do a deadheading tour twice weekly.
- Keep path and terrace areas swept or vacuumed and clear of leaves and dead flowers.
- Prune unsightly growth on shrubs, especially those that flower on long stems.
- Cut out untidy suckers on bougainvilleas.
- Leave large, selected seed heads to ripen for propagation.
- Cut back excessive growth of pond plants to keep a space clear for the fish to surface and feed.
- Cut back hollyhocks once they have finished flowering and collect the ripe seeds.
- Train and tie in climbers on fences and walls.

AUGUST

- Cut back summer lilies and gladioli.
- Keep cutting annuals such as zinnias to prolong flowering.
- Keep up the dead heading.
- Cut sunflowers and hang to dry.
- Maintain summer level of watering if there are no storms.
- Check that no plants show signs of completely drying out.

- Cut off berried ends on lantanas before they drop and squash on terraces and paths.
- Trim climbers to keep them neat and under control and cut out water shoots on bougainvilleas.
- Keep a wary eye open for pests and diseases.
- Cut dead flowers off lavender to tidy the garden.

SEPTEMBER

- Carry out strategic garden review.
- Decide on projects and changes for the autumn and winter.
- Prune and feed roses to re-stimulate flowering for the autumn and Christmas.
- Turn and dampen compost heaps.
- Start to sweep or vacuum fallen leaves. Mix into compost heap or new raised beds.
- Trim and feed annuals to stimula the final fling of flowers.
- Remove all dead annuals and put on compost heat.
- Trim back lantanas and other shrubs such as plumbago and solanum that protrude onto terraces and paths.
- Sow hollyhocks and antirrhinums.
- Give all pot and container plants a tidy up and feed.

OCTOBER

- Prepare new flower beds ready for planting.
- If the rains have come, start to plant perennials, shrubs and trees.
- Take cuttings of succulents and shrubs and propagate.
- Plant Christmas bulbs in pots and place in the dark.
- Bring last year's cyclamens into a north facing porch and start to water and feed.
- Reduce the frequency and extent of irrigation if the weather has cooled down.
- In colder climes, move delicate plants inside or into a greenhouse.

- Prepare and sow new lawns.
- Clean out summer annuals as they finish and replace with pansies.
- Tidy up plants and take cuttings for propagating in the greenhouse or garden frame.
- Give the garden an autumn tidy up but don't fall into the trap of doing a major UK-style garden clean up at this time. If you do, you will have no colour at Christmas. This is why we recommend the major annual cut back and clean up as the number one job for January.

NOVEMBER

- Plant spring bulbs in the garden.
- Construct a rockery or pond.
- Prune rose bushes to stimulate buds for Christmas flowering
- Start sweet peas in pots or ground.
- Wrap the more delicate plants in plastic or frost fleece in colder areas.
- Collect snails and feed on rosemary to prepare for year-end tapas!
- Check ties on trees and shrubs.
- Do an autumn weed and hoe.
- Purchase just-in-bud flowering pot plants for Christmas.

- Complete the autumn planting of perennials, shrubs and trees.

DECEMBER

- Make a last planting of spring bulbs.
- Bring on Christmas pot plants to be at their best during the holidays. Obtain next year's seed catalogues and place orders.
- Sweep up last of fallen leaves, dampen, bag up in black plastic bags (with a few air holes) and leave in a corner to rot down to useful leaf mould.
- Do a pre-Christmas weeding and light tidy up. Leave as many buds and flowers as possible.
- Have tops of palm trees pruned and shaped.
- Arrange a display of colourful flowering plants such as cyclamens, poinsettias, azaleas, kalanchoas and bulbs around the front door,
- Start to build new terraces, paths and walls.
- Ensure that Christmas plants are given sufficient light, kept just moist and out of draughts, and are not baked in centrally-heated rooms.

SECTION SEVEN
HOME GROWN ORGANIC VEGETABLES

HOME GROWN ORGANIC VEGETABLES

HOWEVER SMALL YOUR GARDEN is, try to grow some vegetables, even if the only space available is in a few pots or a trough on an apartment terrace. We started growing vegetables in just 5sq.m and a few containers until we had time to expand to today's vegetable plot (*huerto*) of some 400sq.m.

We had several reasons for expanding our vegetable production:

Local shops were selling less and less local produce, as inherited vegetable growing lands were increasingly planted with fruit trees, while supermarkets sold fewer and fewer loose vegetables, and the prepacked vegetables were not what we wanted for our Mediterranean diet.

More and more vegetables were produced under large plastic houses and not in the fresh air. We wanted a greater diversity of vegetables 365 days a year, and we wanted them to be organically grown. We were prepared to adjust our lifestyle to allocate the extra hours a week necessary for a large vegetable garden for health and exercise benefits.

We recognise that there are an increasing number of like-minded gardeners and therefore outline in this section the way to start small and expand as land and time allow, and as you gain experience in growing vegetables in Spain. It can be very different to growing in cooler and wetter climes.

7.1 THE BENEFITS OF GROWING ORGANICALLY

Growing your own vegetables is fun, good exercise, adds a diversity of readily available fresh vegetables for 9 to 12 months of the year, depending on your summer and winter temperatures, and provides fresh vegetables for eating within minutes or hours of harvesting them, when they are crisp, flavoursome and perfumed, and high in vitamins. You can pick them at the size and in the quantity you need – and of course excess-crops can be frozen, bottled or converted into chutneys.

There are three ways of growing vegetables:

1. Inorganically, using the manufactured inorganic chemical fertilizers, insecticides, fungicides, and weed killers that gradually replaced traditional methods of improving soils and growing vegetables from the 1950's.

2. Organically, using traditional, newly developed, natural and environmentally friendly methods of land husbandry and organic products for the improvement of soil structure and fertility, feeding of crops and control of pests and diseases.

3. A part way house between the above two methods.

We concentrate on describing organic methods in this section of the book for the following reasons:

• Organic fertilizers such as well rotted manures and compost improve the structure and fertility of the soil year by year, while inorganic fertilizers feed current crops but leave little in the soil for follow-on crops, especially when heavy rains leach out some of the residual fertilizer content into the water table.

• Manures and composts add not only minerals but also vital micro- organisms and worms, the latter recycling organic matter into humus, which makes plant foods. They also improve the moisture holding properties of dry soils and drainage of heavy clay soils.

• The total number of varieties of vegetable seed readily available to the amateur gardener has been very much reduced over the last 20 years as seed producers have found it too expensive to meet the EU registration costs for all varieties. However, a wide range of heritage seeds are available from organic seed libraries and clubs that are ensuring traditional seeds never commercialised or not now marketed are not lost.

- The use of traditional non-hybridised varieties means that you can save seed to grow the following year, knowing that you will grow the same variety except for occasional cross pollinations that can lead to some interesting discoveries.
- Organically grown vegetables have no residual chemicals on their surface and are not treated to preserve their freshness between the farm, market, supermarket and home.
- The recycling of kitchen and garden waste through the compost heap reduces the amount of daily waste that is burnt at municipal incinerators or used for landfill, later generating methane gas.
- There can be fewer hazardous chemicals in the tool shed or in the atmosphere where organic insecticides, fungicides and herbicides are used. Your gardening practices are therefore more friendly to yourselves and your neighbours.
- Organic practices are more eco or environmentally friendly to wild life than inorganic methods. Your vegetable garden will enrich the number and diversity of interesting creatures in the garden, adding to the benefits of ponds, hedges, and natural/wild areas of your total garden.
- Home produced organic vegetables will be fresher and less expensive than those purchased in local shops or supermarkets.
- You can grow your own vegetables to their natural, rather than a forced, size. Often this results in tastier, better coloured, and crisper vegetables.

Yes, organic methods will take up more time but exercise is as important for our overall health as what we eat and drink, and it is exercise in a non-chemical environment, except of course when nearby non-organic fruit growers decide to spray on windy days. Unless you are in a truly isolated corner of the countryside, you can never be fully protected, and even then nothing is guaranteed, though wherever you are you will have the satisfaction of knowing you are doing something to protect your local environment in a world of diminishing returns.

7.2 THE SUCCESS FACTORS

Below are ten success factors for gaining the most from growing vegetables organically here in Spain:

1. Improve the soil initially and annually with well-rotted natural manures, composts and dried seaweed. For the initial improvement of a poor soil, aim at working in 25 litres per square metre. This is the equivalent to the capacity of a 40cm diameter black plastic gardener's/builder's bucket.
Supplement the base fertility of the soil by feeding growing crops with supplementary organic feeds. Take account of the particular needs of different types of plants and your crop rotation plan when adding manure and compost after year one. When obtaining manure, look out for well-rotted heaps that are full of worms.
2. Work the soil with worms and hand harrowing, hoeing and raking. Minimise the use of mechanical ploughs and rotovators. This will maintain a healthily growing worm population and minimise the breakdown of the structure of the improving soil when working it.
3. Sow a diversity of types and varieties of vegetables to add interest and health

value to your diet.

4. Use good seed, preferably organic. As at the time of writing there is no Spanish supplier of organic vegetable seeds in small retail packets and the range available to commercial growers is limited.

We either buy organic seed from UK-based suppliers or buy local Spanish vegetable varieties, and allow some plants to seed for use the next year, or obtain local heritage varieties from local villagers and keep some seeds from our organic crops. We also obtain seeds of a range of internationally sourced old varieties by belonging to the following heritage seed clubs:

• The Heritage Seed Library, operated as a section of the HDRA (Henry Doubleday Research Association), *(enquiry@hdra. org.uk)*

• The heritage seed club operated by The Village Guild Ltd. for subscribers to its monthly newsletter. *John@village-guild.co.uk*

• Heritage Gardening Vegetable Catalogue, Ireland *(info@ heritagebulbs. com)*

In this way we can experiment with different varieties of vegetables that are no longer available commercially.

5. Sow to harvest a diversity of fresh vegetables 365 days a year!

6. Grow vegetables for taste, texture, colour, crispness, cleanliness, health benefits and not necessarily size. Over-watered and over-fed vegetables can be very watery and lacking in flavour.

7. Sow and harvest according to the impact of the moon and planet cycles on the growth of plants. We suggest that you obtain one or both of the following lunar calendars each year:

Calendario Lunar, published by Artus Porta Manresa, *(calendario@lunar.info-mail.es)*

Calendario de Agricultura de Agricultura Bionamica, published by Editorial Rudolf Steiner, *(rudolfsteiner@teleline.es).*

Both are available from good book shops. If you have difficulty finding them,

email to ask for your nearest point of sale.

8. Rotate the growing of non-fixed crops to reduce pest and disease damage, and to make best use of the condition of the soil after the previous crops.

9. Water plants when the soil becomes dry with non-chlorinated water if at all possible.

10. Control pests and diseases by the achievement of an eco balance on your vegetable plot and by eco friendly methods or products.

11 Recognise that the advantages of using organic gardening practices are cumulative, and that there are six basic levels of Eco/organic gardening:

Level one: Use only natural and ecological organic soil improvers, fertilizers and plant supplements, starting with the recycling of kitchen and garden waste through a compost heap.

Level two: Use no manufactured proprietary inorganic chemical based herbicides to control weeds.

Level three: Use no manufactured proprietary inorganic chemical based insecticide or organic based insecticides with significant side effects.

Level four: Use only organically produced seeds.

Level five: The development and management of the vegetable plot as a balanced naturally occurring ecological biological system.

Level six: A self-contained system by keeping animals and birds to provide ones own supply of manure.

12. Decide at what level you are able to start and work to move up the scale over a number of years. Naturally if you decide not to follow organic principles, most of what is described in the following chapters is still relevant, except that you will need to use proprietary inorganic chemical fertilizers, pesticides and fungicides.

Every year there are more of these products available.

7.3 STARTING SMALL

You don't need a large vegetable patch to grow a useful selection of organic vegetables. We now have an area of 400 square metres, but only started in Spain with five square metres and few large plant pots. So don't hesitate to have a go, even if you only have an apartment terrace or townhouse patio. Once you have started, you can expand season by season.

You can start off using plastic plant pots and containers, empty milk or fruit juice cartons, water bottles of all sizes with their tops cut off, old chimney pots, plastic containers of all sizes, strong plastic bags and special grow bags can all be used on the terraces of apartments or in a handy corner of the garden.

The plants should be near to the kitchen so that you remember to water and feed them regularly. In the kitchen itself you can achieve an amazing output from a regularly planted seed sprouter.

The easiest crops for containers are lettuces, tomatoes, peppers, peanuts, and salad/culinary herbs such as chives, basil, sage, thyme, parsley, marjoram and rosemary. With a little care and dedication potatoes, radishes, carrots and Swiss chard can also be raised successfully.

More and larger crops can be grown in small raised beds of one to five square metres surface area. Aim for a minimum wall height of 30cm but preferably 40cm. Even higher beds 60 cm high make it possible to work the beds while sitting in a chair.

Build the walls with rocks, bricks or old doors sliced in half. Old baths can also be recycled as raised beds. We grew two kilos of rice in one turned into a paddy field for six months. We then planted rocket and lettuces and it is now planted up with six pineapple plants grown from the leafy tops of pineapples. Disguise them by surrounding them with pots of nasturtiums and marigolds, which will also attract beneficial insects and draw aphids away from the vegetables.

The only constraints on the size of a raised-bed vegetable garden is the area you are willing to allocate to it and the effort required to build two or more parallel units 60 to 80 cm across for ease of working. They can be from 1-20 metres long, or even along the entire back or side wall of the garden, with beans and cucumbers trained up the wall.

7.4 EXPANDING TO A BIGGER VEGETABLE PLOT

A large vegetable plot of 200 to 600 square metres can be fun and very satisfying, and it's amazing how quickly the space fills up. When we expanded our plot from just a few metres to 400 square metres, we thought we would never use all the space – but gradually we did.

Our asparagus bed was expanded, as it is our favourite spring vegetable, and our one-square-metre of comfrey expanded to 30 square metres after splitting it each spring for five years. The one line of raspberries along the edge became three as we transplanted runners each autumn. We collected so many seeds from our sweet peas, we eventually had a 30-metre row, producing enough flowers for all the villagers who pass our huerto for a chat and to find out what the mad foreigners are growing this year.

To their amazement, we have grown over 50 types of vegetables in a year. Some they recognise, but others are from seeds from other parts of Spain and heritage seeds from various parts of the globe.

The only constraints on how large a plot you have are:

1. Time. We probably spend an average of an hour a day on the vegetable plot.

2. The quantity of vegetables you can eat in salads, soups and as vegetables.

3. Irrigation. Beyond a few square metres, a watering or hose can become impractical. So some form of irrigation becomes essential. The most practical method is lines of perforated hoses laid alongside each row of vegetables, fed from the mains or a header tank, and controlled by a battery-operated timer.

The only difficulty is that some vegetables need more watering than others, so the flow control valves at the end of some hoses or a supplementary hosepipe watering may be necessary.

We irrigate by flooding the waterways between crops every seven to ten days in dry periods. The water comes a kilometre across the countryside from a spring, via a complex system of channels, tubes, siphons and tapons (plugs) that need opening and shutting to get the water to go the right way. When the spring dries up, a pump pulls water up from an underground reservoir and feeds the system.

4. Weed control, if you garden organically, and ban the use of weed killers.

5. Obtaining sufficient manure and compost to enrich the soil.

6. Preparing and working the soil.

WORKING THE SOIL

Some advice on the ongoing working of the soil is now needed. Here are some guidelines:

1. Hoe between and around plants to the top 2-3cm to reduce the extent of water evaporation by capillary action, remove weeds and mix in the fine pulverised surface soil caused by periods of heavy rainfall.

2. Hoe, harrow and rake to prepare fine seed beds.

3. Hoe in the evening to stimulate the absorption of overnight dews or in the morning to dry out over-wet soils.

4. Rake earth into ridges between waterways or into flat beds between ridges if watering by flooding.

5. Hoe waterways and walkways to reduce soil compaction and prevent the run off of rain.

6. Maximise the use of worm power to aerate, mix in manures and produce humus. Search out manures rich in worms and cover unused areas of soil with a capping of manure, chopped weeds and compost and cover with an old carpet or black plastic to encourage the working and breeding of worms. Seed the compost heap with worms to improve composting process and breed worms, or start a wormery and add worms to land.

7. Maximise the use of the mattock, hoes and ridge rakes and minimise the use of the fork, spade and rotovator to minimise backache and preserve the soil structure.

8. Work the soil by no-dig methods to keep the goodness in the top 15cm. You will, however, need to rotovate the land every four years to reduce compaction.

9. If you do not use no-dig methods,

rotovate each season before planting.

10. Keep the soil covered with a carpet, black plastic or a green fertilizer crop if not planted with vegetables to prevent erosion.

7.5 WHAT, WHEN AND WHERE TO PLANT

The table entitled "Phased Planting Plan" outlines a suggested phased planting plan, assuming that you are in a situation where it is reasonable to grow vegetables of one sort or another throughout the year. The suggested year-one plantings are for a plot of 100 square metres.

If you want to grow all 40 types of vegetables in one year, a minimum vegetable plot of 200 metres will be required. If you intend to have only a mini vegetable garden – in pots, raised beds or a small plot – select those vegetables that you most enjoy or would like to try, and sow in small quantities closely packed. Even easier, buy some plantlets.

We have started the sowing/planting year in the autumn so that you do not immediately have to cope with the problems of the scorching temperatures and drought of late spring and summer.

As the table indicates, many vegetables can be harvested year round with successive sowings, though some do go to seed faster in the summer. In very hot situations, day time shading with woven plastic can slow down the process of going to seed and daily drying out.

If you garden in a very hot dry area and/or have a summer water shortage, restrict vegetable gardening efforts to winter and spring crops and don't plant for summer or early autumn harvests.

If you live in a frost pocket, this will restrict what can be grown during the winter and how early you can plant in early spring. Plantings will need to be delayed until the final frosts are past, although a green house will enable plantlets of many vegetables to be brought on ready for planting out once

PHASED PLANTING PLAN

YEAR	VEGETABLE NAME English/Spanish	FOR SALADS	AS A VEG.	MANURE NEEDS	WATER NEEDS	PLANT SEEDS A	W	S	PLANT PLANTLETS A	W	S	HARVEST VEGETABLES A	W	S
ONE	POTATOES / Patatas	*	*	H	M	○	○	/				○	○	/
	GARLIC/ Ajo	*	*	L	M	○	/	○	○	○	/	○	○	/
	CHIVES/Cebollino	*		L	M	○	○	○	○	○	/	○	○	○
	ONIONS/Cebollas	*	*	M	M	○	○	/	○	○	/	/	○	○
	LEEKS/Puerros		*	L	M	○	○	○	○	○	/	○	○	○
	SWISS CHARD/Acelgas	*	*	M	M	○	○	○	○	○	/	○	○	○
	SPINACH/Espinacas	*	*	M	M	○	/	/	○	○	/	○	○	/
	SPROUTING BROCCOLI Brecol	*	*	M	H	○	/	○	○	○	/	/	○	/
	PEAS/Guisantes	*	*	L/M	H	○	○	/	○	○	/	/	○	/
	OAK LEAF LETTUCE/ Lechuga rosa	*		M	H	○	○	○	○	○	/	○	○	○
	RADISHES/Rábano	*		M	H	○	○	/				○	○	○
	ROCKET/Oruga	*		M	M	○	○	/	/	○	/	○	○	○
	COURGETTES/ Calabacines	*	*	H	M	/	○	/	/	○	/	○	/	/
	CUCUMBERS/Pepinos	*		H	H	/	○	/	/	○	/	○	○	○
	TOMATOES/Tomates	*	*	H	H	/	○	○	/	○	/	○	/	○
	ASPARAGUS/Espárrago	*	*	H	L/M	/	○	/	○	/	/	○	/	/

PHASED PLANTING PLAN

YEAR	VEGETABLE NAME English/Spanish	FOR SALADS	AS A VEG	MANURE NEEDS	WATER NEEDS	PLANT SEEDS A	W	S	S	PLANT PLANTLETS A	W	S	S	HARVEST VEGETABLES A	W	S	S
ONE	CARROTS/Zanahorias	*	*	L	M	0	0	0	/					0	0	0	0
	BEETROOTS/Remolacha	*	*	L	M	0	0	0	/					0	0	0	0
	PADRON/GREEN PEP. Pimiento dePadron/Verde	TAPAS*	*	H	H	/	/	0	/	/	0	/	/	0	/	/	0
	FENNEL/Hinojo	*	*	H	H	/	/	0	/	/	0	/	/	0	0	0	0
	OGEN MELON/ Melón Ogen	Starter/ desert		M	H	/	/	0	/	/	0	/	/	/	/	/	0
TWO	LETTUCE/Lechuga	*		M	H	0	0	0	/	0	0	0	/	0	0	0	0
	DANDELION/Diente de león	*		H	M	0	/	0	/	/	0	0	/	0	0	0	0
	CHICORY LETTUCE/Escarolas	*		M	H	0	/	0	/	/	0	0	/	0	0	0	0
	BROAD BEANS/Habas	*	*	L/M	M	0	0	/	/					0	/	0	/
	PARSNIPS/Chirivias	*	*	L	M	0	/	0	/	/	0	0	/	/	0	0	0
	CAULIFLOWER/Col de flor	*	*	M	H	/	0	0	0	0	/	0	/	0	0	0	/
	RED/CHILLI PEPPERS Pimentos rojos/picantes	*	*	H	H	/	/	0	0	/	/	0	/	/	/	0	0
	CLIMBING PAELLA BEANS/ Judias verde y rojas alta	*	*	H	H	0	/	/	0	0	/	0	/	/	/	/	0
	ARTICHOKES/Alcachofas	*	*	H	H	/	/	/	0	0	/	0	/	/	0	0	0
	AUBERGINE/Berejenas		*	H	H	/	/	/	0	/	/	0	/	/	/	/	0

261

PHASED PLANTING PLAN

YEAR	VEGETABLE NAME English/Spanish	FOR SALADS	AS A VEG	MANURE NEEDS	WATER NEEDS	PLANT SEEDS			PLANT PLANTLETS			HARVEST VEGETABLES		
						A	W	S	A	W	S	A	W	S
TWO	FRENCH BEANS/ *Judias bajas*	*	*	L/M	H	/	/	0	/	/	0	/	/	0
	PUMPKINS/*Calabazas*		*	H	H	/	/	0	/	/	0	0	/	0
	BUTTERNUT SQUASH/ *Violines*		*	H	M	/	/	0	/	/	0	0	/	0
	TURKS TURBAN/*Calabaza Turquia de adorno*		*	H	M	/	/	0	/	/	0	0	/	0
	WATER MELONS/*Sandias*	Starter/ dessert		H	M	/	/	0	/	/	0	/	/	/
	GINGER/*jengibre*		*	M	M		/	0	/	/	0	0	/	/
	CHINESE LETTUCE/ *Lechuga de China*	*	*	M	H	0	0	0	/	0	0	0	0	0
	PEANUTS/*Cacahuetes*	Tapas		M	M	/	/	0				0	/	/
	SWEET CORN/*Maiz*	*	*	H	H	/	/	0				/	/	0
	KOHLRABI/*Colinabos*	*		H	H	/	0	0				0	0	0

the weather starts to warm up.

The selection of the 40 vegetables listed was based on personal preferences, the desire for a good diversity in our diet, ease of growing, space required and a combined year-round harvesting.

We have grown many other vegetables, so look around for other varieties if our choices in the list do not match your needs and tastes.

WHERE TO PLANT
Not all the above vegetables thrive under the same conditions. Some require substantial amounts of food and others rather less. Some need more watering than others, some have beneficial effects on others and some negative effects. Also, some have a tendency to build up diseases or detrimental insects in the soil.

GROUPING OF VEGETABLES FOR CROP ROTATIONS

Main Vegetable Groups	Includes the following	Soil Fertility needs of group	Constellation group for use of lunar calendar	Best phase of moon for planting/ harvesting	Co-plant as they have similar needs and special benefits e.g.
ROOT ONE – R1	Potatoes	High with new manures	Earth (Root)	When under influence of tauro,virgo and capricorn	
FRUIT ONE – F1	Tomatoes, peppers, melons, pumpkins, cucumbers	High but no new manures	Fire (Fruit)	When under influence of aries, leo and sagitarius	Sweet corn, sunflowers
FRUIT TWO – F2	Beans, peas	High, trench of rotted manure/ compost	Fire (Fruit)	As above	Aubergines, sweetcorn
FLOWER – FL	a. Globe artichoke, brocolli, b. Sweet peas to build up nitrogen in soil	As above	Air (Flowers)	When under influence of gemini, libra and aquarious	
LEAF – L	Lettuce, brassicas, acelga, spinach	High in nitrogen	Water (Leaf)	When under influence of cancer, scorpio and pisces	Onions, fennel, mint garlic
ROOT TWO – R2	Carrots, parsnips, beetroots, onions and garlic	Medium. Dislike new manure and compost	Earth (Root)	As ROOT ONE	Lettuce

CROP ROTATION PLAN

YEAR	SEASONS	SECTOR ONE	SECTOR TWO	SECTOR THREE	SECTOR FOUR	SECTOR FIVE	SECTOR SIX	SECTOR SEVEN
ONE	Autumn/Winter	R1	R2	L	FL	F2	GR	P
	Spring/Summer	F1	R1	R2	L	FL	F2	P
TWO	Autumn/Winter	F2	GR	R1	R2	L	FL	P
	Spring/Summer	FL	F2	F1	R1	R2	L	P
THREE	Autumn/Winter	L	FL	F2	GR	R1	R2	P
	Spring/Summer	R2	L	FL	F2	F1	R1	P

Key to vegetable groups:
R1 = Roots Group 1; R2 = Roots Group 2; F1 = Fruits Group 1; F2 = Fruits Group 2; FL = Flowers Group; L = Leaf Group; P = Permanent Group; GR = Grow a green crop to dig in to enrich soil or leave fallow.

It is therefore wise to practice crop rotation, taking into account the above factors. Divide your planned plantings into the six groupings listed in the table.

Once you have grouped your vegetables for crop rotation, divide your vegetable plot into seven sectors. These might be parallel raised beds, strips divided by pathways or squares of ground.

Allocate one of the end sectors to perennial vegetables such as asparagus and artichokes that need to be kept in one place for a number of years.

Then plan to change the planting area allocated to each of the six groups of vegetables listed in the "Grouping of Vegetables for Crop Rotations" table every six months along the lines in the table above (we plan on the basis that the vegetable gardening year starts in September):

WHEN TO PLANT

There have always been folklore guidelines for when it is best to plant particular vegetables. For instance, potatoes should be planted by St. Patrick's Day, March 17, while

**EXTRACT FROM *CALENDARIO LUNAR*
PUBLISHED BY ARTUS PORTA MANRESA**

indicating the very best days). The days and times relate to the best phases of the moon indicated in the Grouping of Vegetables chart above. Each year the three planting days mentioned above correlate uncannily with the lunar calendar.

A diary-style lunar calendar called Working with the Stars – A Biodynamic Planting and Sowing Calendar is published by the Hawthorn Press *(hawthornpress@ hawthornpress.com)*. Biodynamic gardening suggests that all work in the vegetable garden – sowing, weeding, hoeing, feeding, harvesting, etc. – should be done according to the relationship of the moon to constellations. We suggest that this is too complicated for the average gardener, especially if you are growing a wide range of vegetables versus a simple, single-crop field, though we do suggest you sow, plant and harvest for storage according to the calendar.

HOW TO PLANT

Traditionally, vegetables have been sown in rows, however, there is benefit in planting many vegetables in blocks – for instance, leaf vegetables, root vegetables including potatoes if planted in a raised bed, potato box or heap.

The mass of foliage gives shade to the roots, watering and feeding can be done in a more confined space, and less space is taken up by each sowing. Where necessary, the block can be thinned by harvesting young vegetables for salads to allow the remainder to grow to maturity. A cartwheel design with blocks of different vegetables between the spokes is an excellent idea for a small garden or a children's vegetable plot.

7.6 WATERING

The watering needs of vegetables obviously vary according to where you live in Spain and whether or not you grow vegetables throughout the year. To cater for all situations we suggest the following guidelines:

1. Don't let vegetables dry out at any time.

broad beans must be planted on All Saints Day, November 1, and paella beans four or five days either side of Saint James' Day, July 25. Such dates became custom based on trial error, but in fact there is scientific evidence to back them up.

Various organisations publish an annual lunar calendar that includes guidelines for when to sow and harvest the various groups of plants included in the crop rotation plan. We use the annual calendar published by Artus Porta Manresa *(calendario-@lunarinfo-mail.es)*, reproduced above with their kind permission.

The bottom half of the chart indicates the best days for planting and harvesting the various groups of vegetables (three stars

2. Don't create a swamp or paddy field unless growing water cress or rice.

3. Water just sufficiently to maintain the steady, uninterrupted, healthy growth of your plants.

4. Recognise that some plants need more water than others.

For instance, tomatoes, peppers, pumpkins and lettuces are thirsty plants, while leeks, garlic and melons need less water.

5. Excess water can result in over-sappy crops that can be more susceptible to attacks by insects and fungal spores.

6. Recognise that only a percentage of irrigation water gets to the plants. Much of it evaporates during hot weather or drains away through the sub-soil to the water table.

7. The more you work well-rotted manure and compost into the soil, the more you will build up the humus content and water-retaining properties of the soil. You will then use, and lose less water.

8. In hot weather, keep the surface of the soil around plants loose by hoeing. Invisible holes develop in hard-caked s urfaces and water is lost by capillary action. Also, keep the surface around large plants mulched to reduce evaporation and provide an additional nutrient source.

9. Plant through holes in black plastic sheeting to maintain a high local water table and reduce evaporation. Plant onions, tomatoes, peppers, etc., through rows of small 5cm planting holes and larger plants such as melons and butter squash through well-spaced, larger 20cm holes.

10. Water in the cool of the evening and not during the midday sun.

11. Except for leaf vegetables, water alongside the roots and avoid wetting the leaves.

12. Include appropriate feed supplements in the irrigation water on a weekly basis if required.

13. Well or spring water is better than chlorinated domestic water (unless it is saline) and when energised achieves better yields.

14. There is evidence that energised or reoriented water can stimulate the stronger and faster growth of vegetables. Water can be energised by running it fast through a series of expansion tanks and narrow channels to stimulate the natural stirring up of water in mountain streams (a Moorish style system of channels, bends, drops and siphons can partly achieve the same effect), or using a Vi-Aqua unit as discussed in Section Six.

15. Remove evasive weeds that compete for water. Their roots might end up strangling the roots of your vegetables.

16. We find that the most effective ways of watering vegetables are as follows:

a. For a few pots/containers – a watering can or trickling hose.

b. For raised beds or small plots – a porous hose irrigation system fed from a mains tap, a pump from a well or storage tank or by gravity from a storage tank above the plot. In each case, a timer switch can be a great help in controlling dosages and making sure watering is done at the same time each day.

c. For medium and large plots – a porous hose irrigation system or, where only channelled agricultural water is available, a flooding of the plot on a weekly basis. To achieve the appropriate amount of watering for different types of plants with a channelled water supply system, grow vegetables that need the least water on raised ridges between two water channels that are flooded to water, or grow vegetables that need the most water in flat beds surrounded by raised ridges. The flatbed is flooded when irrigating.

17. Water according to the weather and stage of growth of plants. Water less during the winter months than the summer, less when plants are mere seedlings and more when they are in full growth or at the fruiting stage.

18. Remember at all times that effective watering is about getting moisture to the roots of plants in the amount they need, at the time they need it to sustain the continuous growth of healthy good eating vegetables.

7.7 FEEDING VEGETABLE PLANTS

The soil for growing vegetables needs to be more carefully prepared than for flowerbeds, whether you plan to grow on a small or large scale. Prepare the soil for small-scale growing in pots, containers and raised beds by preparing a 1:3 mix of well-rotted manure/compost with soil, first sieving out any builder's rubble and stones.

If you are planning to prepare a small vegetable plot, double dig it, mixing in one or two 20-litre black buckets of manure/compost into the top 15-20cm per square metre of soil. If it is a large plot, plough it and then rotovate 10 days later, working in the same quantity of manure/compost.

If you can wait six months before planting the first vegetables, cover the area of the future vegetable plot with a thick layer of compost, leaf mould, grass cuttings and manure. Wet and cover with an old carpet or heavy sheet of black plastic. Over the next few months, worms will work the organic material into the soil. After five to six months, all you need to do is to remove the covering and harrow/rake the top 10cm to a fine tilth before starting to plant without the back-breaking job of double digging.

It is worth checking on the acidity of your soil both before and after adding the manure and compost. The acidy of soil is measured on the pH scale of 1 to 14 (1 being very acid, 14 very alkaline and 7 being regarded as neutral).

Most vegetables grow best in a slightly acid soil with a pH of 6.5 to 7. Some vegetables, such as potatoes, grow best at an acidity of around 6. This can be provided for by using fresh manure and pine needles in the planting trench.

One can also use natural sulphur powder to reduce alkalinity. On the other hand, brassicas, excluding cauliflowers, do better in a neutral soil, which is why it might be necessary to add lime to areas where they will be grown. Lime also helps break up clinging clay soils and helps plants unlock the nutritional content of the soil. Comfrey is also very beneficial for the latter.

ADDITIONAL FEEDING WHEN PLANTING

In the areas for planting hungry plants, mix in a further bucket per square metre. For beans, lay this at the bottom of a trench under the place you plan to plant. When planting up asparagus plants, cover the bed with 5-10cm of well-rotted manure and seaweed.

Line the bottom of trenches for potatoes with rotted manure. In the autumn we place a layer of comfrey leaves under the manure. Unfortunately, we rarely have the leaves in time for spring plantings.

FEEDING AFTER PLANTING

The feeds we use are summarised in the "Fourteen Practical Organic Fertilisers" table below. The alternative is to purchase proprietary organic feeds. There are more and more available each year.

FOURTEEN PRACTICAL ORGANIC FERTILISERS

1. SHEEP/GOAT MANURE – collected from animals that graze on fresh grass and herbs on local hillsides, and hay and orange prunings when in the yard. Before using, we compost it for 6 to 12 months, covered with a plastic sheet or old carpet. The manure is very strong, so we try to mix 50:50 with horse manure and compost before using it in the following ways:

- As a liquid feed prepared by fermenting with water in a plastic barrel for two or three weeks. Diluted, it can be used as a foliar feed
- As a mulch around plants such as beans.
- As a layer at the bottom of trenches for planting beans, peas, squash and potatoes.
- In preparing no-dig beds, by mixing with cut weeds and covering with a carpet.
- As a 10-15cm annual layer on the asparagus bed.
- Spread in the autumn and dug in during the spring.
- Mixed with a peat substitute as a potting compost for planting up cuttings.

2. HORSE MANURE – from horses naturally grazed on pastures that have not been chemically treated, or animals that are fed in stables with alfalfa, hay, etc. Prepare and use the horse manure as for sheep and goat manure. It is best mixed with other manures and kitchen and garden waste before composting, as it is not as strong as other animal manures.

3. CHICKEN MANURE – from our free range chicken house where they are bedded on rice husks. As it is very strong, we compost for a minimum of a year and then mix with other manures before using. We then use it as in 1 and 2 above, except not as a liquid feed. Use chicken manure sparingly, as it is very high in nitrogen.

4. RABBIT AND GUINEA PIG DROPPINGS – we mix into the compost heap as an accelerator. Guinea pigs are particularly useful as they eat any green kitchen waste and love palm branches as a treat.

5. COMPOST – prepared in compost boxes from plant waste and weeds from our organic vegetable plot, leaf mould, non chemically treated grass cuttings, fresh uncooked vegetable and fruit kitchen waste, and shredded prunings from the organic flower garden. The final compost is used as 1 and 2 above, except as a liquid feed. We also use it as in seed composts, but only after sieving and sterilizing.

6. COMFREY LEAVES – grown organically on our vegetable plot. Comfrey is very high in potash and also helps plants to extract trace elements from the soil. We use comfrey as a liquid feed for vegetables and flowering plants indoors and outdoors. Prepare the liquid feed by filling a plastic barrel with leaves and then fermenting either dry or with 10 litres water to 1kg of leaves. The latter is the faster method but the former keeps better. We also use comfrey as an underlay when planting seed potatoes.

7. NETTLE LEAVES – cut from clumps untreated with chemical herbicides. We use as a liquid feed to encourage leaf growth, as it is very high in nitrogen, or as a foliar feed to stimulate stronger disease and insect resistant plants. The liquid is prepared by putting the cut leaves in a plastic barrel, covering with water and leaving to decompose and ferment for a couple of weeks and then diluted 20:1 before use.

FOURTEEN PRACTICAL ORGANIC FERTILISERS

8. WORM CASTS – created naturally by worm action in no-dig beds, the compost heap or our kitchen waste composter/wormery. We mix it into seed compost for growing large seed vegetables and in compost for potting up seedlings such as lettuce. Composts including ground worm casts can be purchased.

9. SEAWEED – raked up from local beaches after storms. We use direct as 10cm annual winter mulch on the asparagus bed sandwiched with manure. We also pile it and leave it to rot for several months covered with a carpet and then use as a mulch to improve soil texture. We mix some fresh seaweed into the compost heap as an activator or ferment in water to prepare a liquid spray against aphids and carrot fly.

10. WOOD ASH – saved from our wood burning stove. We use the wood ash in three ways: sprinkled on the soil between crops hungry for potash (e.g., onions and leeks); added as layers in the compost heap; and heaped around plants to deter slugs.

11. LIQUID FROM BOILING OR STEAMING VEGETABLES – we cool, dilute and use as a feed for the seedlings or large seeded plants such as courgettes and pumpkins.

12. GREEN MANURES – rich in nitrogen. We use three types. In the spring we cut back the naturally growing clover (oxalis) that self seeds from nearby orange orchards during the winter. We grow green manures such as alfalfa, and we recognise grass as a natural green manure and not a weed. All are cut and added to the compost heap, mixed with manure and compost on the surface of no-dig beds and also as mulches around our fruit trees and raspberry canes.

13. PROPRIETARY ORGANIC/ECOLOGICAL LIQUID FERTILISERS – that can be used as root and foliar feeds.

14. PROPRIETARY ORGANIC FIBROUS FERTILISERS – which can be used as a general soil enricher when preparing raised beds and seed beds. It can also be mixed into seed and potting composts and as a mulch around plants.

Each of the above natural fertilisers provides the minerals and trace elements required for strong healthy plant growth in varying amounts. They are:
- Nitrogen (N) – which stimulates the development of stems and leaves and their green coloration.
- Phosphorus (P) – in the form of phosphates which stimulate the development of strong root structures, early growth and the steady formation of mature plants.
- Potassium (K) – often called potash essential for the development of drought and disease resistance and the developments of flower buds, flowers, seed heads and fruits. It is essential for achieving the crispness, colour and flavour of vegetables.
- Minerals and trace elements – essential for health and vitality. Some are required in moderate quantities and others to a lesser extent.

The minerals required in moderate quantities are:
- Magnesium – which helps prevent the yellowing of leaves.
- Calcium – essential for cell growth

and resistance to disease.

- Sulphur – for general plant health.
- Iron – which prevents the bleaching of leaves.

   The main essential trace elements are:

- Zinc – which prevents leaves from developing yellow spots.
- Manganese – which prevents yellowing of leaves.
- Boron, copper and molibium – which apparently contribute to cell structures and natural disease control.

In general, we feed vegetables to supplement the general fertility of the soil, recognising that each group of vegetables has different needs

Fruit vegetables such as courgettes, tomatoes and peppers benefit from a fortnightly feed high in potassium once they start to flower. This helps develop large healthy fruit and also drought and disease resistance. We use comfrey liquid diluted with water 1:10 if it was prepared using the wet method and 1:100 if the dry method was used.

Leaf and stem vegetables such as spinach, acelgas, leeks and asparagus benefit from a fortnightly feed high in nitrogen. This helps green growth. We often use a nettle liquid feed.

Root vegetables, such as carrots and beetroot, do not normally require extra feeding. However, if they are slow to grow, a diluted liquid feed made from compost and farmyard manure can be beneficial. An occasional comfrey feed can stimulate deeper colourations and storing qualities.

Flower vegetables, such as artichokes and broccoli, benefit from a general feed once a fortnight. We use a dilute feed made from seaweed, nettles, comfrey and manure in water.

If at all possible, include a patch of comfrey on your vegetable plot. The leaves are rich in potassium, containing three times as much as animal manures, and it also contains significant amounts of nitrogen, phosphorus and trace elements. The leaves can be used in a number of ways:

- Digging into the ground.
- Laying in trenches before planting potatoes and peas.
- As a mulch around young seedlings. When the leaves rot they add fertiliser to the soil but, more importantly, they are an excellent natural snail and slug repellent.
- As a concentrated liquid feed alone or in combination with other natural fertilisers in a general fertiliser cocktail.
- As a compost heap accelerator.

Comfrey (consuelda) is a perennial herb and grows best in a damp fertile soil. It is normal to cut it back to the ground three times a year, but do allow some late autumn growth before it dies back in the winter. The best variety to grow is Bocking 14, otherwise known as Russian comfrey, which does not flower so profusely or self seed as some other varieties. Half a dozen plants will soon cover a square metre and they can be split annually in the autumn or spring.

Liquid feeds can be mixed with water in a watering can or, if you are watering by flooding, by adding a little at a time to the water as it flows.

Some soils might lack calcium and as a result brassicas, such as cabbages and broccoli, can develop club root. The addition of lime to the surface of the soil before planting can be of help. However, although this was our normal practice before coming to Spain we have not found it necessary here.

Naturally occurring sulphur is generally insufficient to prevent mildew and fungal diseases on fruits such as courgettes, pumpkins, peppers and tomatoes therefore, dust all such plants fortnightly with sulphur powder, dusted lightly from an old sock.

Natural fertilisers, liquid or solid, are not as strong as manufactured inorganic chemical fertilisers. The rate of growth of vegetables can therefore be better controlled, particularly in respect of the amount of nitrogen added to the soil. Plants fed too much nitrogen and water grow too fast, too big and are watery and sappy. Not only is the taste lost but sappy plants can be vulnerable to attacks by disease and pests.

By only feeding a supplementary fertilizer to half of a crop initially and then to the other half several weeks later, you can extend the harvesting season.

7.8 DISEASE AND PEST PREVENTION AND CONTROL

We have fewer problems with diseases and pests on our vegetable plot in Spain than we had in the UK and Ireland, as we have more time to try out ecological prevention and control methods. We now recommend the following approach:

1. Don't sow diseased or infected seeds.
2. Only plant out strong/healthy plantlets.
3. Grow healthy, unforced plants at a natural rate rather than accelerated ones with large amounts of unnatural inorganic growth stimulators and excess water.
4. Grow a diversity of vegetables in close proximity rather than one huge crop.
5. Season by season, rotate crops to prevent the build up of latent pests and fungal diseases.
6. Do companion planting to deter or attract bugs (e.g., marigolds, nasturtiums and fennel).
7. Do sacrificial plantings to attract insects away from your more valuable vegetables to less valuable ones that you don't mind them eating (e.g., sweet corn).
8. Physically protect plants. For instance:
- Cover recently planted peas with a netting to prevent pigeons from picking out the seeds and eating them.
- Cover young plants with mini cloches made from the plastic water bottles.
- Place 60cm high plastic mesh fences around carrots to deter roaming carrot flies.
- Place plastic cloches or tunnels to pro-

tect early plants or force early crops.
- Erect strong mesh fences against rabbits and wild boar.
- Split circles or squares of cardboard, felt or old natural carpet around the stems of brassicas to deter the cabbage root fly.
9. Sow seeds at the right time. For instance, plant all peas before Christmas so that they are germinated and up by the time field mice come out of hibernation in early spring and are harvested before late spring mildew.
10. Use non-chemical deterrents for slugs and snails. Use slug pellets only as a last resort.
11. Spray susceptible vegetables, or those that have already been attacked, with biological eco sprays, either home made sprays as illustrated in the "Natural Insect Inhibitors and Fungicides" table or purchased proprietary sprays.
12. Pick off beetles and caterpillars by hand and squash them.
13. Pick out any tips of broad beans infected with black fly.
14. Dust sulphur powder, shaken gently through a sock, over the leaves of pumpkins, melons, cucumbers and courgettes and the leaves and fruit of tomatoes and peppers to prevent fungal diseases.
15. Make a scarecrow with hanging pieces of cloth that flap even in light breezes to distract birds that might dig up seeds or seedlings. Alternatively, tie strands of fine string with a line of attached mini- aluminium foil kites or old CD'S.
16. Wind short lengths of copper wire round the stem of tomatoes to prevent fungal diseases.
17. Allow your vegetable plot to develop as a balanced self-sustaining eco system. Allow some weeds to grow to attract beneficial insects such as ladybirds, centipedes, hoverflies, ground beetles, and snakes that then attack and feed on the harmful insects. Within three years of starting our present 400-square-metre

NATURAL INSECT INHIBITORS AND FUNGICIDES

Most common vegetable garden pests and diseases	Main plants affected	What to look for	Causes	Suggested ecological treatments baseD on our personal practices
Asparagus Beetle	Asparagus	Black and orange beetle with six square white patches on back, young shoots or summer foliage.	Natural attractor	a. Pick off. b. Interplant with a few tomato plants in spring. c. Spray with solutions of potassium soap, nettle or Neem.
Ants (Hormigas) NB: Ants are also very beneficial as they feed off aphids	Attack red worms in compost heap. Remove newly planted seeds (e.g., carrots, radishes)	Trails in compost heap or seed beds.	Looking for food and moisture	Find nests and pour hot water down holes
Aphids (Pulgones) a. Greenfly	Beans	Tiny sticky insects on stems, leaves and buds. Usually ants feeding off them.	Natural attractor. Too much nitrogen producing fleshy plants	a. Spray twice weekly with solutions of potassium soap, nettle or Neem.
b. Whitefly	Broccoli and other brassicas	Tiny white insects covering plant with sticky substance.	Natural attractor	a. As above b. Interplant French marigolds as an insect repellent. c. Hang yellow bottles along lines. (Swill bright yellow paint in a 1.5 litres empty water bottle). They dislike the yellow glare!
c. Blackfly	Broad beans, spinach, artichokes	Tiny black insects on upper tips and stems of broad beans. Base of stems of spinach. Flower heads and stems of artichokes.	Natural attractor	a. Pinch out tops of broad beans when first beans have formed. b. Spray twice weekly with solutions of potassium soap, nettle or Neem. c. Interplant spinach and acelgas with mint in pots to deter flies. d. Feed with liquid seaweed to develop stronger plants which are more resilient.
Bean and pea weevils	Peas and beans.	Holes in pods and damaged fruit.	Natural attractor	a. Rotate crops yearly. b. Remove and burn any badly affected plants.

NATURAL INSECT INHIBITORS AND FUNGICIDES

Most common vegetable garden pests and diseases	Main plants affected	What to look for	Causes	Suggested ecological treatments based on our personal practices
Cabbage white butterfly	Cabbage, cauli-flowers and other brassicas.	White butterflies nearby and green caterpillars eating leaves.	Natural attractor.	a. Pick off eggs and caterpillars daily. b. Sprinkle wood ash over plants. c. Spray twice weekly with solutions of potassium soap, nettle or Neem. d. Spread cut sage between rows regularly as a deterrent.
Cabbage root fly	Mainly cabbage, Brussels sprouts and cauliflower.	Flies lay eggs at base of stem and white maggots attack roots.	Natural attractor.	a. Plant healthy strong plantlets. b. Don't plant deeper than in seed boxes. c. Don't earth up. d. Cut out 10cm slit square of carpet, carpet underlay or card-board and fit round base of stem to stop flies laying eggs.
Carrot fly	Carrots	Small holes and maggots in roots.	Smell of carrots attracts flies.	a. When weeding or thinning, disturb as little as possible. b. Surround with planted onions. c. Interplant a couple of small rosemary plants and put cut sage in between rows. d. Enclose in 75cm high mesh fence.Carrot flies are low flying! e. Sprinkle powdered seaweed along rows.
Colorado beetle	Potatoes	Striped fleshy orange and black bugs eating the underside of leaves Yellow patches of eggs.	Natural attractor	a. Pick off and squash . b. Wipe off any newly laid eggs.
Grasshoppers	They can eat greenery.	Jumping grasshoppers in mid to late summer.	Natural habitat	Catch them if you can or leave them to the frogs!
Shield bugs	Cabbages, bras-sicas and other green leaves.	Triangular shaped green bugs. Others orange and red.	Natural attractor	a. Pick off and squash. b. Let fennel and coriander plants seed. Bugs congregate there rather than eat plants.
Slugs and snails	Young seedlings, melons, courget-tes, lettuces, artichokes, raspberries, strawberries, redcurrants	Eaten leaves. Slimy snail trails and missing plants.	Natural attractor	a. Remove at night with torch. b. Put down beer traps. c. Surround young plants with comfrey leaves. d. Spray around plants with garlic solution.

NATURAL INSECT INHIBITORS AND FUNGICIDES

Most common vegetable garden pests and diseases	Main plants affected	What to look for	Causes	Suggested ecological treatments based on our personal practices
Spider mite	Beans, peas, tomatoes, cucumbers, pumpkins.	Yellowing leaves. Tiny spiders with silk like webs covering underside of leaves.	High temperatures. Too much nitrogen. Lack of water.	a. Where possible wipe off. b. Twice weekly spray with solution of potassium soap, nettle or Neem.
Wireworm	Various plants.	Hard, thin, slow moving, shiny, wormlike.	Natural attractor.	a. Crop rotation prevents the problem building up. b. Add a little sulphur to fertilizers to improve hygiene of soil. c. We haven't had a problem and accept them. If you use liquid ground insecticide you will kill off the red worms that are the invaluable workers of the soil!

FUNGAL DISEASES

Mildew	Tomatoes, potatoes, vines.	Pale yellow blotches and white powder on leaves.	Damp conditions and high temperatures.	a. Don't wet plants when watering. b. Dust lightly fortnightly with sulphur. In winter dust vines once or twice. d. Tomatoes – twist 10cm length of copper loosely around stem to protect against fungal diseases. e. Feed liquid seaweed to develop more resilient plants.
Neck rot	Onions, garlic.	Rotting off at ground level.	Hot damp conditions. Over-watering.	a. Don't over-water. b. Ensure good drainage. c. Rotate crops yearly.
Oidio	Courgettes, pumpkins, beans, melons, cucumbers, peas.	White powder on leaves.	Damp conditions, over-watering and fluctuating temperatures.	a. Dust lightly with sulphur fortnightly from initial planting. b. Avoid wetting plant when watering. c. Peas planted in November should have no problems.
Rust	Onions, leeks, garlic, beans.	Orange/brown pustules on leaves.	Damp conditions.	a. Don't over-water. b. Don't wet leaves when watering. c. Spray in spring with solutions of horsetail or Neem.
Club root	Brassicas (except cauliflowers)	Roots swollen and knobbly.	Fungus in the soil caused by high acid and poorly draining soil.	a. Sprinkle the surface of the soil with lime before planting. b. Improve drainage.

vegetable plot from scratch, we had very few problems with bugs. All down the food chain, insects, reptiles and birds fed off each other rather than off our vegetables.

18. As a first step, construct a pond and rockery between the flower garden and vegetable garden to attract families of frogs and toads. They can do a great job of reducing the number of slugs and unwanted insects.

The above list might raise fears that growing vegetables in Spain is a constant battle. It definitely is not, so don't rush out to purchase chemical warfare sprays at the first sign of insects or fungal disease. Remember that most problems are minor and that the loss of a few beans, tomatoes or lettuces are unlikely to be significant compared with the remaining healthy vegetables you harvest.

Notes:

Where possible use non chlorinated water when preparing sprays. Potassium soap is now often referred to as insecticidal soap and in Spain as *jabón negro*.

7.9 WEEDING (AND BENEFICIAL WEEDS)

Organic vegetable growing implies that no chemical weed killers can be used. Weeds are therefore inevitable and some vegetables will self-seed, so that after a few years the vegetable plot can start to look like a patchwork, old-fashioned, cottage garden. Some readers will welcome this and others not.

If you are a fanatic for a totally tidy garden, then weed the vegetable plot several times a week and put all weeds on the compost heap but remember this will be time consuming, especially in the spring.

Most vegetable gardeners will want to take a more laid-back approach to the problem and perhaps make maximum use of the beneficial properties of many weeds. We therefore suggest the following practical, less time consuming approach.

1. Recognise and accept that weeds are inevitable and that keeping them totally under control – except when growing

---

OUR TOP 10 SNAIL AND SLUG CONTROLS

SNAILS:

1. Provide "homes" and catch by hand. Place a square metre of black plastic sheeting over a brick or damp soil and weigh down, or place a number of 20cm lengths of 5cm diameter plastic tubing around the plot.
2. Plant a circle of comfrey plants around the vegetable plot. Snails will gorge themselves on the leaves and get no further.
3. Places circles of comfrey leaves around blocks of seedlings or around individual plantlets.
4. Lay a sharp stone-chipping path around the vegetable plot.
5. Stick in a line of shiny surfaced canes into the soil. Young snails climb up them overnight to drink the condensed dew on the surface. Then pick off.
6. Place cabbage leaves over piles of bran around the plot. Collect the snails in the morning. Works best if leaves placed under large roofing tiles.

SLUGS:

7. Lay upside-down grapefruit and orange skin halves to attract slugs overnight.
8. Lay beer/bran traps. Empty and top up as necessary.
9. Place lines of dry bran around vulnerable young plants.
10. Attract frogs and toads to the plot with a small pond.

vegetables intensely on a small scale – may be counterproductive.

2. The first priority is to remove weeds adjacent to shallow rooted crops such as lettuces and onions or blocks of plants such as young carrots. If you leave the weeds, they compete for moisture and food and eventually for space, but wait until seedlings have put down firm roots and weeds are big enough to grasp easily to avoid unearthing young plants.

3. Shallow-rooted weeds around established deep rooted plants can provide shade for the top of roots and reduce water evaporation.

4. The second priority is to remove deep-rooted perennial weeds. These are difficult to remove when they mature and if bits of root are left in the ground they re-grow and compete with deeper-rooted vegetables and seed profusely.

5. The third priority is to hoe off the grass and weeds in unplanted areas. Having done this we cover them with a layer of well-rotted manure and an old natural carpet and leave the worms to prepare an enriched seed bed over the next three months.

6. When we take the carpet off to prepare a seedbed, we first harrow and rake and then leave for a week for any seeds to germinate. We then hoe again before planting. Seedbeds can be de-weeded using a flame gun or infrared burner, but there is a danger of killing off useful micro organisms and shallow worms.

7. The planting of seedlings through holes in plastic mentioned in the last chapter not only conserves water but also stops most weeds from growing. Use a heavy grade of black plastic, as thin plastic lets a degree of light through and weeds can grow under the plastic, pushing it up.

USEFUL USES OF TRADITIONAL WEEDS

WEEDS	Adds taste to salads	Makes tasty soups	Steamed as a tasty tapas or vegetable	Boiled with potatoes as tasty tapas or vegetable	Fried as tapas or vegetabe	Good rabbit food	Add to compost heap	Steep in water for use as liquid fertilizer	Infused in water for insect deterrent (ID) or fungicide (F)
Wild asparagus	●	●	●		●				
Wild rocket	●					●	●		
Dandelion	●		●			●	●		
Chicory	●		●			●	●		
Fennel			●	●			●		
Borage			●				●		
Poppy			●	●			●		
Horsetail									● (F)
Nettles		●						●	● (ID)
Wild Garlic	●	●	●		●				

8. Put all weeds except deep-rooted perennials on the compost heap. Once rotted down, they can be recycled as compost, and the compost will include the minerals and trace elements that weeds took from the soil, plus carbon taken from the air by photosynthesis. Weeds then become a useful crop!

9. Recognise that some weeds (out of place wild plants) have additional uses. Borage plants are good for attracting pollinators, marigolds for attracting black fly and fennel flowers for attracting a variety of insects from other plants and larger insects that devour the smaller ones.

10. Burn deep-rooted perennial weeds, especially if they have seed heads. Biodynamic gardening institutes suggest that useful weed inhibitors/killers can be prepared by burning weed seed ash at different periods of the lunar/cosmic calendar. For information contact: in Spain *rudolfsteiner@teleline.es*, in the UK *bdaa@biodynamic.freeserve.co.uk*

11. Some weeds also have even wider uses as illustrated in the table above. Make use of them before weeding out the remainder and composting.

7.10 HARVESTING VEGETABLES

Here are a few basic guidelines to harvesting vegetables:

1. Start to harvest vegetables when they are young. Enjoy them in salads and as nouveau cuisine mini vegetables. This way you will be able to harvest them in good condition for a longer period of time. The picking of young courgettes for instance will encourage the plants to produce more flowers and, hence, a larger crop. Similarly, the thinning of carrots will give more space to those remaining to grow larger for the main harvest.

2. Only harvest enough for the next meal or two. Eat them while they are fresh, at their crispest, most tender, most flavoursome and when they have the most natural vitamins.

3. Recycle what is not used into the compost heap. It's better to eat fresh vegetables daily than end up with inedible plants going to seed.

4. Wash and wrap leaf vegetables for storing in the refrigerator for the day in a clean damp cloth or kitchen towel paper.

5. Hang hot peppers in bunches or strung along strings to dry in the sun and then hang them up in a dry cool place until used.

6. Harvest excess vegetables before they are past their best. Freeze or bottle in brine what can't be eaten today or use to produce chutneys or jams (e.g., tomato).

7. Leave excess root crops such as carrots and parsnips in the ground. In Spain they keep better than in a box of peat in a cellar or garage.

8. Clean the earth off onions and garlic before hanging up in bunches to dry.

9. Harvest pumpkins and other squash and melons when the stalk dries and withers. Store them on shelves in an airy cool place.

10. Check weekly anything you store in baskets or boxes or on shelves, and immediately throw away anything that is starting to rot.

7.11 EVALUATING YOUR EFFORTS

You have probably spent much time and effort in the vegetable garden but it is unlikely that it will be totally organic/ecological for the first few years, if ever. The two audits that follow are designed to help you evaluate your efforts and learn from your relative successes and failures:

SELF AUDIT OF ORGANIC/ ECOLOGICAL PRACTICES

Complete the questionnaire below, add up your scores and reflect on the observation guidelines. Then prepare a note of the changes in practices that you plan for the year ahead.

The following are observations on

your scores:

28 to 35 – You have become a full and competent organic gardener.

19 to 27 – You are obviously well on the

BEST PRACTICE	HOW WOULD YOU DESCRIBE YOUR CURRENT PERSONAL PRACTICES?	SCORE FOR ANSWER	PERSONAL SCORE
Improve the structure and fertility of the soil using only natural/ecological materials	1 Only use proprietary inorganic chemical fertilizers. 2. Use above plus peat and peat substitutes. 3. Now use some compost and have cut back on the use of chemical fertilizers by half. 4. Use well-rotted manure and compost but may include some non-organic materials. 5. Use only well-rotted manure and compost from organic sources. 6. As above plus the use of seaweed.	0 1 2 3 4 5	
Self production of the materials used for enriching the soil and producing natural feeds	1 Buy proprietary mixes in bags. 2. Buy in bags but have started a small compost heap. 3. Now have a large compost heap and have reduced what is purchased. 4. Now have two compost heaps, a source of well-rotted manure and some compost from local eco park. 5. As above, but now have a few rabbits, guinea pigs and hens that produce useful manures. 6. Have purchased a few sheep and goats that keep the orchard tidy. Now totally self sufficient from own animals, birds, compost heaps and productive worm farm.	0 1 2 3 4 5	
Feed crops with natural/ecological plant feeds during the growing season	1 Use only proprietary inorganic manufactured chemical feeds. 2. Still use above but have started to use proprietary organic/ecological feeds. 3. Now use mainly proprietary feeds but have started to prepare own. 4. Now use only own produced feeds but not sure that all manure used is organic. 5. As in 4, with all organic manures and plants, but only feed the soil. 6. Have a planned programme for using a variety of own organic feeds as soil and foliage feeds.	0 1 2 3 4 5	

BEST PRACTICE	HOW WOULD YOU DESCRIBE YOUR CURRENT PERSONAL PRACTICES?	SCORE FOR ANSWER	PERSONAL SCORE
Use non-chemical methods to control weeds	1. Still use proprietary weed killers extensively. 2. Have started to cut back use of above and now do some weeding by hand and hoe. 3. Hand pick, hoe, and mulch but still use weed killers in the spring. 4. Hand pick, hoe and compost. Some weeds fed to animals. Rest on compost heap. 5. As in 4, plus smothering with eco carpets and plastic sheeting. 6. As in 5, plus preparing biodynamic natural weed killers.	0 1 2 3 4 5	
Use natural/ ecological insect deterrents and pesticides and companion planting for pest/disease prevention and control	1. Still use chemical sprays. No companion planting. 2. Use 80% chemical, 20% natural. 3. Use 60% chemical 40% natural, started companion planting. 4. Use 20% chemical 80% natural, and much more companion planting. 5. Use only proprietary and some own natural sprays and substantial companion plantings. 6. Use only own natural plant sprays and sulphur but extent very reduced as natural predators and extensive companion planting solve most problems.	0 1 2 3 4 5	
Plant ecologically and organically produced and protected seeds	1. Use only regular seeds. 2. Use regular seeds with 20% organic seeds. 3. Use 50:50 organic and regular seeds. 4. Use 80% organic seeds. 5. Use 100% organic seeds. 6. Use 100% organic seeds, 30% own seed.	0 1 2 3 4 5	
Development and management of naturally balanced eco system	1. Sterile plot without worms or wildlife. 2. Worms appearing, and beneficial wildlife starting to visit. 3. Worms are breeding. Frogs, toads and lady-birds are resident. 4. Many worms, snakes are in residence and birds nest nearby. Companion and sacrificial planting are working. 5. Plot is now a haven for a range of natural wildlife that control all serious infestations. 6. As above, but now have a number of sheep and goats that keep the orchard tidy, and all edible weeds plus household waste fed to rabbits and guinea pigs. We are now self sufficient in manures and composts.	0 1 2 3 4 5	

way to becoming a totally organic gardener.

10 to 18 – You appear to believe in the
benefits of organic gardening and are
making progress.

0 to 9 – You appear to have no real
interest in organic methods at present.
Review what you have against organic
principles. Reread the first chapter in
this section and consider changing over
to some organic/ecological practices
during the next year.

Whatever your scores consider what
changes or improvements would be of most
benefit during the next year and commit
yourself to introducing them.

REVIEW OF CROP
SUCCESSES AND FAILURES

Before finalising a planting plan for the
next year, reflect on your successes and failures during the past year. The following
series of questions will help you do this
systematically:

*What crops were the greatest successes in
terms of quality and yield?*

Why do you consider them as successes?

*Were these crops also amongst your greatest
successes for the previous year?*

What crops were your greatest failures in
terms of quality, yields, pests and diseases?

*Were they also amongst your greatest failu-
res the previous year?*

*Why do you consider these crops to have
been failures?*

*Can you think of any fundamental reasons
why some crops were worse than others?*

Were there differences between the
way in which you grew the excellent and
poor crops? For instance, were their
differences in:
- The preparation of the soil and beds?
- The source, variety and age of the
seeds?
- The plantlets used – the source and
variety?
- The locations on the vegetable plot?
- The fertilizers used and frequency of
feeding?
- The pattern of watering?
- The pattern of sun and rain and day
and night temperatures?
- The density of weeds?
- The types and extent of insecticides and
fungicides used?
- The use of greenhouse, cloches and
mulches?
- The planting dates, time of moon and
pattern of weather?
- The accuracy of planting by the lunar
calendar?
- Effects of adjacent varieties?
- The pattern of crop rotation?
- The vicinity of companion plantings?
- The extent of pest or disease damage?
- The use of a new or old part of the
vegetable plot?
- A new or established raised or no dig
bed?
- The acidity of the soil?

Overall, what did you change from previous years when the poor crops or similar
crops were more successful? What did you
forget or not have time to do thoroughly?

Which of the differences or changes
were the most likely causes of crop failures?

Should you change your approach to
growing vegetables in any way for the next
planting season?

7.12 A VEGETABLE GARDEN CALENDAR

The calendar starts in September, as that is the most practical month, for gardeners new to Spain, to commence vegetable growing. Making first plantings in October will enable you to have fresh vegetables for Christmas and the spring and to get used to your soil before facing the problems of irrigation during a long hot summer. Having said that, for gardeners on the high meseta that has heavy winter frosts and, it would be best to start in March.

SEPTEMBER

If you are starting from scratch:
- Decide on the size of your vegetable garden and where to locate it.
- Depending on the size of the plot, double dig, rotovate or plough the area.
- Mix well-rotted manure and compost into the top 15cm of the soil.
- Harrow and rake the soil into a series of ridges and hollows if irrigating by flooding, or rake level if planning to use perforated irrigation tubing.
- If you start on a small scale in containers or raised beds, fill them with a 1:3 mix of well-rotted manure and compost and a reasonable soil.
- Collect a pile of manures to rot down for the spring.

If you have been growing crops through the summer:
- Continue to feed peppers and tomatoes to prolong their fruiting as long as possible.
- Harvest and store pumpkins, squash and melons.
- Convert excess crops of peppers, tomatoes, onions and courgettes into chutney.
- Pick out ends of flowering shoots on butter beans to stimulate the formation of larger beans.

OCTOBER

- Plant seeds for winter salad and green crops such as spinach and sea kale beet.
- Plant winter root crops – carrots, parsnips, beetroot and radishes.
- Chit a few potatoes and plant them to produce new potatoes for Christmas.
- Cut back asparagus bed and plant out new plantlets.
- Plant seeds of useful companion plants such as marigolds and nasturtiums.
- Sow the first batch of broad beans, peas and mange tout for the spring.
- Plant onion, leek, broccoli, cauliflower, cabbage, spinach, seakale beet and lettuce plantlets and remember to take precautions against slugs and snails.
- If possible, plant according to the most preferable days in the lunar calendar.
- Continue to harvest over-summered crops such as carrots, tomatoes, peppers and beans.
- If there are no autumn rains, install an irrigation system.

NOVEMBER

• Plant comfrey plants around the vegetable plot if you can obtain them. If not, do this in the spring.

• If you have an existing comfrey patch, make a last cutting and put in a barrel to produce liquid manure.

• Plant a line of sweet peas, as their flowers attract pollinators in the spring and enrich the soil with nitrogen.

• Sow a second batch of broad beans, peas and onions as well as some leeks for planting on in the spring.

• As summer crops finish, give the plot a good clean up. Put remains of vegetable plants and annual weeds on the compost heap and have a bonfire for perennial weeds. Don't forget to get a licence for the bonfire first.

• Earth up potatoes that should be up by now.

• Harvest the last butter beans, paella beans and young fennel and spinach.

• Make and put up a scarecrow.

• Collect all good used canes and support in a cane rack to keep them dry and strong for reuse next year.

• Cap any unused areas with well-rotted manure and compost and cover with carpet to produce seedbeds for vegetables that like a newly manured soil.

DECEMBER

• Make last winter sowings of broad beans and peas. Also plant garlic cloves.

• Transplant thinings of beetroots.

• Harvest lettuce, rocket, purslane, potatoes, salad onions and chives.

• Sow some oak leafed lettuce, carrots, parsnips and beetroot under plastic tent cloche.

• Immediately after sowing, sprinkle some dry wood ash, and what comfrey leaves you have, as a circle around the area sown to deter snails that can be at their most active at this time of year. Also, set up other deterrents to slugs and snails.

• Give brassicas a nettle foliar feed, which will also deter any white fly that may be present.

• Cover newly-planted broad bean and pea seeds with protective netting against hungry pigeons.

• Build a new raised bed and fill with a mixture of fallen leaves, compost, manure and seaweed. Dampen and cover with a carpet or sheet of heavy plastic until February, then plant potatoes as a first year crop.

• Cap the asparagus bed with 10cm of manure and seaweed.

• Give the plot a good weeding.

• Ensure that all new plantlets and seedlings are not allowed to dry out.

JANUARY

• Watch for black fly on broad beans and spray if necessary.

- Place yellow painted bottles on sticks between brassicas to deter whitefly.
- Cut and put new canes in a drying rack.
- Support growing peas with twiggy sticks. Long thin prunings from fruit trees are ideal.
- Dig up rest of winter potato crop before first frost.
- Look out for seed potatoes and chit them in a dark dry place.
- Sprinkle wood ash around onions and leeks.
- Plant out more leek and onion plantlets.
- Give leaf vegetables a nitrogen feed.
- If there is a warm spell, harvest the first asparagus.

FEBRUARY

- Spring clean the greenhouse and garden frame.
- Turn over last autumn's compost heaps, sieving what is nice and crumbly to prepare compost for seed trays and pots for large seeded varieties.
- Sow trays of lettuce, annual herbs, tomatoes, courgettes, pumpkins and water melons in greenhouse.
- Plant more onion and leek plantlets.
- Spray peas with horsetail solution to protect against mildew on pods.
- Plant potatoes, if in a frost free location. If not, plant in second half of March.
- Earth up potatoes as the first leaves appear and spray earth with horsetail solution to prevent fungi.
- Sow more spring crops in greenhouse.
- Overhaul and improve the irrigation system.
- Give comfrey a dressing of chicken manure.

MARCH

- Sow last squash, pumpkins, tomatoes, aubergines in the greenhouse or cold frame. Also, plant pumpkins and squash directly in the ground under plastic cloches.
- Plant/sow out beneficial companion plants such as roses, borage, marigolds and nasturtiums.
- Harvest asparagus, peas, mange tout, broad beans, broccoli, etc., while young and tasty.
- Plant another bunch of onion plantlets for summer harvesting and winter storage.
- Control weeds as the weather warms up.
- Put down a number of pieces of heavy black plastic, raised up by two bricks and kept damp underneath, as a good snail trap. Collect the produce twice a week and feed on rosemary for three weeks before cooking Asturian-style.
- Give a comfrey feed to all fruit vegetables currently growing on the plot.
- Tie in vigorously growing sweet peas and tall growing peas.
- Give artichokes a good soaking and feed with a liquid nettle, manure and comfrey cocktail or a general ecological fertilizer.
- Keep asparagus weeded during the main cropping period.

APRIL

- Collect nettles and steep in water for a useful, high nitrogen feed.
- Prepare cane supports for tomatoes, peppers, aubergines, climbing beans and cucumbers.
- Plant out first summer salad plantlets and squash, melon, peppers and tomatoes. Protect them with plastic cloches if still cold.
- Make final sowings of carrots, parsnips and beetroots.
- Take a first cutting of comfrey and add to barrel.
- Place comfrey in circles around new planted plantlets and new sowings to protect against snails.
- Take in main harvest of broad beans and peas. Freeze the excess while still young.
- Plant out giant pumpkins, lettuces, artichokes, sweet corn, French beans and runner beans, early tomatoes, water

melons and sunflower seeds and plants.
- Plant herbs such as dill, coriander, basil and parsley in the greenhouse.
- Dig first spring new potatoes.

MAY

- Plant peanuts and the last carrots before the summer.
- Plant out courgettes, rest of tomatoes, gourds, melons, peppers and aubergines.
- Select large pods of tasty peas and beans and mark them for growing to maturity for next year's seed.
- Pick out side shoots on tomatoes and tie them to supports as they grow.
- Weed or hoe beds regularly before they go to seed. Add dampened weeds to the compost heap.
- Watch for black fly on artichokes and treat before they get into the heads.
- Harvest last of over-wintered onions and garlic and hang up to dry in semi shade.
- Make successive sowings of climbing and dwarf beans.
- Sow sweet corn and plant out sunflowers plantlets to provide windbreaks and to support climbing beans.

- Be on the alert for snails, as they are very active in the spring, especially after watering.

JUNE

- Plant out leeks, cucumbers, gherkins, butterbeans, dwarf beans and last tomatoes.
- Start to dust the leaves of courgettes, pumpkins, gourds, tomatoes, peppers, cucumbers, beans with sulphur powder once a week and continue through until September.
- Plant broccoli, cauliflower and cabbage seeds in trays to produce plantlets for planting out in the autumn.
- Clean out broad bean and pea beds when they have finished cropping.
- Harvest bean and pea pods for seed when dry, and dry further in the sun before storing.
- Increase frequency and quantity if watering as the weather warms.
- Tie up tomatoes, peppers, aubergines, climbing beans and cucumbers as they grow.
- Take a second cutting of comfrey.
- Feed globe artichokes with comfrey

to stimulate more edible flower buds.
- Watch out for blackfly on artichokes and spinach, and spray them.

JULY

- Increase watering as the temperatures rise, and feed plants weekly.
- Watch for infestations and spray as soon as you see them.
- Hoe around plants to keep soil loose and weeds under control, and to reduce capillary evaporation.
- Dig out any perennial weeds before they flower and put them in a heap for burning.
- Remove any annual weeds before they flower and seed, and add to the compost heap.
- Plant climbing beans for autumn harvest.
- Don't forget to continue dusting with sulphur.
- Sow onions, leeks, cabbage, cauliflower, brussel sprouts, broccoli, spinach etc., in seed boxes to produce plantlets for planting out in the autumn.
- Mulch tomatoes, peppers and aubergines with well-rotted compost to help retain moisture.
- Check that the compost heap is damp and not drying out. If necessary, turn and water the layers with a dilute comfrey solution. Comfrey is a good accelerator.

AUGUST

- Harvest onions, melons, pumpkins and squash for storage in a well-ventilated cool place. Before storing onions, dry them for a week in the semi shade before hanging up in bunches or plaits. Check your lunar calendar for the best harvesting days.
- Pull or dig out finished plants and put stems and roots on the compost heap.
- Hoe or lightly dig the used beds. Cover with 5cm of well-rotted compost or manure and then cover with an old carpet or black plastic. The beds should be well worked by worms for planting in October and November.
- Keep on top of perennial weeds. Pull or dig them out before they seed.
- Keep watering and feeding. If you nurse tomato plants, they can continue fruiting until November.
- Remove and pot up any self-seeded tomato plants from flower pots, raised beds or around the compost heap. Put them in the greenhouse to raise tomatoes for Christmas.
- Dig up peanuts. Wash the soil off the shells and dry thoroughly in the sun. Store in shells until eaten fresh or baked in a low oven.
- Update your vegetable record chart.
- If starting a new vegetable plot or planning to enlarge it, clear the area of weeds ready for ploughing or rotovating in September.
- Review the success and failures of the last vegetable gardening year and prepare a planting plan for the next 12 months from September.

HOME
GROWN FRUIT

HOME GROWN FRUIT

NO SPANISH GARDEN should be without at least one or two fruit trees, even if they are only orange and lemon trees. They add a Spanish touch, can provide fresh fruit 365 days a year, add evergreen screening, ever useful summer shade and some are among the best spring flowering trees.

What fruit trees you can plant will be dictated by five factors: the size of your garden, it's height above sea level, the protection of the garden from cold winds, whether it is in a frost belt, and the rainfall and availability of water for irrigation.

If you have a very sheltered coastal garden, it may well be practical to concentrate on growing tropical and sub-tropical fruits. This would not be possible if your garden is above the frost line, but citrus and many other fruits can withstand temperatures well below zero, though in some years a heavy night frost can seriously damage leaves and fruit buds. On the other hand, raspberries grow exceptionally well at almost 2000 metres in the mountainous region of the Alpujarras in Andalucia.

8.1 40 POPULAR FRUITING TREES, BUSHES AND PLANTS

The tables below should help you select one or two trees for a small garden or plan a comprehensive orchard. When you visit a nursery or garden centre, you will find a range of different varieties and cultivars. Ask the nurseryman what will be best for your specific location and which flower and fruit early and late. Oranges, for instance, can be harvested from November until June with the right mix of varieties.

The maximum heights indicate that these fruits have been seen growing at these heights in sheltered situations. The flowering and fruiting times are typical along the costas and in coastal mountains. They could be two weeks early or two weeks later than indicated if you are in a very favourable or poor situation respectively.

40 POPULAR FRUITING TREES, BUSHES AND PLANTS

NAMES ENGLISH - SPANISH Botanical	FORM	TBT	THT	TPT	TYPICAL PLANTING HEIGHTS ABOVE SEA LEVEL (METRES)					DR	FR
					< 200	< 400	< 800	< 1200	> 1200		
ORANGE/*Naranjo* Citrus sinensis	Tree	Mar, Apr.	Nov. Jun.	Spr.	•	•				•	•
MANDARIN/*Mandarino* Citrus reticulata	Tree	Mar, Apr.	Oct, Jun.	Spr.	•	•				•	•
GRAPEFRUIT/*Pomelo* Citrus paradisi	Tree	Mar, Apr.	Aug, Dec.	Spr.	•	•				•	•
LEMON/*Limonero* Citrus limon	Tree	Cont ***	Cont	Spr.	•	•				•	•
OLIVE/*Olivo* Olea europea	Tree	Mar, Apr.	Nov, Feb.	W	•	•	•	•	•	•	•
ALMOND/*Almendro* Prunus amygdalus	Tree	Jan, Mar.	Aug, Sep.	W	•	•	•	•		•	•
WALNUT/*Nogal* Juglans regia	Tree	Mar, Apr.	Aug, Oct.	W	•	•	•		•	•	•
QUINCE/*Membrillo* Cydonia oblonga	Tree	Apr., May	Sep, Oct.	W	•	•	•			•	•
APPLE/*Manzano* Malus communis	Tree	Mar, Apr.	Aug, Oct.	W	•	•	•	•		•	•
PEAR/*Peral* Pyrus communis	Tree	Mar, Apr.	Aug, Oct.	W	•	•	•	•	•	•	•
PEACH/*Melocotonero* Prunus perica	Tree	Apr., May	Jun., Sept.	W	•	•					•
PLUM/*Ciruelo* Prunus sativa	Tree	Mar, Apr.	Jun, Jul.	W	•	•	•	•			•
APRICOT/*Albaricoquero* Armeniaca vulgaris	Tree	Apr., May	May	W	•	•				•	•

1. Orange
2. Tangerine
3. Nectarine
4. Banana
5. Apple

40 POPULAR FRUITING TREES, BUSHES AND PLANTS

NAMES ENGLISH - SPANISH Botanical	FORM	TBT	THT	TPT	TYPICAL PLANTING HEIGHTS ABOVE SEA LEVEL (METRES)					DR	FR
					< 200	< 400	< 800	< 1200	> 1200		
NECTARINE/*Nectarina* *Prunus persica*	Tree	Apr., May	May, Jul.	W	•	•				•	•
PARAQUAYA/*Paraguayo* *Prunus paraquaya*	Tree	Apr., May	Jul., Aug.	W	•						
CHERRY/*Cerezo* *Prunus avium*	Tree	Mar, Apr.	Mar., May	W	•	•	•			•	•
MEDLAR/*Nispero* Loquat	Tree	Apr., May	Sep., Oct.	W		•	•	•			•
NÍSPERO/*Nispero de Japón* *Eriobotryra japonica*	Tree	Oct., Nov.	Apr., May	Spr	•	•					•
PERSIMON/*Kaki* *Diesphros kaki*	Tree	Apr., May	Sep., Dec.	W	•	•	•			•	•
KUMQUAT/*Naranjo China* *Fortunella margarita*	Bush	Feb., Mar.	Nov., Mar.	W	•	•	•			•	•
CUSTARD APPLE/*Chirimoya* *Chirimoya anona*	Tree	Mar, Apr.	Aug., Oct.	W	•						
KIWI/*Kiwi* *Actinidia chinesis*	Vine	Apr., May	Aug, Oct.	W	•	•					•
BANANA/*Platanera* *Musa paradisiaca*	Tree	Apr., Jun.	Aug, Oct.	W	•	•					
MANGO/*Mangero* *Mangifera indica*	Tree	Apr., Jun.	Aug., Sep.	Spr	•						
AVOCADO/*Aguacate* *Persia gratisoima*	Tree	Jan., Mar.	Oct, Jun.	Spr	•	•					•
FIG/*Higuera* *Ficus carica*	Tree	-	Aug., Oct,	W	•	•	•			•	•

6. Papaya
7. Lychee
8. Pomegranate
9. Fig
10. Mango

40 POPULAR FRUITING TREES, BUSHES AND PLANTS

NAMES ENGLISH - SPANISH Botanical	FORM	TBT	THT	TPT	TYPICAL PLANTING HEIGHTS ABOVE SEA LEVEL (METRES)					DR	FR
					< 200	< 400	< 800	< 1200	> 1200		
MULBERRY/*Morera* *Morus negra*	Tree	Apr., May	Jun, Jul.	W	•	•	•				•
PAPAYA/*Papaya* *Cariaca papaya*	Tree	Mar, Apr.	Jun, Nov.	W	•						
POMEGRANATE/*Granado* *Punica granatum*	Bush	May	Oct., Feb.	W	•	•				•	•
SWEET CHESNUT/*Castaño* *Castaño sativa*	Tree	Apr., May	Sept, Oct.	W		•	•	•		•	•
HAZEL NUT/*Avellano* *Corylus avellano*	Tree	Apr., May	Aug., Oct.	W		•	•	•	•		•
PISTACHO/*Pistacho* *Pistacia vera*	Tree	May	Sept, Oct.	Spr	•	•					•
GRAPEVINE/*Vid* *Vitus vinfera*	Vine	Apr., May	Jun., Oct.	W	•	•	•	•		•	•
PASSION FRUIT/*Granodillo* *Passiflora caerviea*	Vine	Apr., Oct.	Jun., Oct.	W	•	•					•
STRAWBERRY (Cultivated)/ *Fresón* Fragaria aranassa	Plant *	Jan., Oct.	Jan., Aug. ****	W	•	•	•			•	•
WILD STRAWBERRY/*Fresa* *Fragaria vesca*	Plant *	Apr., Jun.	Mar., Sep.	W	•	•	•	•		•	•
RASPBERRY/*Frambuesa* *Rubus ideas*	Cane	May, Nov.	May, Nov.	W		•	•	•	•		•
RED CURRANT/*Grossellero* *Ribes silvestres*	Bush	Apr., May	May	W				•			•
BLACKBERRIES/*Zarza* *Rubus fruticosus*	Vine **	May, Sep.	Jun., Sep.	W	•	•	•			•	•
BLUEBERRIES/*Arándano* *Vaccinium*	Bush	May, Jun.	Jun., Sep.	W		•	•	•			•

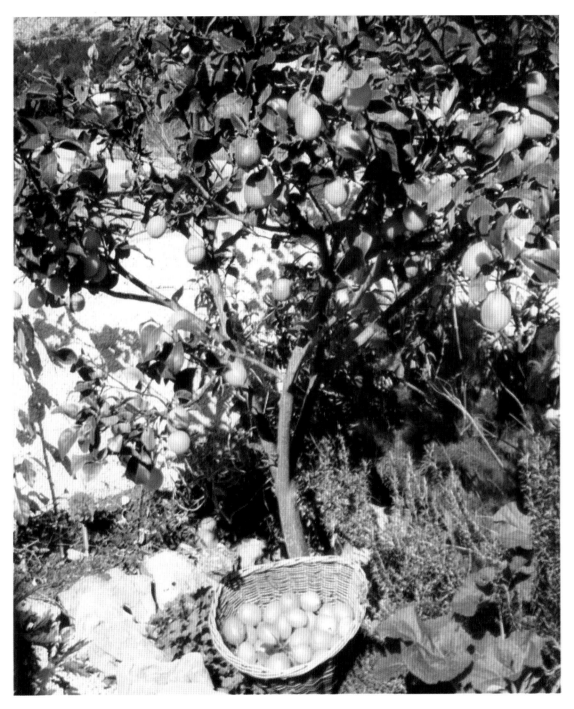

CODES:

* = Actually grown from runners from mature plants. ** = Best trained as if they were vines. *** = The "lunar" variety flowers every 6 to 8 weeks and therefore the tree has maturing fruit throughout the year. **** = Early fruit if forced under plastic cloches.

TBT = Typical blossom time (months), THT = Typical harvest time (months), TPT = Typical pruning time(season), DR = Reasonably drought resistant, and FR = Reasonably frost resistant.

8.2 WHAT, WHERE AND HOW TO PLANT

Think carefully about what you want to plant. Consider how many trees you can fit into the garden, whether you can fit in full-sized trees or whether it would be best to seek out varieties on dwarf root stocks that will be rather smaller when mature. If you want to plant a few in pots and are a patient gardener, consider growing them from seed.

Most importantly, decide which fruits you like. If you are not used to eating some of the fruits listed in the previous chapter, buy some to try before finalising your choice of trees. There is no point in having an orchard full of fruit that you are not going to eat. If you have a special liking for a particular fruit, try to buy both early and late fruiting varieties. Above all, aim to have something that you can harvest on every day of the year.

WHERE TO PLANT

Decide where to plant when designing the overall garden layout. Some of the possibilities are:

1. Individual trees within flowerbeds or terraces.
2. Trees trained espalier, cordon or fan style on walls, fences or internal post and wire supports.
3. An orchard area at one side or an end of the garden, or around the boundary of a larger garden as a screen and wind break.
4. Dedicated soft fruit beds.
5. Wild strawberries as a useful ground cover/mulch in shrub beds.
6. In containers (e.g., citrus trees in large pots on terraces or strawberries in a terracotta strawberry barrel.
7. Vines trained along wires between posts, on fences or walls, over a wire pergola in front of a south facing doorway, or allowed to ramble over old buildings. If you plant kiwis, you will need to plant a male plant to every two or three females to achieve pollination.

PLANTING

The following are general guidelines for planting:

Fruiting trees do best in a deeply dug, rich, slightly acid, well- draining but reasonably water-retaining soil. They do not, however, like to be waterlogged.

If you are planting a dedicated orchard area, or an area which will be essentially a flowerbed, prepare the soil a few weeks before by digging or rotovating in well-rotted compost or manure. If planting a few scattered trees, prepare the planting holes in advance for flowering trees. Fruiting trees are hungry trees, so don't take short cuts. If short of compost or manure, work in a handful of an organic fertiliser high in potash into the planting hole. Ensure that trees are securely and safely staked and tied.

If possible, plant fruit trees, bushes and plants during the autumn or winter, except for the more delicate varieties that should be planted in the early spring after the last frost is expected. An early planting will help trees start to develop a good root system before the new growth of leaves, buds and branches starts in the spring.

If you decide to plant trees in containers, purchase a larger size container that looks balanced with a small tree to allow for five or more years of growth. Fill it with a rich planting compost.

When transporting a young tree from a nursery or from one part of the garden to another, try to plant the tree so that the side that was facing south continues to do so in the new position.

If you buy bare-rooted trees or bushes, take special care when planting to spread the roots out well in the planting hole and water especially well for the next three months. Soak the roots in a bucket of water for 24 hours before planting.

When planting, fill up planting holes twice with water and then let it soak away before commencing to plant. If the water does not soak away, break up the soil at the bottom of the planting hole until it does, or dig larger planting holes.

If transporting trees from a nursery to your house on the back of a truck, or through the sunroof of your car, wrap the exposed parts in plastic to prevent them from being dried out by super-evaporation on a hot day, or by a cold wind on a cold day.

There is evidence that fruit trees take off best if planted at the time of a descending moon. If you garden by the lunar calendar, you can be more accurate by planting on a fruit day.

8.3 WATERING AND FEEDING

We recently read in the national press that the recommended amount of water required by mature orange trees – the thirstiest of trees – to achieve their maximum yield and quality is 6000 cubic metres a hectare (10,000 square metres) of fruit trees. This equates to 15 litres per square metre a day.

This is three to five times the normal rainfall in most parts of Spain. Allowing for the rainfall, you would need to water your three-metre diameter orange tree with around 120 litres of water a day on average, approximately six watering cans! Most established deciduous fruit trees will survive well on merely a watering at the time they are forming fruiting buds and one when they are setting fruit.

Decide whether you want average slow-growing trees that give architectural shape, a reasonable amount of fruit and may live for a century or more, or fast-growing, spreading and high-fruiting trees of commercial orchards that can outgrow themselves within 20 to 30 years and then need replacing.

The ideal condition of the roots of citrus trees is that the earth around their roots is just damp and is not allowed to dry out. When the latter is allowed to occur, the roots harden and the damage is often irreversible. For a small garden and family, you may

well be happy with controlled size, sub-optimal trees.

Rake a watering ring around trees after planting and give a good deep soak. Then, preferably, install a computer-controlled drip irrigation system to each tree. Water young trees throughout the year, increasing the volume during the spring and summer, and at flowering and fruiting times. Once established, cut back on the autumn and winter watering unless there are long dry spells.

If you plant trees in an area that can only be watered by flooding from a channelled distribution system, flood the area in the spring as soon as flower and leaf buds start to swell and once the fruit is set. A monthly flooding during the period they have fruit on the tree will help achieve bumper crops. If your lone avocado tree or lemon tree is anywhere near the outflow of the septic tank, you may achieve unusually large crops.

As a tree spreads, water it at the drip line to encourage a widening ring of roots.

Following are some rules for feeding:

a. Mulch each autumn and rotovate grass and weeds, especially the valuable yellow flowered oxalis, into the top five centimetres of the soil.

b. Add a fruit tree fertilizer to the irrigation water or onto the soil just before watering.

c. Mulch above the roots of raspberries and currants with well-rotted compost, manure and grass cuttings. Give them an occasional comfrey/nettle feed or a general fruit fertilizer feed during the fruiting season.

d. Ensure that trees in containers are watered weekly, more in the spring and summer, and fed monthly. In all cases, a weak frequent feed is preferable to a strong infrequent feed.

e. If you have prepared your soil well before planting, fertilizing will not be a big issue until the growing trees have almost used up all the initially available nutrients. You then need to at least replace what is extracted annually.

Realise that a large good fruiting tree will need more than a small one, so increase the feed levels accordingly and fertilize at the drip line.

f. Give maturing citrus trees an annual foliar feed in the spring before the flower buds open. If the trees are caught by frost and many buds or flowers are lost, an immediate foliar spray may stimulate a second budding and flowering. There is benefit in incorporating an insecticide into the spray liquid.

g. Basically, young trees need a potassium feed to stimulate the development of strong tree structures, nitrogen to develop greenery and a potash feed to aid the development of large fruits. If you are near poultry farms, or keep a few chickens, sprinkle chicken manure around the trees, as it is high in nitrogen.

h. Mature trees need more potash and potassium to maintain steady growth and crops. Excessive nitrogen can stimulate excessive new growth and reduce the yield of fruit.

i. Kiwis need regular watering and feeding, while grape vines can create good harvests in poor soils with little water. Watering grape vines can lead to excessive sappy growth and fat juicy grapes, both vulnerable to fungal attacks. Although larger fruits may result, they may be lacking in flavour.

j. Ensure that all manure used around fruit trees is first well- rotted down, as still-decomposing lumps can attract fungal diseases and pests.

k. Water and feed soft fruits weekly during the harvesting season to stimulate long harvests. We enjoy raspberries from May until November on one variety of canes.

8.4 PEST AND DISEASE CONTROL

It makes sense to plant fruit trees that are normally grown in your area. Exposing trees to unusually hot dry summers or winter frosts can result in weakened plants that will be more susceptible to diseases and plagues.

When you are buying fruit trees, always check whether virus-free varieties are available. Recognise that some fruits give more problems than others. Figs, persimmons, almonds, cherries and olives are amongst the easiest, while apples, pears, peaches and kiwis are amongst the most difficult in the Mediterranean climate. Kiwis grow best in cool, wet Galicia.

If you develop a natural ecological garden where chemical sprays are never used, there is a good chance that few serious infections will occur, especially if you have a good mix of types rather than an orchard of only one type of fruit. Fewer pests will appear in a mixed orchard and at the same time there will be more natural predators – such as birds, frogs, toads, ants, ladybirds and other insects – around to feed on them.

If you have a large orchard in a commercial fruit-growing area where programmed chemical spraying from the ground or air is the norm, you will probably have to do likewise, as few natural predators will make it to your land, but do look for ecological natural products, which are increasingly available. Check out the products stocked by your local horticultural shops and agricultural cooperative. If they stock very few natural products, get a copy of the Organic Gardening Catalogue, published by Chase Organics in conjunction with H.D.R.A., the premier UK organic organisation open to the amateur gardener (email *chaseorg @aol.com,website www.OrganicCataloque.com*).

If you do use hazardous sprays, ensure you wear a face mask, rubber gloves and rubber boots as well as long-sleeved clothing. As agriculturalists become more safety conscious, "space suit" sprayers are becoming a regular feature of rural Spain but they don't always use a warning flag or stop spraying when you walk by. Try to be socially responsible and stop spraying even when cars go by because the windows could be open.

The table below summarises some of the

most common problems as well as some organic/ecological solutions. Where appro- priate, wear a mask, boots and gloves, and don't spray on windy days or in the full sun.

SOME COMMON PESTS, DISEASES AND SOLUTIONS

DISEASE OR PEST	TYPICAL FRUITS ATTACKED	WHAT TO WATCH OUT FOR	SUGGESTED SOLUTIONS
SLUGS AND SNAILS	Raspberries and strawberries.	Their presence and signs of fruit being eaten.	• Remove by hand. • Place beer traps by/amongst plants. • Surround bed by line of gritty sand, prickly oak leaves, pine needles or comfrey leaves. • Spray along bottom of raspberry canes with garlic solution.
	Oranges and kiwis	Presence and young leaves being eaten.	• Be vigilant and remove by hand. • Place beer traps under trees. • Use slug baits as last resort.
BIRDS	Red currants	Birds eating fruit buds, and bunches thinned.	• Cover with fruit cage or netting.
	Strawberries	Holes in fruit.	
	Fruit trees	Birds eating fruit buds.	• Hang bird scarers in trees.
POWDERY MILDEW	Apples, pears, quince and strawberries.	White coating on leaves and branches.	• Plant resistant varieties. • Cut out and burn. • Keep soil moist when leafing up. • Don't wet leaves. • Spray with proprietary fungicide or horsetail solution.
FUNGAL ATTACKS	Strawberries	Fruit going brownish grey and rotting. Plants rotting off.	• Place mats around stems of plants. • Place straw under leaves and fruit. • Avoid wetting plants when watering. • Keep plants under ventilated cloches. • Spray with horsetail infusion. • Remove and burn.
	Any tree at soil level.	Bark splitting or signs of fungus.	• Cut off loose bark and diseased wood and spray well with a fungicide or horsetail infusion. • Seal damaged area with pruning sealer. • Keep soil around trunks free of manures, herbage and rotting fruit. • Always clear fallen fruit. • Make watering circle as a moat with the soil around the trunk kept up above the highest water line as an "island" to prevent trunk becoming water logged.

SOME COMMON PESTS, DISEASES AND SOLUTIONS

DISEASE OR PEST	TYPICAL FRUITS ATTACKED	WHAT TO WATCH OUT FOR	SUGGESTED SOLUTIONS
FUNGAL ATTACKS	Grape vines	Withering/ rotting of branches and fruit.	• Prune affected parts and burn. • Dust vines from February to April with sulphur powder shaken through an old sock or stocking. • If it rains when grapes are at final swelling and changing colour, they are very vulnerable. Spray with dilute copper sulphate.
MEALY BUGS/WOOLY APHIDS	Citrus fruits and apples	Sticky white blotches on branches covering aphids, and ants going up trunk to feed.	• Scrub off with an old toothbrush and potassium soap solution. • Spray with strong jet of potassium soap solution.
SCALE	Citrus	Hard black scales on bark.	• Scrub off with potassium soap. • Spray with Neem oil in autumn/winter. • Spray with potassium or insecticide soap solution.
RED SPIDER MITE	Citrus and apricots	Speckled leaves and leaf fall.	• Spray with water or potassium soap solution. Could also try Neem.
MINERO PLAGUE	Citrus	Curling of leaves and small holes in leaves followed by hardening of branch.	• Encourage predators. • Set free neutered moths. • Hang moth traps on trees in spring. • Spray in Feb/Mar and Oct/Nov with Neem or the latest recommended insecticide.
CORAL SPOT	Raspberries	Branches dying back and orange spots on dead wood.	• Cut out and burn. • Spray bush with horsetail infusion.
MEDITERANEAN FRUIT FLIES/ MOTHS	Stone fruits, including olives	Leaf curl. Young fruit falling off. Maturing fruit with small holes in flesh.	• Spray preventively pre- and post- flowering with Neem or another light oil or potassium soap solution. • Clean up fallen fruit and do not put on compost heap. • Grease or glue bands around trunks during winter and spring. • Hang traps in trees.
CODLING MOTHS	Apples	Moths around trees, rotten cores of apples and excreta hole of larvae.	• Hang traps in trees. • Spray in winter and spring with Neem oil or a proprietary winter oil wash.

SOME COMMON PESTS, DISEASES AND SOLUTIONS

DISEASE OR PEST	TYPICAL FRUITS ATTACKED	WHAT TO WATCH OUT FOR	SUGGESTED SOLUTIONS
LEAF CURL	Peaches, nectarines and cherries.	Blistering, curled-up leaf	• Spray with strained water, pigeon dropping, nettle mixture. • Copper sulphate spray. • Clean up fallen leaves. • Cut off affected branch ends. • Give tree a nitrogen foliar feed.
VINEGAR FLIES	Fleshy, stone fruits	Flies feeding on fermenting fallen fruit.	• Clean up fallen fruit. • Spray soil and undergrowth around trees with Neem or potassium/insecticide soap solution..
WASPS	Stone fruits at ripening time.	Wasps around trees and feeding on ripest fruit.	• Use wasp traps. • Find and destroy nests with care. • Clear up fallen fruit.

Note: Potassium soap is now often referred to as insecticidal soap and, in Spain, as jabón negro.

8.5 HARVESTING AND STORING FRUIT

The main purpose of growing your own fruit is to be able to enjoy eating it at its tastiest and juiciest, so do just that. Leave the fruit on the tree, bush or ground plant until it is ready to eat that day.

Obviously, if you have more than a few fruit trees and varieties, it will be impossible to consume every piece of fruit at its best. It will be necessary to pick most of the fruit for storage a week or two early, when not yet ripe, or when almost ripe for bottling, jams, chutneys or freezing.

Many unripe fruits can be stored in news-paper-lined trays in a cool cellar, or in boxes in a spare refrigerator. You can increase the storage life by first washing the fruit with a water-soluble, edible wax and then drying before storing.

The produce of the fruit trees listed in the table at the beginning of this section offer the possibility of many tasty single or mixed fruit jams jellies – so dig out the old recipe books and have a go. Try making quince

---

**HOME PICKLED OLIVES ARE EASY TO PREPARE.
HERE IS A RECIPE WE USE TO PRESERVE THEM:**

1. Pick olives when ripe.

2. Soak in a bucket of water (preferably non-chlorinated) for four to six weeks, changing the water every two to three days. This removes most of the bitter taste.

3. Prepare a brine. Dissolve salt in cold water by stirring vigorously. Every so often, put a fresh egg in its shell in the brine. When it floats to the top, it is the correct strength.

4. Collect some small-leafed pebrero thyme and fill jars or a large earthenware container with alternative layers of olives and a twig of thyme.

5. Fill the jars with brine and float two or three carob leaves on the surface. This is good for preventing mould. You can process green and black olives separately or together.

6. Seal the jars or cover the earthenware container with a sheet of plastic and store in the cellar for three months before starting to use.

7. A speedier processing can be achieved by squashing the olives lightly with a wooden mallet or slitting them with a knife before putting in brine.

8. When ready, open a jar, drain the liquid, and fill the jar with fresh water twice, to rinse off excess salt, and then place in an olive jar or bowl in olive oil, to which a few rosemary twigs have been added and, if you wish, a garlic glove. Leave a couple of days and the olives are ready for tapas or a salad.

9. Alternative finishes include adding a little picante red pepper, anis or a salted anchovy to the olive oil.

10. Alternative starting ingredients include adding slices of carrot, onion, garlic, a chilli pepper, a slice of lemon or orange, a bay leaf, fennel seeds, and a little cider vinegar to the starter brine in the jars. Try your own experiments. You can get a large harvest from just one tree.

11. If there is a little mould on the carob leaves and surface when you open the olives, simply discard it.

(*membrillo*) jelly, to enjoy with cheeses, and red currant jelly, to enjoy with lamb.

Some fruits freeze well. Frozen raspberries and strawberries can be used as fresh desserts and stoned fruit such as apricots and plums make wonderful tarts or pies.

Nuts need drying in the sun before storing in boxes in a cool cellar. Shelled almonds can keep for a number of years. Unfortunately walnuts do not seem to store as long.

If you have many olives, you can also take them to local olive presses to extract your own olive oil. Five or six kilos will yield a litre of oil. If you have a genuine date palm, eat the dates directly from the tree or glaze them in syrup. Figs are good when fresh and are even better when cooked gently in an earthenware dish with honey and anis. You can ripen avocados by wrapping them in newspaper and putting them in a dark place.

8.6 PRUNING FRUIT TREES, BUSHES AND PLANTS

Pruning is an art, and most trees, bushes and plants benefit from it. The pruning of young, newly-planted trees should be minimised to allow the tree to concentrate on developing strong, far- reaching root structures rather than new energy sapping growth.

There is an ongoing debate between commercial growers who prune heavily and ecological fruit growers who minimise pruning. There are many reasons for a domestic annual winter pruning and summer thinning of fruits:

1. To improve the shape of the tree as a feature, to give better shade, to open up a vista, or to train the tree to hide the house next door.

2. To create special formats such as cordons, umbrellas and standards. The traditional possibilities are illustrated below.

3. To reduce the height of fruiting branches to make harvesting possible without a ladder.

4. To reduce the stress on the root system if the tree is in bad soil.

5. To improve garden hygiene by cutting out dead, diseased or pest-covered branches and leaves.

6. To stimulate fruiting side shoots and fruit buds.

7. To improve the size of fruit by diverting rising sap from the creation of new growth to swelling fruit and by reducing the number of fruit left on a tree to maturity.

8. To allow ventilation between branches and around ripening fruit by cutting out crossing branches.

9. To let the sun shine on ripening fruit by cutting out the centre and excessive leaf cover on the end of branches.

10. To allow space between trees or between a tree and path or terrace.

11. To prevent long branches from breaking from the over load of fruit or strong winds.

12. To give other plants light.

The main pruning is done during the winter months when a tree is dormant or just when the sap is starting to rise and buds starting to swell.

Summer pruning is restricted to thinning fruit, removing diseased growth, stimulating fruiting side shoots for the next year and maintaining ornamental shapes.

Over pruning can upset a tree's balance between growth supported by nutrients extracted from the soil and those from the air by photosynthesis.

Poor pruning and hacking at a tree can allow diseases to enter. Seal wide diameter cuts with a proprietary pruning sealer or clay

Prune with good fruit tree pruners, sharp secateurs and a sharp pruning saw. An extendable pruner will be helpful for tall trees. Don't climb into trees to prune, use

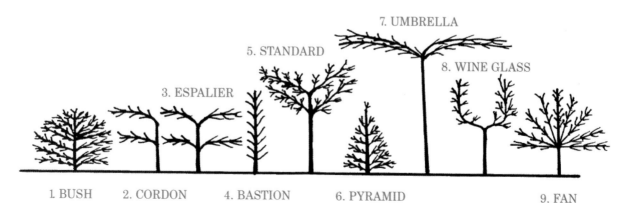

5. STANDARD

7. UMBRELLA

8. WINE GLASS

3. ESPALIER

1. BUSH   2. CORDON   4. BASTION   6. PYRAMID   9. FAN

GUIDELINES FOR PRUNING FRUIT TREES, BUSHES & PLANTS

TYPE OF FRUIT TREE	E.G	FRUIT FORMS ON...	TYPICAL PRUNING SHAPES...	ANNUAL PRUNING REQUIRED. *Prune during winter months unless indicated.*
STONE	Plum	One or two year branches.	Flat umbrella, wine glass, fan or cordon.	Light pruning to keep shape, to stimulate fruit buds and to keep height down for picking. Cut out suckers at base.
	Cherry and apricots	Side shoots and one year wood.	Open wine glass, fan or free growing.	Neither like pruning, especially of the thicker branches. Heavy pruning can cause gum disease. Cut out dead wood and dangerous branches. Cut out main shoots on cherry trees when 1 to 1.5 metres long to encourage side branches. For apricots lightly trim and shorten old branches to stimulate forks
	Peach and nectarine	One year fruiting shoots and main branches.	Wine glass, fan shape or free.	Cut out fruited shoots. Leave one-year growth and trim to shape.
	Olives	On young branches.	Standard with 1, 2, 3 or 4 trunks as per local tradition.	Cut back after harvesting to stimulate new fruiting branches. Often cut back very hard to keep tree low to ease harvesting. If allowed to grow freely, it can reach a very large size and live for two thousand years.
	Níspero	One year laterals and tips.	Wine glass or standard.	Prune lightly to remove crossing branches and shape. Thin out forming to produce large fruits.
	Avocado	On maturing wood.	Free form standard	Cut out crossing and damaged branches.

GUIDELINES FOR PRUNING FRUIT TREES, BUSHES & PLANTS

TYPE OF FRUIT TREE	E.G	FRUIT FORMS ON...	TYPICAL PRUNING SHAPES...	ANNUAL PRUNING REQUIRED. *Prune during winter months unless indicated.*
PIPED	Citrus	One year branches and new shoots.	Standard, bush,wine glass or bastion as a hedge.	Oranges, mandarins and grapefruits. In January or February cut out suckers, trim old branches and woody-fruited side shoots. Cut out centre every two or three years to improve aeration. The continuously fruiting varieties of lemon are best pruned at the end of a crop cycle as the next batch of flowers are appearing. Grapefruits will produce larger fruits if you trim back ends of fruiting branches to fruit buds and thin fruit when formed.
	Pears	On ends of new shoots and side shoots.	Cordon, espalier, fan or pyramid.	Cut back woody branches to stimulate fruiting side shoots. Trim to fruit buds.
	Apples	Same as above.	Same as above	Cut out suckers and small crossing branches. Trim back to fruit buds
	Membrillo	One year growth and side shoots.	Standard	Prune lightly back to fruit buds.
SEEDY	Fig	At the leaf nodes on new and one-year growth.	Freeform standard, wine glass, fan on wall, or flat umbrella.	When young, cut out central shoot to encourage future horizontal growth. Cut out old wood to reduce height and stimulate fruiting forks and branches. Can be ruthless with an old tree to reshape.
	Kaki	Young branches less than one year old.	Free form standard.	Prune to reduce crop after fruit has set to stimulate larger fruits.
	Kiwi	One-year growth.	Cordon or espalier.	Cut out fruited branches, and in early spring reduce the amount of excess vegetation.

GUIDELINES FOR PRUNING FRUIT TREES, BUSHES & PLANTS

TYPE OF FRUIT TREE	E.G	FRUIT FORMS ON...	TYPICAL PRUNING SHAPES...	ANNUAL PRUNING REQUIRED. *Prune during winter months unless indicated.*
SEEDY	Grapes	On new growth.	Cordon, espalier or umbrella	During summer, cut out excess green growth below forming fruit, non-fruiting growth and weak leaders, and thin forming bunches. Cut vines back to four buds per framework branch in February/March after frosts.
NUTS/ BEANS	Almonds	On one-year growth and side shoots.	Standard	Cut out unnecessary main branches in December to create a well-shaped tree with airy centre. Prune out one-year growth and older side shoots with no flower buds just as buds begin to swell. This will vary from December in the south to February or even March if high up in the north.
	Walnuts	On fruiting side shoots.	Standard	Normally left to grow naturally.
	Carob	One year growth and side shoots.	Standard or columnar.	Carob trees were traditionally pruned as fat columns with equal width and height of foliage. The effect can be very attractive.
SOFT	Strawberries	On new growth.	Tidy plants.	Cut out dead leaves and stems as they appear. Cut off runners in the autumn and transplant to replace three-year plants.
	Raspberries		Cordons.	Cut out dead fruiting canes during the winter. Trim any frost burnt tips in the spring.
	Recurrants	On new canes. On old wood.	Bush or Cordons.	Cut out crossing branches to let air and light into bush. Trim back to stimulate fruit buds on old wood.
	Blackberries	On new growth.	Cordons, fan or espalier.	Cut back fruited branches back hard and remove weak suckers.
OTHER	Banana	On flowering central stalk.	Left to grow-naturally.	Cut out old leaves and fruited stalks. Leave to grow as a clump or split of plantlets.

a stepladder instead. A rung ladder placed against branches can do damage.

Clean away all prunings from under trees. The longer, straight prunings will be useful in the vegetable garden to support peas etc., and shorter ones, once dried for a year, can be used as kindling in a wood burning stove.

Cordons and espaliers are trained along wires and fans against walls or trellis. Wide umbrella fig, carob and walnut trees can be trained by hanging weights to weigh young branches down. The weights are increased gradually as the branches thicken, and all upward growing branches kept short to provide a central canopy.

It is preferable to remove fruit from a new tree for two or three years until it has grown a good root system and a substantial network of branches. Well-prepared and planted trees will develop a natural form and growth rate appropriate to your microclimate.

8.7 SOIL MANAGEMENT

The first step in soil management is to prepare the area or, as a minimum, the planting holes, as described for flowering trees in Section Six. Secondly, each year work the top 5cm of the soil under and around the trees to prevent compaction, minimise water evaporation, the harbouring of pests in any grass or weed cover, and to enable rain, irrigation water and fertilizers to get down into the soil to be extracted by the tree roots rather than by vigorous weeds.

There are four possible ways of doing this, each having benefits and risks:

a. Rotovate the ground around the trees each spring and autumn to a depth of five centimetres to loosen the compacted surface and work the surface grass and weeds into the soil; add nutrients to improve the moisture-holding capacity of the soil; bury and kill any aerobic pests that were lurking in the grass; and bury any decaying remains of fallen fruit.

All that is positive, but there is the danger of damaging roots near the surface. Ensure that you work the soil no more than 5cm and clear the last metre around young trees by hand. Excess rotovating can also damage the soil structure and build up an impermeable layer in poor soils just below the depth of the blades.

b. Kill the weeds in the orchard once or twice a year to clear the grass and wild flowers. This does not prevent pests feeding on leaves and fallen fruit, so you will need to add an insecticide to your weed-killing spray, not altogether an ecologically friendly approach.

c. Mulch deeply around the trees to reduce the growth of grass and weeds and reduce moisture evaporation from the soil. Pests may, however, harbour and breed in the attractive humid microclimate of the compost used as a mulch, and fungal diseases may attack the trunks of trees. You will, therefore, need to mulch in the autumn and roto-vate the mulch into the soil well   befo-re the trees bud or, in the case of citrus fruits, flower. Again, do not rotovate more than 5cm deep.

d. Cover the area around the fruit trees with porous black plastic and cover with 5cm of stone chippings, except for a circle around each fruit tree. This will keep a small orchard area tidy, reduce weed growth and reduce the evaporation of moisture, although fallen leaves and fruit will need to be cleared as they build up.

8.8 THE FRUIT GARDEN CALENDAR

JANUARY/FEBRUARY
- Winter pruning of fruit trees.
- Winter oil wash of summer fruiting trees and fix grease/glue bands.
- Clean up all leaves and fallen fruit under trees.
- Clean up strawberry beds, put mats and straw down and plant new plants.
- Cut out dead raspberry canes and cut back new growth by a third.
- Tighten training wires and tie up canes.
- Prune currant bushes.
- Spray citrus trees with insecticide befo-re flowering.
- Weed or kill off weeds around bushes and trees.

MARCH/APRIL
- Thin out non-fruiting and crossing branches on fruit trees.
- Fix traps for minero moth on citrus trees.
- Cut out any frost damage on citrus and semi tropical/tropical fruits.
- Give damaged trees a foliar nitrogen feed.
- Give strawberries a feed.
- Clean up banana plants and use leaves as a high-in-potassium mulch.
- Start to dust grape vines with sulphur.
- Mulch raspberries with well-rotted compost and manure.
- Give all trees and plants a good soak if there are no spring rains.
- Watch for early leaf curl and spray.

MAY/JUNE
- Thin out forming fruit on citrus, peach, plum and nectarine trees to stimulate larger fruits.
- Clean up early fallen fruits such as apricots and cherries.
- Rotovate all growth under trees.
- Plant out young banana and papaya plants.
- Thin out bunches of grapes and cut out excess non-fruiting growth on vines and continue to dust with sulphur.
- Water citrus trees to swell the fruit.
- Freeze or make jams with surplus strawberries, currants, cherries and apricots.
- Feed and water kiwi, blackberry and loganberry vines.
- Watch for slugs and snails on strawberries, raspberries and currant bushes.
- Watch for snails on citrus trees.

JULY/AUGUST
- Dust grape vines with sulphur as fruit swells and colours.
- Keep cleaning up any fallen fruit.
- Hoe summer weeds under fruit trees.
- Harvest almonds and dry in sun before storing.

- Freeze or bottle surplus peaches and nectarines.
- Prune apple and pear trees.
- Ensure you water kiwis, papayas, bananas and mangoes copiously.
- Water and feed raspberries to stimulate autumn fruiting.
- Hang wasp traps on fig trees.
- Don't worry about your almond tree losing leaves. This is normal.

SEPTEMBER/OCTOBER

- Harvest apples and persimmons and tray for storage.
- Give fruit trees an autumn feed.
- Prune out excess growth from kiwi vines.
- Prepare ground for new fruit trees and bushes.
- Plant out new strawberry runners and remove old plants.
- Cut back bananas after fruiting.
- Pick quince and make jelly.

- Pick excess lemons and store in cool cellar or fridge.
- Freeze last raspberries for Christmas.
- Give fruit trees a spray with Neem.

NOVEMBER/DECEMBER

- Plant new kiwi vines and fruit bushes.
- Harvest first olives and prepare for pickling in brine.
- Plant bare rooted or container fruit trees.
- Cover strawberries with cloches for forcing.
- Start to harvest first mandarins and oranges.
- Plant new raspberry canes.
- Prune currant bushes and blackberry and loganberry vines.
- Weed around strawberries and raspberries.
- Harvest last persimmons and store.
- Protect papaya and mango trees from frost and cold winds.

MANAGING YOUR GARDEN

MANAGING A GARDEN

IN THIS SECTION WE LOOK at a number of general issues important to the management of your garden in Spain, issues that could make or break the fun and enjoyment you get from a garden developed by following the ideas and guidance of the earlier sections.

9.1 DO I NEED A GARDENER?

This is a very personal question. It needs to be considered objectively against the background of your own situation.

Retirees moving to Spain with plenty of leisure time often have an interest in a variety of activities, including gardening. For some it is their main hobby and for others it is of limited interest. Younger persons who come here to work may have little time for gardening, whether interested or not and there are those of all ages who are physically unable to garden

Every expatriate has genuine ambitions for a new lifestyle in Spain and many will need a gardener, either for a short time, to establish the garden, or on a permanent basis, to maintain it as well.

It is very easy to let your enthusiasm for creating a wonderful garden get out of hand and to assume that every thing can be done in a year. It can, of course, if you take on a landscape gardener to do the whole job for you, but this could be costly.

ACTIVITIES REQUIRED TO DESIGN, CONSTRUCT AND MAINTAIN A GARDEN	DO WE REALLY WANT TO DO THIS?			OR SHOULD WE GET A GARDENER?	
	YES	PARTIALLY	NO	PARTIALLY	TOTALLY
• Design of garden • Landscaping, including construction of paths, terraces and walls • Development of special features • Selecting plants • Purchasing plants • Planting plants • Watering and feeding • Raising new plants: – from seed – from cuttings • Ongoing maintenance: – flower garden – fruit garden – vegetable garden • Care of greenhouse and garden frame • Winter cut back • Ongoing maintenance: – Lawn cutting – Flower garden – Vegetable garden – Fruit garden – Pool/jacuzi maintenance					

Many will prefer to have the fun and satisfaction of creating a new garden from nothing, or perhaps improving an existing one. In either case, creating a garden that satisfies all their needs will take a good number of years.

It is important to be honest with yourself. Before deciding whether you need a gardener, analyse what you, your partner and close family would like to do in the garden, what you are capable of doing, and how much time you will be able to dedicate to the garden.

Based on this analysis, decide whether you need:

1. No gardener.

2. A gardener to help do an initial cleanup of an existing neglected garden.

3. A gardener to design and develop a garden that you will then maintain.

4. A gardener to design, develop and maintain your garden.

If you are going to be an absentee gardener, decide if you want a gardener to tend the garden 52 weeks a year, whether you are in Spain or not, or whether you want him to do only a major tidy up just before each of your visits and during your stay.

There may be a gardener who goes with the property you have bought. In this case, consider whether he or she has the knowledge, experience, physical fitness, motivation and time to create and maintain the garden you want – or whether you need to find a new gardener. If it is the latter, make the change as early as possible.

If you are lucky enough to inherit a good gardener, make sure you don't lose him or her. In some areas, they are like gold.

9.2 FINDING THE RIGHT GARDENER

Now you have to decide what type of gardener you need. There are several choices. It could be a landscaping contractor, an experienced and knowledgeable gardener, a trainee gardener on a local gardening course who has to do six months practical work to gain a final diploma, an enthusiastic amateur new to Spain who needs to make a living, or an odd-job man or girl Friday.

Draw up a short list of possible gardeners, including your inherited gardener, if you have one. Spend a few weeks asking around, reading the services column in the local newspaper or putting an advertisement in the newspaper or on the notice board in your local store.

Don't rush into hiring the first person who puts a leaflet in your post box or the first one you see working down the road. This is an important decision and many of you have never employed a gardener before coming to Spain.

Having drawn up a short list, ask each of them to come for a chat. Then evaluate each in turn, taking into account the following factors:

- **Previous experience:** What gardens do they currently look after and have looked after in the past? What style of garden and size? Have they developed a garden along the lines that you envisage? How long have they been gardeners in Spain?

- **Pride in work:** Do you get the impression that he or she takes pride in their work and could become enthusiastic about your garden?

- **Client satisfaction:** Are current and past clients happy with the gardener's work? Are they willing to let you see their gardens? A visit will tell you a lot.

- **Aesthetics:** Do other gardens suggest that the gardener has an eye for beauty? Are the designs and materials used in keeping with the location, style of garden and most importantly the style and colour scheme of the house?

- **Knowledge:** Does he or she have a good knowledge of the local nurseries, know what plants are best for your location and style of garden, and how to propagate in order to expand the number of plants in the garden economically? If you want to garden organically, does he or she know about organic fertilizers and insecticides and believe in not using weed killers? Does he or she believe in improving the soil before planting, and know where to obtain organic compost or manures?

- **Contacts:** Does the gardener have good contacts with specialists if he or she is unable to carry out all the work you need doing (e.g., tree surgeons, bricklayers and tilers)?

- **Communication:** Does he or she speak English, Spanish or both? Does he or she have a history of listening and contributing to other house owners? Do you feel that you could establish a good partnership to develop and maintain the garden on an ongoing basis?

- **Reliability:** Do you feel that you can trust the gardener to get on with agreed tasks in your absence and with keys to the property. Have other clients found the gardener reliable in completing jobs on time, tidily and within estimates?

- **Equipment:** Does the gardener have the tools for the job or are you expected to provide them? Are they productive Spanish-style tools suited to hard soils?

– **Availability:** When can he or she start? What hours are possible without creating complaints from other clients? Are the hours sufficient to carry out the work you want carried out in the short and long term? Can the summer maintenance work be fitted in to suit the times that you wish to use the garden privately?

– **Legality:** If a foreigner, is he or she working legally in Spain?

– **Cost:** What will be charged, and how? Is this realistic and in line with local prices for both initial design and landscaping work and for ongoing maintenance?

Having made your analysis of each gardener available, make an objective choice and negotiate a realistic verbal or written contract.

MOTIVATING YOUR GARDENER

The following guidelines are suggested for getting the most out of your gardener:

1. Negotiate a realistic and fair contract and pay on time. in many cases it is preferable to pay the gardener on the basis of:

- A monthly or quarterly retainer rather than on an hourly basis for the ongoing maintenance and minor improvements.

- An agreed budget for the purchase of plants, garden materials, fertilizers and sprays, etc.

- An agreement as to whether the gardener has the right to pick flowers, almonds, olives, other fruit and vegetables for his or her own use.

- Agreed additional payments for the initial landscaping of the garden and major changes in an existing one. You may well use a landscaping company for the latter and then a private individual for the ongoing maintenance work.

– Whether you should increase the rate of pay in line with inflation each year.

2. Share your vision for the garden. Agree realistic milestones for the development of a new garden or changing an

existing garden. Tell the gardener what you think and what visitors thought of the results of his or her efforts. Evaluate by results, not hours worked. A good gardener will achieve much in a relatively few hours. The limited results of a poor gardener will soon be obvious.

3. If you plan to work on the garden with the support of a gardener, avoid misunderstandings by:

– Involving the gardener in the planning phase.

– Asking for ideas to supplement your own before making final decisions.

– Agreeing how to share out the work required.

– Agreeing what should be composted and what will go to the refuge tip.

– Visiting garden centres together to choose and purchase plants.

4. If you become dissatisfied with your gardener, be fair before making a change. Make an objective evaluation and then discuss your major misgivings with him. See if you can find out what is causing things to go wrong and try to agree on an improvement plan for the next month or two before making a final decision.

9.3 EVALUATING YOUR GARDENER

September is probably the best time to evaluate the contribution and performance of your gardener in relation to the creation and maintenance of a garden that suites your site, environment and lifestyle.

You will have just spent, hopefully, a summer in a wonderfully colourful and perfumed garden. Memories and perhaps photographs remind you of the best features of the garden last Christmas and in the spring, and the current state of the garden will give an impression of how it will look during the autumn.

If you have changes and new projects in mind, the autumn and winter are the best times of the year to implement them. September is the most appropriate time for a review to ensure that they will be in knowledgeable, capable, productive and trustworthy hands, especially if you are an absentee owner and are shortly to depart for some months.

Likewise, if you have just returned from spending the summer in cooler climes, take a close look at the garden. Does it look good? Does it look as if you have not been away. And if the property has been rented, have there been any complaints or praise from tenants or the letting agency?

9.4 EFFECTIVE CHANGE OVER OF GARDENERS

Most of us have experienced at some time in our working life a poor handover from the previous incumbent when starting a new job – the inevitable "dropped baton" which is sometimes as disastrous in the working environment as in a relay race.

The same often happens when gardeners are changed, and the result is a lack of continuity in the development and maintenance of a carefully nurtured garden. If you have to make a change, ensure that this takes place with the minimum disruption to the gardening calendar.

The following check list covers the information that needs to be handed over to the new gardener:

1. The extent to which the owner likes to be involved or whether he/she leaves the gardener to do what they think is best.

2. The owner's general vision for the garden and specific likes and dislikes.

3. The current programme for the development/improvement of the garden, e.g., new terraces, flower beds, rockeries etc.

4. Any urgent jobs planned for the next few months.

5. Recently planted plants and any special care they need until established.

6. Provisional planting plans for the next autumn/winter including cuttings required for propagation.

7. The regular programme of watering and feeding plants, trees and lawns.

8. The normal schedule of weeding, hoeing and weed killing (if allowed) and the areas where weeds are normally killed, and with what.

9. The normal frequency and height for cutting the lawn.

10. The range of machinery (mower, strimmer, shredder etc.) and tools provided by the owner, and servicing arrangements.

11. How the watering system works and the normal seasonal settings. Who to contact if there are problems with the electronic controls on a complex system. The owner's attitude to the cost of watering.

12. The normal programme for the winter cleanup in January/February.

13. Facilities for disposal of garden waste, e.g., compost heap, bagging for tip or the ordering of a skip for the winter cleanup.

14. The owner's policy re organic/ecological versus inorganic manufactured fertilizers, insecticides and herbicides.

15. Programme for pruning, watering and feeding fruit trees. Whether the gardener is expected to harvest crops and allowed to take some for his/her own use.

16. Whether the gardener is expected to develop and maintain a productive vegetable garden.

17. Location and types of spring and summer bulbs in flowerbeds to ensure that they are not disturbed or damaged.

18. Owner's desire for displays of annuals in containers or beds.

19. Owner's budget for new plants and any agreed re-plantings.

20. Ownership of hedges and owner's policy re height and depth of hedges.

21. Owner's pet plants and names.

22. Who has the responsibility for maintaining the swing, slide, sand pit etc., in the children's play area.

23. Where tools and chemicals can be stored securely.

24. Who is responsible for repair of steps, paths, terraces, walls, repainting of terrace walls, garden furniture etc. Is there a regular handy man as well as a gardener?

25. What special things need to be done in the week before each of the owner's visits, if the owner is not resident, or if the property is let.

26. Who is responsible, you, the gardener or the cleaner, for sweeping paths and terraces.

27. If the gardener is to maintain the pool, how the pool system works, what pool chemicals are used and where they are purchased and stored.

28. How and when to submit bills for work carried out, and expenditures on behalf of the owner.

29. How and when the owner likes to be contacted.

Clarifying these issues on day one will go a long way to preventing hiccups and demonstrate that you take a great interest in the garden.

9.5 SPANISH GARDENING TOOLS

The soil in most Spanish gardens is initially very unforgiving. Except for a day or two after rain, it can be rock hard, even in the winter. The use of an inappropriate or ergonomically inefficient tool can cause unnecessary hard work and can even lead to injury, especially to backs, shoulders, elbows, wrists and knees.

When we first came to Spain, we soon found that most of the tools we used regularly in the damper climate and the generally more friable soils of northern Europe were no match for traditional Spanish tools.

TRADITIONAL SPANISH TOOLS

Our collection of Spanish tools has been built up over the years by observing how Spaniards work the land and watching out for regional tools as we travelled around.

1. A range of mattocks (*azadones*).

a. Small size with a 5 or 6cm wide blade on a short 15cm handle – essential for easy close work such as weeding, hoeing, making seed drills and small planting holes.

b. Medium double-ended on long handle. We use two types as illustrated. The first has an 8cm flat mattock blade on one side and a U-shape on the other side of the head. The other has a flat mattock blade on one side and a pointed blade on the other. The first is a general-purpose tool used daily. We find it is very useful for taking the strain out of heavy weeding, making medium diameter and deep planting holes. The second is especially useful for weeding between closely planted plants.

c. Single larger, 10cm wide, light blade on short handle. Very useful for weeding between rows.

d. Large heavy 12cm head on long handle. Mainly used for digging large planting holes, trenches and clearing irrigation channels, and for removing the tap roots of large rooted weeds, shrubs and trees.

Note that the medium and large sizes often come with handles too short for tall persons. If you have this problem, buy longer handles separately.

2. Heavy ridging rake *(bilbadora)* with a 28cm wide saw edged head. Comes on a long handle and makes easy work of jobs such as levelling soil, making planting ridges and irrigation channels on the vegetable plot, preparing seed beds, earthing up potatoes and removing bean and pea plants after the last harvesting.

3. Small pruning secateurs *(tijeras de podar)*, used in the fruit orchards. Ergonomic and very useful for light detailed pruning, cutting flowers for the terrace or house table and deadheading.

4. Long extendable pruners *(tijeras de podar extendible)*, indispensable for cutting back high climbers and thinning out/pruning the highest branches of trees.

5. Short and long handled, straight and curved pruning saws *(sierras)* with an extendable handle, essential for pruning palms, large cacti, shrubs and trees.

6. Traditional Spanish long-bristle brooms *(escobas)*, light and handy for all sweeping-up jobs, except when paths are heavily encrusted with sand or earth after construction projects, when a shorter tougher bristle head is more effective.

7. Several sizes and shapes of *capazos*, the plastic buckets used by Spanish builders and gardeners. They are inexpensive, long lasting, easily cleaned and used for a wide variety of tasks such as holding a plastic sack open when weeding and pruning, moving sand, manure and earth, and mixing small quantities of mortar. We use one together with a wheel barrow for heavy loads.

8. Traditional, woven baskets *(capazos)*, good for harvesting and storing vegetables and hard-skinned fruit.

9. A good pair of kitchen scissors *(tijeras)* for cutting leaves from perpetual salad crops, trimming onion seedlings before planting and cutting raffia, plastic and string ties.

10. A strong cane *(caña)* to knock down almonds.

11. Various sizes of sprayers *(pulverizadores)*. It's handier to have small and medium-sized hand-held sprayers than a larger twelve-litre backpack version.

MODERN MULTI HEAD TOOLS
Several brands and designs are available,

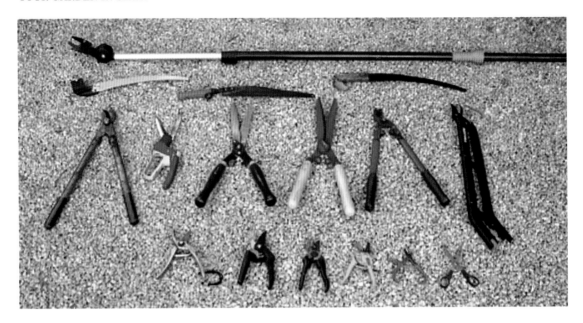

with a long standard handle and a variety of easily attachable tool heads. We use the following heads:

1. A double sided hoe, swoe, *(azada)* with a sharp wavy head, very effective for removing annual weeds in hot weather when the soil is rock hard, both around shrubs and between the rows of vegetables. Also good for loosening the top 2cm of soil when damp to prevent water loss by capillary action.

2. A three-pronged harrow *(grada)*, used to lighten the surface of damp, no-dig beds before planting. It is also used in wet weather to remove weeds when it is more effective than the swoe.

3. Two flexible metal rakes *(rastrillos)*. A narrow, 10cm wide, five pronged version is the best tool for raking around plants in densely planted beds to remove dead leaves and loosen the surface soil. A wider, 35cm pronged head is excellent for raking up leaves, etc.

OUR NORTHERN EUROPEAN TOOLS

We still use some of our northern European tools, but less frequently than before coming to live in Spain. The ones we still use are:

1. Small trowel *(desplantador)* for digging planting holes for infill small plants and bulbs in densely planted beds and the rockery, but the small mattock is better on the wrists.

2. Small fork *(horca)*, for weeding densely packed beds and the rockery, but, as above, the small mattock is normally more versatile with less effort.

3. Lawn rake *(rastrillo)* for clearing leaves from areas covered with stone chippings and levelling after periods of major use.

4. Traditional garden fork *(horca)*, for digging up plantlets for transplanting and root vegetables when the soil is too dry to pull up by hand and for turning the compost heaps and loading well-rotted manure into plastic buckets for carrying to where required.

5. Traditional shovel *(pala grande)*, for shovelling sand and stone chippings into the wheel barrow, though a broad mattock is more useful and less strain for mixing mortar or cement.

6. Light-weight wheel barrow *(carretilla)* with inflatable tyre, for for transporting rocks, stone chippings and soil – and as a cement mixer for smaller quantities

when building walls, laying paving slabs, etc.

7. Our old hedging shears *(tijeras de jardín)*, sharpened whenever a traditional afilador passes through the village, for tidying up and shaping evergreen hedges, shrubs and herbs.

8. Ancient pliers *(alicates)*, always useful for cutting, straining and tying wire supports for sweet peas, roses, climbers and raspberries.

ELECTRO-MECHANICAL AIDS

We find the most useful machines are:

1. An electric shredder *(trituradora)*, used for the annual winter cutback, when we shred as much as possible to add to the compost heap.

2. An electric strimmer *(destrozadora)* for trimming the only patch of grass we have – 10 square metres under an almond tree – and rough grass along one side of the vegetable patch, which we cut and dry for hay for the rabbits and guinea pigs.

3. An electric hedge trimmer *(cortasetos de cuchilla)* to trim the sides of a conifer hedge.

4. A rotovator *(moto azada)* to clear new areas and lighten consolidated soils.

5. If you have a lawn then you will need a lawnmower *(cortacésped)*.

6. An electric blower/vacuum cleaner *(aspiradora)*, for blowing leaves into piles before sucking them up. Also good for cleaning up stone chipping paths and terraces.

7. If you have a large piece of ground that is rock hard, it may be worth getting someone to work it with a plough *(arado)*.

These are the tools we use. Like many gardeners, we learned the hard way but soon realised that in Spain one follows local tradition or strain the body unnecessarily – definitely not a good thing to do as we get older. If your local nursery or horticultural shops do not stock the tools we describe, search out the nearest agricultural cooperative. Just one warning: be careful when you use mattocks as they have sharp edges.

Buy lightweight tools when possible. They take much of the toil out of gardening and reduce the risk of aching backs, legs and arms. Look after your tools. Dirty handles cause warts and blunt edges double the effort required to use them. Good tools make maintenance work easy and give enjoyable exercise.

9.6 MAKING YOUR GARDEN SAFE

Every year many accidents occur in gardens. Most could be avoided by careful design, construction and safe gardening practices. The following guidelines are based on our own experience and observations:

DESIGN AND CONSTRUCTION

Walls:

• Ensure that boundary walls are on secure foundations and sufficiently strong to withstand the forces exerted by climbing plants, gale force winds and vibrations of passing lorries.

• Ensure that retaining walls are strong and stable enough to support the infill behind, especially during and after heavy rains.

• Ensure that retaining walls and boundary walls have sufficient and large enough drainage pipes to allow the release of retained water.

• Ensure that dry stonewalls are wide enough and sufficiently well stacked to withstand their own weight and the weight of the retained earth. And be sure the top stones are cemented to make them safe to stand on.

Paths and terraces:

• Build paths and terraces with none slip surfaces.

• Ensure easy slopes, steps and curves

for all ages.
• Regularly clean off the winter build up of slippery algae and moss, especially under trees.
• Repair loose slabs and cracks as soon as they appear that could cause trips.

Steps:
• Construct with equal rises and treads to reduce the risk of tripping.
• Ensure that the edges of the treads are totally secure. Loose and broken edges can be lethal.
• Use nonslip materials.
• Install handrails alongside.

Electricity:
• Install a separate trip for the garden circuit.
• Use armoured cables and strong plastic conduits. Sink them a minimum of 20cms deep and cover with slabs of concrete. Mark where they are to avoid hitting them when digging down with a fork, spade, pick axe or mattock.
• Use special waterproof fittings and immediately change anything damaged.
• Use low voltage solar lights and pond pumps.
• Use a qualified electrician.

Fences:
• Ensure that all fence posts for wire mesh and panelled fences are strong and secure as well as the fixings for the wire and panels. Check them after heavy storms and gales.
• Keep the weight of accumulated growth of climbers down by an annual thinning out of the undergrowth that often dies back, otherwise fences can become top heavy.

Swimming pools and Jacuzzis
• Ensure that all surrounding terraces are nonslip and have no sharp edges.
• Check regularly for any loose tiles and sharp edges in the pool.
• Check that diving boards and slides are

firm and that no bolts have worked loose.
• Only use plastic glasses and tableware in these areas to avoid breakages and slivers of glass falling into the pool or Jacuzzi.
• Fence in the pool and Jacuzzi to prevent unattended young children from using them or falling in.
• Clearly mark the depths of both the shallow and deep ends.
• Store pool chemicals securely.
• Consider changing to non-chemical cleaning methods.

Ponds:
• Locate ponds away from main paths and terraces.
• Fence off or cover when young children are resident or visiting.
• Ensure that the surrounding terrace and rocks are secure.
• Store pond chemicals securely.

SAFE GARDEN PRACTICES
Plants:
• Avoid prickly plants or, if you have them, site them back from paths and terraces and keep them under control. Especially cut off the spiky points of yuccas and palms to reduce the chance of eye and head injuries.
• Use strong gloves and thick trousers and long sleeved tops when pruning palms, yuccas, cacti, blackberries, etc.
• Be aware that certain plants are poisonous (e.g,. datura, morning glory and oleander). Either avoid them or locate them away from main paths. Prune them with care and always wear gloves. Warn the family and visitors about the dangers of these plants.
• Take special care when cutting off and carrying palm fronds. Avoid the spikes at any cost.
• Fell dying trees and cut off dangerous branches before they fall.
• Don't touch processionary caterpillars that come down from pine trees in the spring and don't let your pets near them.

Avoid dangerous points:
- Ensure that the ends of all wire ties are tied in tightly.
- Prune back low branches on palms, ornamental and fruit trees to the trunk. Don't leave dangerous ends at head height.
- Ensure that the ends of canes and supporting posts are blunt or covered over with tape to avoid eye injuries when leaning over plants.

Avoid glass:
- Use plastic rather than glass for cloches, garden frames and greenhouses.
- Don't use glass jars or jugs in the garden.

Protective clothing:
- Wear appropriate protective clothing when handling fertilisers, insecticides, pesticides and herbicides, and especially when spraying with chemicals.
- Purchase a good quality protective hat, goggles, face mask, gloves and gardening shoes. Keep them clean and wash after handling chemicals. Disposable gloves and masks are a good idea when spraying.

- Always use tough topped shoes when digging, raking, hoeing and cutting grass.
- Wear thick gloves when pruning prickly and spiky plants.
- Wear a protective mask and clothing when using a strimmer and goggles and gloves when using a shredder.

Chemical storage:
- Store all garden chemicals in a secure place on high shelving or in secure bins away from pets and children.
- Ensure that all chemical containers are sound with secure tops, no leakages and clear labels.
- Dispose of out-of-date chemicals in the appropriate container at a local eco park.

Use ecological solutions:
- Change from manufactured chemicals to less hazardous natural/organic/ecological solutions.
- Start to grow and use beneficial plants, especially in the vegetable garden, such as:
a. Comfrey and nettles for liquid fertilizers.
b. Garlic, nettles, lavender, rosemary, and scented geraniums for insect deterrents.

c. Horsetail as a fungicide.
d. Rosemary, borage, sweet peas, roses and sunflowers to attract pollinators.
e. Coriander, nasturtiums and fennel to attract bugs away from vegetables.
f. Chives, garlic and marigolds as insect repellents.
g. A pot of basil or rue by the door to repel flies.

Animal and stinging insects:
• Locate and destroy the nests of wasps and hornets.
• Spray wasps around the pool with a dilute mix of ecological washing-up liquid and water, using a small sprayer. Also leave bowls of the liquid around when wasps first appear.
• Watch out for scorpions, adders, processionary caterpillars and biting spiders.

Control bonfires:
• When clearing out an overgrown garden or doing the annual winter cutback, avoid bonfires by shredding most material for the compost heap, putting in eco bins, selling to a local compost making eco park or as a last resort use a skip.
• If you do have a bonfire, first obtain the necessary local license and follow local safety bylaws.
• Control the size of bonfires by burning in an oil drum or breeze block screen. One often sees the latter being used in the orange groves.
• Don't leave a bonfire unattended. Always have a working hosepipe or buckets of water nearby to get fierce or spreading fires back under control.
• Put out and dampen down any fire before leaving it.

Tools and equipment:
• Purchase good tools and keep them clean.
• Repair or replace any loose or broken handles or parts immediately.
• Ensure that guards and safety catches on machines are operable, secure and used.

• Don't leave sharp-edged tools lying around.
• Use safety catches on secateurs.
• Ensure that rungs, legs, rubber feet and catches on ladders and stepladders are safe.

Avoid strains:
• When buying tools, choose ones that are ergonomically designed.
• Use the right tool for the job, especially when trying to prune thick branches.
• Avoid lifting heavy rocks, sacks, etc., without help.
• Avoid overloading the wheelbarrow or plastic baskets.
• Don't mix too much mortar or concrete at any one time.
• Warm up, especially in cool weather, before doing heavy jobs.
• Don't overdo it by working long hours day after day. We are in Spain to enjoy life! What is an extra month or two if the completion of a DIY project is extended?

9.7 THE HISTORY OF MY SPANISH GARDEN

This chart is included to help you maintain a record of the evolution of your Spanish garden from the day you took over a bare plot or an established garden to the day you achieved your vision of what it should become. Naturally you may achieve this within a year or two through an instant garden planted up with mature plants by an expensive contract witha landscaping company. But the average gardener coming to Spain will take longer whether working solo or with the support of a gardener. We therefore provide space for a record of the first five years of your garden. By then you should be nearing your dream garden as plants mature and blend together in harmony, with only a minimal amount of maintenance required.

No	**IMPORTANT EVENTS** Record the most important initiatives, projects, events and achievements.	20....				20....				20....				20....				20....			
		S	S	A	W	S	S	A	W	S	S	A	W	S	S	A	W	S	S	A	W
e.g.1																					
2																					
3																					
4																					
5																					
6																					
7																					
8																					
9																					
10																					
11																					
12																					
13																					
14																					
15																					
16																					
17																					
18																					
19																					
20																					
21																					
22																					
23																					
24																					

VOCABULARY
AND INDEX

A GARDENER'S VOCABULARY

350 PLANT NAMES ARE LISTED
IN SECTION FOUR, pages 110 to 173

40 VEGETABLE NAMES ARE LISTED
IN CHAPTER 7.5, pages 262 to 264

40 FRUIT TREE AND PLANT NAMES ARE
LISTED IN CHAPTER 8.1, pages 292 to 297

GARDEN TOOL NAMES ARE LISTED
IN CHAPTER 9.5, pages 320 to 323

GARDEN NOUNS

Garden – *el jardín*

Gardener – *el jardinero*

Bonfire – *una higuera*

Cloche – *una campana.*

Compost heap – *un montón de abono vegetal*

Copse – *un bosquecillo*

Fence – *una cerca*

Flower bed – *un cuadro, un macizo*

Fountain – *una fuente*

Garden frame – *un mini invernadero*

Greenhouse – *un invernadero*

Hedge – *un seto*

Hose – *una manguera*

Lawn – *un césped*

Moon calendar – *un calendario lunar*

Orchard – *un huerto*

Path – *una verda*

Pergola – *una pérgola*

Plant – *una planta*

Plant pot – *una maceta*

Pond – *un estanque*

Rain – *la lluvia*

Rockery – *un jardincito*

Seat – *una silla*

Seed bed – *un semillero*

Seed box – *una caja de semillas*

Shade – *la sombra*

Shrub – *un arbusto*

Shubbery – *los arbustos*

Sun – *el sol*

Swimming pool – *la piscina*

Terrace – *una terraza*

Tool – *una herramienta*

Trellis – *un enrejado*

Vegetable plot – *el huerto*

View – *una vista*

Water butt – *una tina para agua*

Watering can – *una regadera*

Wall – *un muro*

Watering system – *un sistema de riego*

Weed – *una mala hierba*

Wildlife – *la fauna*

Window box – *una jardinera de balcón*

SPANISH GARDEN MEASURES

English acre – *un acre* – 0.405 hectares – 4047 square metres.

Foot - *un pied* – a third of a metre.

Hectare – *una hectárea* – 10,000 square metres.

Henegade – *un henegada* – 833.33 square metres, a twelfth of a hectare.

Metre – *un metro*

Kilo – *un kilo*

Litre – *un litro*

Ton – *una tonelada*

GARDEN MATERIALS

Cane – *una caña*

Chippings – *la gravilla suelt.*

Compost – *el abono vegetal*

Fertilizer – *un abono*

Fungicide – *un funguicid.*

Grit – *la arena gruesa*

Herbicide – *un herbicida*

Insecticide – *un insecticida*

Lava pulverised – *la lava pulverizada*

Manure – *el estiércol*

Mulch – *un mantill.*

Netting – *la red*

Peat – *la turba*

Pesticide – *un pesticida*

Post – *un poste*

Rainwater – *el agua de la lluvia*

Rock – *una roca*

Sand – *la arena*

Seeds - *las semillas*

Slab of rock – *un bloque*

Soil – *el suelo*

String – *la cuerda*

Water – *el agua*

Weedkiller – *un herbicida*

Wire – *el alambre*

PARTS OF PLANTS

Bark – *la corteza*

Blossom – *las flores*

Branch – *una rama*

Bud (flower) – *un capullo*

Bud (leaf) – *una yema*

Cutting – *un esqueje*

Flower – *una flor*

Flower head – *un arriate*

Fruit – *una fruta*

Leaf – *una hoja*

Perfume – *un olor*

Pollen – *el pólen*

Root – *la raíz*

Rootstock – *un rizoma*

Seed – *una semilla*

Seed head – *una cabezuela*

Seedling – *una plántula*

Spray of flowers – *una ramita*

Stem – *un tallo*

String of onions – *una ristra de cebollas*

Texture – *la textura*

Trunk – *el tronco*

Twig – *una ramita*

TYPES OF PLANTS

Annual – *un anuario*

Bamboo - *un bambú*

Bulb – *un bulbo*

Cactus – *un cactus*

Corm – *un bulbo*

Fruit tree – *un árbol frutal*

Grass – *la hierba*

Ground cover – *un progresivo*

House plant – *una planta de interior*

Herb – *una hierba aromática*

Palm – *una palmera*

Perennial – *un perenne*

Rambler – *una enredadera*

Shrub – *un arbusto*

Shrub (climbing) – *una trepadora*

Succulent – *un suculento*

Tree – *un árbol*

Tree (evergreen). – *un árbol de hoja perenne*

Tree (deciduous) – *un árbol de hoja caduca*

Vegetable (green) – *una verdura*

Vegetable (general) - *una legumbre*

Vegetable (pulses) – *una leguminosa*

GARDENING VERBS

Axe – *hachear*

Bind – *atar*

Burn – *quemar*

Buy – *comprar*

Cascade – *caer en cascada*

Change – *cambiar*

Choose – *eligir*

Clean up – *limpiar*

Construct – *construir*

Cover over – *cubrir*

Create – *crear*

Cultivate – *cultivar*

Cut – *cortar*

Cut back – *recortar*

Cut down – *talar*

Deadhead – *descabezar*

Decide – *decidir*

Design – *diseñar*

Develop – *desarrolar*

Dilute – *diluir*

Dig – *cavar, cultivar*

Dig a hole – *excavar*

Dig in – *añadir al suelo*

Dig over – *recavar*

Dig up – *desarraigar*

Divide – *dividirs.*

Dry – *secar*

Employ - *emplear*

Fertilize – *fertilizar*

Garden (general) – *trabajar en el jardín*

       (vegetable plot) – *cultivar un huerto*

Graft – *injertar*

Grow – *cultivar*

Hammer – *clavar*

Harrow – *gradar*

Harvest – *cosechar*

Hoe – *azadonar*

Irrigate – *regar*

Level – *nivelarse*

Kill off – *exterminar*

Maintain – *mantener*

Maximise – *maximazar*

Minimise – *minimizar*

Mix – *mezclar*

Mix in something – *añadir algo*

Mow – *cortar*

Open – *abrir*

Open up – *abrir*

Pinch out – *quitar con dedos*

Plan – *planear*

Plant – *plantar*

Plough – *arar*

Propagate – *propagar*

Protect – *proteger*

Prune – *podar*

Rain – *llover*

Raise plants – *producir*

Rake – *rastrillar*

Rotovate – *trabajar con motorcultor*

Saw – *serrar*

Select – *escoger*

Separate out – *apartar*

Screen – *tapar*

Shade – *proteger del sol*

Sieve – *cribar*

Shear – *cortar*

Shelter – *resguardar*

Sow – *sembrar*

Spray – *pulverizar*

Stake – *rodrigar*

Stimulate – *estimular*

Strim – *desbrozader*

Sweep up – *barrer*

Take out – *quitar*

Thin out – *entresacar*

Tidy up – *arreglar*

Tie up – *atar*
Till – *cultivar*
Top up – *llenar*
Transplant – *transplantar*
Trench – *excavar*
Water – *regar*
Weed – *deshierbar*

GARDENING ADJECTIVES

Colourful – *lleno de color. Vivo*
Bright – *brillante*
Burnt – *abrasado*
Clammy – *pegajoso*
Cloudy – *nublado*
Cold – *frío*
Comfortable – *comfortable*
Cool – *fresco*
Cosy – *amistoso*
Damp – *húmedo*
Dead – *muerto*
Deciduous – *de hoja caduca*
Dry – *seco*
Dull – *sombrío*
Evergreen – *de hoja perenne*
Flooded – *inundado*
Frost bitten – *congelado*

Gritty – *arenoso*
Frozen – *congelado*
Hot (climate) – *cálido*
Hot (weather) – *caliente*
Humid – *húmedo*
In flower – *florecido*
In fruit – *da fruta*
Level – *a nive*
Muddy – *lodoso*
Natural – *natural*
Organic – *orgánico/ecológic.*
Inorganic – *inorgánico*
Perfumed – *perfumado, aromátic.*
Prickly – *espinoso*
Rainy – *lluvioso*
Saline – *salino*
Shady – *sombreado*
Sloping – *inclinado*
Spiky – *puntiagudo*
Sunny – *soleado*
Sub tropical – *sub tropical*
Temperate – *templado*
Young – *joven*
Warm – *caluroso*
Water – *acuático*
Weeding – *escardar*
Well draining – *bien drenado*

INDEX